From Bumper to Bumper
Bob Sikorsky's Best Automotive Tips

TAB BOOKS
Blue Ridge Summit, PA

For Rich and Pam

FIRST EDITION
SECOND PRINTING

© 1991 by **Robert Sikorsky**.
Published by TAB Books.
TAB Books is a division of McGraw-Hill, Inc.

Library of Congress Cataloging-in-Publication Data

Sikorsky, Robert.
   From bumper to bumper : Bob Sikorsky's best automotive tips / by Robert Sikorsky.
      p.   cm.
   Includes index.
   ISBN 0-8306-2134-2 (H)   ISBN 0-8306-2131-8 (P)
   1. Automobiles—Maintenance and repair.   2. Automobile driving.
3. Automobiles—Purchasing.   I. Title.
TL152.S52313   1991
629.28'722—dc20   91-17960
                                          CIP

TAB Books offers software for sale. For information and a catalog, please contact TAB Software Department, Blue Ridge Summit, PA 17294-0850.

Acquisitions Editor: Kimberly Tabor
Book Editor: April D. Nolan
Director of Production: Katherine G. Brown
Book Design: Jaclyn J. Boone   TAB1

Contents

Acknowledgments

I WOULD LIKE TO THANK the New York Times Syndication Sales Corporation for permission to reprint the columns that appear in this book. I would also like to thank my various syndicate editors who have helped me hone my writing with their dogged attention to detail. To Max Horowitz, Anne Harnagle and Barbara Gaynes, all editors *par excellence*, thanks gang.

My gratitude to Paula Reichler, former New York Times Syndication Sales Corporation Vice President who took the chance and signed me on. To Carl Horwitz, former Syndication Sales President, and John Brewer, current syndicate President, thanks for putting up with me. I am especially indebted to all the sales and promotion people—especially Dan Barber, Connie White, and Sue Sawyer, who worked diligently at making my automotive columns some of the most widely read in America.

And lastly, a special thanks to Frank Johnson, former Executive Editor of the Arizona Daily Star in Tucson, Arizona, for giving me the opportunity to write the columns that eventually led to my syndication and to this book.

I would also like to thank the following organizations, companies and individuals who contributed in some way to this book:

Environmental Protection Agency, National Highway Traffic Safety Administration, Federal Trade Commission, Arizona Energy Office, Connecticut Department of Transportation, Illinois State Police, United States Department of Transportation, American Petroleum Institute, Society of Automotive Engineers, Automotive Information Council, Mothers Against Drunk Driving, Ohio Insurance Institute, Automotive Service Association, Automotive Service Councils, Motor Vehicle Manufacturers Association,

Chemical Specialties Manufacturers Association, Bob Bondurant School of High Performance Driving, Volkswagen AG, Ford Motor Company, General Motors Corporation, Chrysler Motors, Saab Cars USA, Range Rover of North America, Inc., McDonnell Douglas Corporation, Phillips Petroleum Research Division, Champion Spark Plug Company, Pennzoil Products Company, LOOC Corporation, Beverly Hills Motoring Accessories, Armor All Products Corporation, Allparts, Inc., Allen Testproducts, Bridgestone (U.S.A.), Inc., Norfolk Southern/Amoco Motor Club (Operation Lifesaver), Fred Willis Motors, Barrett-Jackson Auction, Reader's Digest Association, Automotive Engineering, Automotive News, Associated Press, The California Independent, Jackie Stewart, Jim Conners, Donald A. Randall, Thomas H. Hanna, and members of my High Mileage Club.

Introduction

BUMPER TO BUMPER, that's what this book is all about. It covers every part of your car from bumper to bumper, including the person behind the wheel. For the past six and a half years, I have been a syndicated automotive columnist with the New York Times Syndication Sales Corporation. My two columns, "Drive It Forever" and "Ridin' In Style," appear in newspapers throughout the United States, Canada, Japan, and Europe and are read by millions each week.

This book, a compilation of a number of my "Drive It Forever" car-care columns, covers just about everything you'd want to know about cars. It goes beyond basic car care and maintenance and covers such important subjects as correct driving techniques—a number of them from such experts as Jackie Stewart, three-time former world champion Formula 1 racecar driver; "gas saving" gadgets; emissions and the environment; how to get more miles per gallon; how to store a car properly; and even how to keep from getting ripped off at the repair shop. It also includes a chapter on my High Mileage Club, featuring readers whose cars have gone at least 100,000 miles without a major repair. Through the years, over 2,000 readers have joined this exclusive club. My current reader longevity record: 580,000 miles—without a single major repair!

And there's more. If you're in the market for a new or used car, chapter 16 will be of special interest. It's loaded with practical information that will help you get the best car at the best price. It will also alert you to many consumer protection devices you can use to your advantage when purchasing a vehicle.

My two-part series on solid lubricants, included in chapter 3, was one of my most popular ever. Tens of thousands of readers sent me SASEs for my list of brand names of solid lubricants I tested and found to be valuable aids for extending engine life and increasing gas mileage. (That same list is yours for the asking.)

You'll also learn how to choose the best oil and gasoline for your car; techniques for breaking in a new car or a rebuilt engine; why engines and transmissions wear and how to prevent it; and the often overlooked importance of the cooling system and how it affects both engine longevity and fuel economy.

Turn to chapter 13 and you'll take a ride down tire lane. There, you'll find out how to buy tires that will last and be safe and how tires affect handling, fuel economy, performance, and much more. In chapter 20, you'll see that car care, Sikorsky-style, can be fun. A number of my personal favorite columns occupy that chapter.

As I do in all of my columns, I have tried to keep technical language to a minimum so that *everyone* can benefit. Whether you're a new or experienced driver, have owned many cars or just bought your first one, you're sure to find loads of helpful information between the covers. Just turn the page to start your Bumper To Bumper journey.

1

The cold start:
A tough way
to get going

FOR MOST INDIVIDUALS, an automobile is the second-most expensive possession, ranking only behind their home. Car owners are universal in their longing to protect this investment. They want it to last as long as possible, give good gas mileage, be trouble-free, and bring a fat trade-in allowance if and when they choose to buy a new car.

It can't be done, you say? An automotive engineer's dream? A "2001" fantasy? The answer is no, to all of the above.

Hang on now for a trip over the mounds of automotive garbage and misinformation, through the maze of mechanical confusion, past the traditional signs of automobile senility, and into the land of trouble-free, long-lasting, more efficient, money-saving cars.

For any vehicle, there is no time as crucial as the first few minutes after a cold engine is started. (A cold engine is one that hasn't run for at least four hours.) During this short time, the engine labors under severe conditions of minimal and sometimes nonexistent lubrication, maximum fuel consumption, and copious fuel waste. It's the time when every engine must bite the bullet. This period is so wear-intense, in fact, that up to a full 90 percent of the total mechanical wear the engine experiences occurs during cold starts. By mechanical wear, I mean the actual removal of metal as one engine part rubs on another, the classic conception of wear as the parts become smaller and literally begin to "wear out."

Engineers at the McDonnell Douglas Corp. transportation department in Long Beach, California, give a dramatic example of this cold-engine wear:

Say your car is parked in the driveway and has had time to cool off. Before retiring for the night you decide to pull the old buggy into the garage, reasoning that it will be better protected and, too, that's what your dad did, and he usually knew best.

It takes about 30 seconds to start the car, pull it into the garage and turn off the engine. You feel good about it, knowing the car will be snug for the night. What you wouldn't feel good about—if you only knew—is that you have just caused as much wear on the engine as a 500-mile trip!

Driving the car those few yards with a cold engine wears it out as much as driving a long distance with a warm engine. Think of it—nine hours of driving 55 mph vs. 30 seconds. It seems incredible that the two are comparable, but in terms of the mechanical wear the engine experiences, the bottom line reads the same. Was putting the car in the garage worth it?

This dramatic example drives home the point of how rapidly an engine wears when it is operating under cold conditions. What does this mean to you, the car owner?

A little foresight, planning, and common sense can help you hold these cold starts to a minimum. For instance, when you come home after work or whatever, and you don't anticipate using the car again that evening, pull it directly into its night resting place, whether it be the garage, a carport, or the street. By doing it then and not later, you avoid one extra cold-engine start—and the accompanying wear.

Warm-up Tips for Cold-Weather Driving

I received the following note from a reader in Bellingham, Washington. It is typical of the confusion motorists face when confronted with the question, "To warm up or not to warm up?" And, indeed, that is the question now that winter is upon us.

> Dear Bob:
> My neighbor races her car (on both cold and warm mornings) for 5 minutes before moving it. My mechanic says, "Start the car, let it idle for 30 seconds—do not race or gun the engine—and take off slowly (less than 45 mph) for the first 2 or 3 miles, then gradually build up to higher speeds." Who is right? I would like to see your comment on this.

Answer: It looks as if your mechanic has been reading my column because he, not your neighbor, is right. It's funny how many of us still labor under the misconception that a car should be warmed thoroughly before it is moved in the morning or after it has been sitting a long time. That mentality is a hand-me-down from old Uncle Jack, who used to rev and roar his engine on those cold mornings. Then he would turn on the heater and let it idle until the interior was warm. Nice for Uncle Jack—bad for his car. It's one of the reasons his car was always in the shop.

New-car manufacturers have recognized what I have been preaching for years: A car that is in proper running order—and I want to emphasize that last point—needs no more than a few seconds of warm-up before it can be moved. The owner's manuals of almost every new car made today recommend brief warm-up periods.

One of the major objections I have had to this technique is that many cars just don't want to run unless they are warmed up. OK, I know that.

But many won't run because they aren't tuned properly. That's easily remedied and, in fact, a pre-cold-weather tune-up is a wise winter precaution. But even if they are tuned, some cars still won't run without a prolonged warm-up. It's the nature of some beasts. What to do then?

Use the "least-possible" rule: Idle the engine the least amount of time necessary to get the car moving smoothly, safely, and without stalling. It might be a minute or two, but that is better than having it chug and gasp for 5 minutes like the neighbor's car.

But why, some ask, is it bad to idle the car to warm it? For one thing, cold idling is the least productive and slowest way to warm the engine. You get no real payback when the car is sitting still. The engine becomes a contaminant breeding station, coughing up copious quantities of unburned fuel, producing varnishes, condensation, and a variety of ill-boding engine non-goodies.

But when the car is in gear and moving, albeit slowly at first, it is getting something for the gas it is burning: It is moving down the road and warming up much faster than if it were sitting. The engine and the entire car—transmission, rear axle or transaxle, tires, and heater—warm and become more efficient and wear-resistant.

The mechanic is right: Keep the speed low for the first mile or two until all car parts have had time to warm, then gradually increase to your desired speed. Hey, the car will be much happier, and in the long run so will you. Warming the car by moving it is one cold-weather fuel-economy and anti-wear technique that will boost winter mileage and car life.

Just keep in mind that cold idling is the most inefficient engine mode of operation. Look at it this way. Santa doesn't ask his reindeer to run 100-yard dashes at the North Pole to warm up before that long trip. He just gives an "On Dancer, On Dasher" and away goes the whole shebang. And I've yet to hear anything about Santa not making it the whole way or breaking down because of an improper warm-up. So do like Santa does and those little elves are less likely to bother your car on cold mornings.

Engine Heaters Turn Cold Starts Warm

If you're a regular reader of my column, you know I've written a number of times about the wear that takes place during and immediately after an engine is cold-started. The wear of internal engine parts is intensified when a cold engine is started at below freezing ambient temperatures. A study conducted by engineers at Volkswagen AG has helped confirm—in a back-door sort of way—what I have emphasized (some might say belabored) through the years: Cold starts are nasty things.

VW engineers measured the amount of oil actually flowing and lubricating when an engine is cold-started at a rather mild temperature of 20 degrees Celsius. The study noted: "When the engine was started, nearly 80 percent of the oil supplied by the (oil) pump flowed through the bypass, which was open as a result of high start-up oil pressure." Only a third of the available oil reached the cylinder head area.

The VW study—conducted with a 1.3-liter Volkswagen engine—also vividly demonstrates the major role engine oil viscosity (how thick or thin the oil is) plays during the cold start-up. When a cold engine is started in below-freezing or near-freezing temperatures, the motor oil is heated mainly through contact with various friction points inside the engine—in particular, the piston area, the walls of the combustion chamber, and the cylinder-head area. Oil flowing in and around those areas is much hotter than the oil still in the oil pan or sump.

What this study is saying in layman's terms is that when you start your cold-engine car, the engine might have as little as one-third of the oil in the crankcase available for lubrication. And because the cold oil is so viscous (thick) it creates a high internal-engine oil pressure that triggers the bypass to open, temporarily diverting the remainder of the oil back to the crankcase. Because much of the oil flows through the bypass, it isn't heated, thus prolonging the engine's agony. We now know that nearly 90 percent of an engine's mechanical wear happens during the cold start-up.

So what can we do to offset or minimize this cold-start treachery? Again we must go back to something I have said for years, but it is worth repeating. First, select a multigrade oil of the lowest viscosity permitted in your owner's manual for the range of outside temperatures anticipated before the next oil change. For winter driving, manufacturers typically call for either a 5W-30 or a 10W-30 grade oil. This thinner-when-cold oil will not be as viscous and will circulate more freely than a heavier oil, so more oil is available for lubrication quicker, and the entire oil content of the engine will heat more rapidly.

The other method is one I have used for years, even though I live in Arizona where morning temperatures, even in winter, aren't really that cold. I use an engine heater that is timer-set to come on about three hours before I use the car in the morning. I also use an oil dipstick heater if the anticipated temperature is to be around freezing.

Many kinds of engine heaters are available—ranging from tank heaters that heat and circulate the coolant, to oil dipstick heaters, and even battery warmers. All will help beat the cold-start, wear-me-down blues.

No matter if you live in Florida or Alaska you can benefit from these heaters. As the VW study showed, cold oil just doesn't flow efficiently, and it will not warm fast because much of it can be diverted back to the sump. But engine heaters keep the oil and other engine parts warmed and ready to go so your engine doesn't have to pay the maximum wear penalty inherent in starting a cold engine with cold oil.

My suggestion: Outfit your car with an engine-tank heater that can be installed in the car's coolant system—usually at the lower radiator hose—in conjunction with an oil dipstick heater or a magnetic heater that clamps on the bottom of the oil pan. In severe cold, a battery warmer of some type can also be helpful.

Quick, fuel-efficient starts with greatly reduced wear and tear on the engine are just some of the benefits you will reap. Your heater will also be effective sooner, and you can get moving faster because the car won't stall as readily.

Engine and engine oil heaters are available at larger automotive supply stores. Note: Some new car manufacturers offer engine heaters as options. Their cars have an area built into the engine block that will accept a manufacturer-made engine heater. Check if yours is one of these before adding an aftermarket type heater.

2

Engine wear: How it happens, how to prevent it

ENGINES AND OTHER MECHANICAL PARTS of an automobile are subject to certain inescapable processes. They all wear out, some sooner than others, but eventually time takes its toll on all. Virtually all mechanical parts are subject to a fast, then slow, then fast again, wear process.

When a part is new, its wear rate is very high as it tries to find an ideal mating surface with adjoining working parts. This high rate of initial *break-in wear* isn't something to get worried about; in fact, it is beneficial if implemented correctly. Trying to slow down or even do away with the initial wear process in the benign hope that it will lead to longer life of the engine or mechanical parts is foolhardy. If an engine or other mechanical part is broken in properly—and that means allowing accelerated wear to take place—it will be able to spend much more time in the second, or slow, wear stage.

Once an engine or transmission or axle is broken in, it enters a blissful state of *near non-wear*—an automotive Nirvana. Parts work and move with a minimum of friction and wear. Clearances between the parts, established by the break-in, are near perfect and allow for maximum lubricant circulation. In this stage mechanical parts can run almost forever if proper maintenance and driving habits are cultivated: changing of lubricating fluids at proper intervals, and not subjecting the parts to a type of service they weren't designed to handle (using a 2-wheel-drive vehicle as a 4-wheel-drive, for instance).

But any part will eventually wear out, no matter how much care it is given. When it begins that final stage, wear comes fast and often without warning. Sometimes the part itself fails, and this is known as *catastrophic wear*. Each of us has probably been a victim of catastrophic engine wear—a part breaking, an engine seizing.

Keeping these three wear stages in mind, let's look at the four major ways an automobile engine can wear once it has been broken in. Each of these contributes to the final and rapid wear stage we discussed above.

Internal engine rusting With the advent of high-quality unleaded gasoline, internal engine rusting has been almost eliminated. Older cars that still use unleaded gasoline are more susceptible to internal engine rusting, but all cars used in non-Sun Belt areas (most of the United States) are still subject to internal rust processes if cheap gasoline is used and the oil isn't changed frequently. Other causes of internal engine rusting are poor-quality oil; frequent short trips, especially in cold weather; neglected pollution-control devices; and the simple fact that some engines are more likely to rust than others.

Mechanical wear Mechanical wear involves the removal of metal from one part by another. Most of this wear takes place during the first 30 seconds or so after an engine is started. The best ways to reduce the effects of this kind of wear: Eliminate as many unnecessary engine starts as possible, drive slowly after a cold start until the engine has warmed, and use a low-viscosity oil (5W-30, 10W-30) in cold weather.

Corrosion Corrosion of internal engine parts is caused by acid buildup in the oil. It can be triggered by a number of factors, but the most prominent is infrequent oil changes. Acids build up in old oil and eat at the metal parts, much like rust eats at the outer skin of a car. Fresh oil in the crankcase, especially in cold weather, ensures that a good supply of acid inhibitor is available in the oil, and the inhibitors neutralize the acid buildup. But remember, these additives deplete with use, and if the oil is not changed, acids gain the upper hand and begin to eat at engine parts.

Abrasive wear Abrasive wear might easily be the most common cause—and the most easily avoided—of engine wear. It takes place when foreign particles that are harder than the metal parts find their way into the engine and begin to scrape, abrade, and wear down the parts. There is nothing fancy here; everyday dirt—in the form of sand, dust, and grit, combined with hard metallic oxides that are produced in the engine itself—does the damage.

The best way to keep abrasives from their dirty work is to have efficient and clean filters in the oil, fuel, and air-intake systems. Stay away from dirt and dusty roads if possible, and change filters on schedule, or before, if unusually dirty or dusty driving is your norm.

Be on guard against these four "demons" of engine demise and you will prolong the slow rate of wear and postpone the eventual onset of the catastrophic stage.

Still at the Same Old Grind?

I have hammered on the topic of the accelerated wear a car undergoes after a cold engine is started and have advised on how to minimize that wear. I write about this so much because it is important for any car owner who wants long life from his or her vehicle. I get letters from readers who complain that their cars have trouble starting when cold and ask if this, too, can cause wear even though the car isn't moving or the engine running. Take, for example, this brief excerpt from a letter from a reader in Fayetteville, North Carolina.

> I own a 1979 Buick Skylark that shows 66,000 miles, and I am reaching for 100,000. However, I have my doubts because I am unable to find a mechanic that can tune it properly. As a result, there is too much grinding on the first start of the day. After that, it's the same baby doll of a car it has always been.

Let's consider "there is too much grinding away on the first start of the day." Way too many cars suffer from the cold grinding syndrome while their owners wail and gnash their teeth, praying the car will start. They will also suffer from the depleted pocketbook syndrome if the grinding isn't stopped. Miraculously, halting the grinding will also halt the wailing and gnashing.

The point of this is that grinding should be saved for nightclubs and not for your car's starter. It's obvious that something is wrong if the car won't cold-start on the first or, at most, second attempt at turning the key. Each subsequent and unnecessary attempt subtracts from the starter's overall longevity, especially if the driver is impatient and keeps whirring away.

If you insist on grinding, then the least you can do is give the starter a minute's rest between grinding intervals of no longer than 15 seconds. Almost all manufacturers recommend this procedure to keep the starter from overheating and dying.

But the starter is only one part that suffers when you go through the same old grind. It's obvious your battery is taking a beating too, wearing itself out before its time. Consider also what is happening inside your poor engine. It's the pits. Even though the oil pump is working and doing its best to get lubricant to distant engine parts it doesn't succeed very well at this task. Only limited amounts of oil find their way into such critical places as the upper cylinder areas or around the main bearings.

Then add another disturbing factor: During all this futile grinding, gasoline is being pumped into the engine. And what happens to that gasoline if it is not being burned? You guessed it. It finds its way into the upper cylinder area of the engine where it washes away what little lubricant protection the oil pump is providing.

If you have been putting off tuning the engine or replacing the battery or fixing whatever it is that is causing your hard starts, that is plain dumb. Just because you can't see the damage being done doesn't mean anything is happening. I'll guarantee *you* will have to pay the piper sooner than your neighbor, who turns his key and is off even on the coldest morning.

Don't Start Until You're Ready

Never start your car's engine until you are ready to go. Sounds reasonable, right? And logical. But many drivers ignore this simple gas- and engine-saving maxim. Take stock of your starting procedure. How many times a day do you start your engine before you are ready to leave? My money says it is almost every time you turn the key.

Most drivers agree with the logic of not starting the engine too soon, but they do it anyway. For some reason we have a tendency to start the engine once the door is closed. It is hard for a driver to sit behind the wheel without the engine running. I think there may be some deep-seated psychological reason for this that has to do with horses.

That's right, horses. When our ancestors sat on a horse it was always ready to go; when we get into a car we want the horsepower ready to go, too. But a horse didn't wear and use gasoline while it waited; a car does. It costs you money to start that horsepower churning before its time.

How many times have you gotten behind the wheel, started the engine, then lit a cigarette, arranged packages, fastened seat belts, adjusted mirrors and seats, tuned in a radio station, or waited for someone who was still in the house—all while the engine was running?

Why not do these things first, then start the engine. Simple? You bet, but it will take practice to get over the bad habit and replace it with a fuel- and wear-efficient one.

Before turning the ignition key make sure of two things: Conditions inside the car are "go," and conditions outside the car permit immediate exit from where you are parked. If you can remember "inside" and "outside," that should cue you to cut out unnecessary idling. You can save gallons of gasoline with this simple procedure. If you cut just minutes a day of unnecessary idling from your driving, they could add up to 30 hours a year. A medium-size V-8 engine can use up to 1 gallon of gas for each hour it idles. Multiply that by 30 hours per year and you have saved 30 gallons of gasoline.

That's a nifty saving for breaking just one of your old driving habits, and it doesn't include an even more important saving—the wear you eliminate by cutting out one of the most severe engine operations, warm or cold engine idling.

Severe Service: Hazardous to Your Car's Health

In all automotive literature, no two words are more important than "severe service." This term does not mean Marine Corps boot camp, the severe service I am talking about is a more insidious kind, one that can play havoc with your car's longevity and performance.

What, then, does severe service mean, and how does it affect your car?

The American Petroleum Institute (API) defines severe service as car operations that are more severe than others and that place greater demands on the motor oil and car. The API considers the following to be severe-service operations:

○ Trips that are less than 10 miles

○ Driving in dust or sand

○ Cold weather, which prevents complete engine warm-up

○ Idling for extended periods

○ Pulling trailers

○ Operating in any other heavy-duty manner.

That last one is a bit confusing, but it means driving conditions that taxis, delivery vehicles, or police cars encounter.

Car manufacturers also consider the following hazardous to your car's health:

○ Chrysler says severe-service conditions include "more than 50 percent operation at sustained speeds over 70 mph during hot weather."

○ Volvo says "sustained hill climbing" should be considered a severe-service operation.

○ Nissan adds "Driving in areas using road salt or other corrosive materials; driving on rough and/or muddy roads; and driving in high-humidity areas or in mountainous areas."

These severe-service operations sum up the automotive industry's thinking on what types of operations are toughest on your car. If prolonged, any one of them will put the grim reaper on early standby.

Let's listen to API again: "Severe service operations represent the type of driving done by most motorists. One of the most frequent and severe types of driving is short trips with many stops and starts. For his protection, the motorist should recognize these severe-service operations and follow the recommendations of the manufacturers."

What are these recommendations? The most important is changing the motor oil more frequently. If you spend considerable driving time in any of the above conditions (or any combination of them), the oil should be changed according to the manufacturer's oil-change schedule for severe-service operations. The "ideal" change schedule should be ignored. The other major recommendation is to avoid driving in as many of the severe-service conditions as is practical.

Study these severe-service operations. Get to know them. Whenever possible, try to eliminate them when you drive. Remember that frequent oil changes are your first line of defense.

Pedal to the Metal Wreaks Havoc with Your Engine

On an episode of the old television show "The Dukes of Hazzard" (No, no, I didn't really watch it!), the inimitable Boss Hogg growled at Sheriff

Roscoe that he'd better "put the heel to the steel." Roscoe glanced at Boss and stuttered, "That's pedal to the metal, Boss."

Either way, "heel to the steel" and "pedal to the metal" mean flooring the accelerator pedal. The antics of Boss and Roscoe aside, it's bad news for your car and your wallet.

If a car is standing still or moving at a slow speed and the accelerator is suddenly floored (the epitome of a classic jackrabbit start), the engine undergoes a trauma not unlike an overweight person trying to break 10 seconds in the 100-yard dash. This simple action wreaks havoc with any engine, big or small, and puts tremendous strain on the transmission and rear axle.

The highest temperatures and pressures an engine will experience come about as the result of sudden flooring of the gas pedal. Vital wear-preventing engine oil is literally squeezed from between the moving parts; in the worst cases, metal-to-metal contact occurs and instantaneous welds are formed. In extreme cases, the engine will stop operating.

The engine oil itself is placed under severe conditions, and the additives in the oil have their backs to the walls—the cylinder walls, that is. This is when many motor oils fail, because the additives are not of sufficient quantity or quality to respond to the rigors of sudden acceleration. Under sudden, full-throttle acceleration, the polymers incorporated in motor oils to prevent wear actually stretch themselves to their limits and, because of the tremendous pressures and temperatures, they break apart and just quit, their preservative qualities used up.

Sudden acceleration also demands the most from your gasoline. Octane requirements skyrocket, and the engine labors, knocks, and pings as the gasoline tries to catch up.

Why put your car to this test? Why do it if it isn't necessary? Impress your pocketbook and not your friends. Save those full-throttle accelerations for emergencies, and you will take a giant step in preventing automobile senility.

A Cricket? Nah, It's Your AC

Listen! You can hear them all over town: "Buzz, buzz; chirp, chirp; click, click; hummm, hummm; clatter, clatter; whir, whir . . ." The sounds seem to come from everywhere, echoing from parking lots, reverberating off downtown building walls, droning from bank and fast-food drive-in lanes.

Yep, it's summertime, and those sounds are as familiar as the hot weather that accompanies them. Crickets? Toads? Cicadas? Nope, it's not the sound of dormant insect and animal life aroused by the summer rains; it's the sound of cars idling with their air conditioners on.

A car, AC on, idling unnecessarily in the heat, is a car whose owner isn't interested in its well-being. Engineers consider any idling car to be laboring under severe service conditions. Idling with the AC on in the heat is much worse. It qualifies for the special category of "super-severe service." It is one of the most stringent forms of punishment that can be inflicted upon an engine.

Idling with the AC on in high outside heat causes the internal engine temperature to skyrocket. The engine's efforts to cool itself are handicapped by the extra horsepower it must produce to run the AC. This is particularly crucial for small, four-cylinder cars in which the air conditioner gobbles a disproportionate amount of the engine power available.

Now, I'm not advocating driving around without the air conditioner on; there are better places to take a sauna. I am suggesting sensible use of the AC, especially when the car must sit and idle.

Are you aware that in many cars, you can turn off the AC, but the blower will continue to furnish residual cool air to the driver's compartment? Take advantage of this free cool air when you are in situations where you cannot shut off the engine (traffic lights and other mandatory stops or slowdowns). If you anticipate a delay, turn the AC off but leave the blower on. This eases the load on the engine and allows it to run cooler and more efficiently, and you will still get cool air for a minute or two. When you start moving again, turn the AC back on.

Once the car is moving, the bite of the AC is much less painful because the engine has built up sufficient rpms to offset the additional power necessary to turn the AC unit. In fact, at highway speeds the AC (although still taking a chunk out of your gas mileage) will inflict little or no wear on the engine.

If the car must idle, always ask yourself, "Is running the air conditioner really necessary?" Many drivers lock their cars and leave the engine and the AC on while they dash to the post office or convenience store. The car is nice and cool when they return, but the engine is broiling and pays a dear price for the owner's brief respite from the heat. Park in the shade when you can, turn off the engine and AC when you can, walk when you can, and use the AC on/off method when you can't do any of the above.

And leave the chirping, humming, and buzzing to the summer creatures.

Scouting Reports

In the old days it was common practice for the cavalry to send Indian scouts ahead of the troops to prepare an advance report on what conditions could be expected. Information about a wide or deep river, precipitous cliffs, hostile Indians, little or no water, and other conditions that would affect the main party was vital.

Lewis and Clark had their scouts, and the Lone Ranger had Tonto. You can be your own scout to help you and your car work better. A scouting report on conditions around your car supplies valuable information even before you open the door.

Look around the car before getting in. Are there going to be any problems pulling out? Is there a telephone pole, a sign or a low wall nearby that might be hard to see from the driver's seat? Is another driver getting ready to pull out? Noting this could save you a bumper-to-bumper confrontation.

If you are parked on a busy street, check the traffic flow before getting in and starting the car. No sense letting the engine idle if you know you can't pull out. If it is dark and you are parked in an unfamiliar area, there is no better time to check conditions around the car. It has saved me a dent or two. There are many other examples, but you get the idea.

Checking out the situation is something anyone can do. No mechanical knowledge is necessary, just common sense and an observant eye. A minor thing, you say? Not by a long shot. Remember, you start your car several thousand times each year. If you take a few seconds to do advance scouting, you and the car will be better for it.

By practicing this simple technique you will eliminate hours of unnecessary idling and cut down measurably on engine wear. You will reduce fuel costs and boost your average miles per gallon. Your car will spew less pollution. You will cut your chances of getting involved in a parking-lot scuffle with another car or backing into an otherwise hard-to-see object. On a thoroughfare, you will have a much better idea of when it is safe to pull into traffic.

All of this will make your insurance company happy, too, and your rates should reflect its glee. You will become a safer, healthier, more efficient driver because you took a few seconds to scout around before getting into the car.

3

Motor oil, additives, & solid lubricants

WHICH IS THE BEST OIL FOR YOUR CAR? Motor oil is one of the most common automotive products, yet it is also the least understood and most mysterious. Knowing what the oil is and what it does can help owners choose the right one for their cars. We see oils every day: at the gas station, in supermarkets, at convenience stores. But how much do most people know about them other than the car needs oil to operate?

The most important physical property of a motor oil is its viscosity, which is the measure of how thick or thin—or, if you prefer, how heavy or light—the oil is. It is a numerical indicator of how easily the oil will flow. High-viscosity oils (high numbers) are thick, flow slowly, and have a honeylike consistency. Low-viscosity oil (low numbers) are thin and flow more readily—like milk, if you will.

Printed on top of every oilcan is information you should know. Let's look at a typical oil found in today's market. A glance at the top of the can reveals that it is an SAE 10W-30. What does this mean?

The letters "SAE" stand for Society of Automotive Engineers, the group that started the viscosity-classification system. The numbers and letter immediately following SAE refer to the viscosity of the oil in the can.

Single-grade or single-"weight" oils are the simplest to grade, because they have only one number. Currently, these range from 5W (the thinnest) to 50 (the thickest). If the designation SAE 40 appears on a can, it means that the oil is a 40 viscosity—nothing more, nothing less. It is important to know that the SAE system defines the viscosity *only* and gives no other information about the oil. If a "W" appears after a number it signifies that the oil is especially suited for winter use, the "W" denoting winter.

Multigrade oils also fit into the SAE classification. Multigrade means that the oil is capable of assuming different viscosities under different temperatures. In the case of the SAE 10W-30, it is a 10W when cold and becomes a 30 upon warming. A single-grade oil (one number only) cannot change viscosities; it is stuck with the one number for life. Multigrades can and do change; they are the Jekyll and Hyde of motor oils.

Current available multigrade oils range from a 5W-15 to a 20W-50, the former used in extremely cold climates, the latter for hot-weather driving.

Multigrades have the ability to offer engine protection over a whole spectrum of temperature variations, whereas a single-grade oil is quite limited.

The SAE viscosity-classification system is simple, direct, uncomplicated. The lower the number, the thinner the oil; the higher the number, the thicker. Multigrades (more than one number in the designation) can be both.

Read Any Good Oilcans Lately?

Read any good books lately? How about a good oilcan? You might not want to curl up in bed with a good oilcan, but read it you should. Let's dig out a typical oilcan and see what is printed on top of the can. Besides being an SAE 10W-30 (we talked about this viscosity classification system in an earlier column), we see that this particular oil is rated "API Service SG/CC."

API stands for American Petroleum Institute, the group that began this grading system. The word "service" means that the oil satisfies requirements of a particular service category—in this case, SG/CC.

SG means the oil is a service "G"-rated oil. CC shows that the oil also meets the additional commercial "C" requirements, thus the CC.

This system originated with the SA category of oils, which were nothing more than straight mineral oil. Next came SB. These oils had a few engine-protection additives, allowing for their higher rating. SA and SB oils were the original non-detergent oils. SC oils were the first "detergent" oils available to the public, and this rating qualified them to provide warranty protection for all new 1964-67 automobiles. In other words, if you bought a new car during those years, you were required by the manufacturer to use an SC oil to maintain the new car's warranty.

SD oils were a step above the SCs, providing extra protection against engine deposits, rust, corrosion, and wear. These were introduced in 1968 and afforded warranty protection for 1968-70 model year cars. Again, these oils offered additional engine protection when compared with their predecessors: SA, SB, and SC.

SE took its bow in 1971 and was required for warranty protection in cars bought between 1971 and 1979.

SF oils provide warranty protection for 1980-to-1989 vehicles. They contain extra antiwear and oxidation additives, not found in the SE oils. SG oils are the latest category and offer warranty protection for 1989 to present car models.

Any oil that is listed higher alphabetically can always replace a lower one: SG oils can be used in place of SE or SF oils, for instance, but the reverse is not true; an SE or SF cannot replace an SG. Using a lower-rated oil can void a warranty and seriously damage the engine.

Some current oil containers might be marked something like "API Service SD, SE, SF, SG, CC, CD." This is just the oil company's way of making the oil look impressive, but all it really means is that the oil is an SG/CC and is capable of replacing all the lower indicated categories. Be concerned only with the highest rating on the can.

So what about the CC stuff?

Any C designation means the oil is also suited for commercial use; translated, this means for use in diesel-engine cars and trucks. These also start with the lower CA rating and go up to a CE. The same rules apply: Never replace a higher category with a lower one and vice versa. CE is the latest "diesel" category and contains extra engine-protecting additives when compared with any of the prior commercial-rated oils.

So the "API Service SG/CC" designation means that the oil is a Service G-rated oil, which also meets the commercial C requirements. This means it can be safely used in all gasoline engines and in certain diesel engines that call for a CC-rated oil.

Closer scrutiny of the top of the can might reveal further information. The words "energy conserving," "friction modified," or "fuel saving" might be there. These designations mean that the oil has additional friction modifier (compared to conventional oil) that will help the engine run more efficiently and save fuel.

Other lettering might also appear—for instance, "Mil-L-46152" or "GM 6048M." These are military (Mil) or car manufacturer's (General Motors, in this instance) tests the oil has met. For our purposes, pay them no heed; they are window dressing on the can. Any oil that meets the SG/CC-CD requirements will automatically meet any military or car-manufacturer's specifications.

A Can of Oil Is Not Campbell's Soup

A can of oil contains more than just oil. A lot of other ingredients—the absence of which would cause most automobile engines to wear rapidly—are in that can. Unlike Campbell's Soup, the ingredients won't be listed on the can's label. Unfortunately, there is no truth-in-labeling law for oil.

You can't tell how much or how many of these ingredients are in the can; you can't compare Brand A with Brand B for content. You are caught between the oil company's blandishments and your own personal experimentation in deciding on an oil for your car.

All current motor oils (except SA-rated) contain additives. The additives can account for anywhere from 1 percent to more than 33 percent of the total volume in the can. No two manufacturers blend the same additives in the same amounts. Each has it own closely guarded secret blending arrangement. Oils that meet current American Petroleum Institute SG requirements (we explained the API system in a recent column) have varying amounts of some or all of the following additives; the better oils have them all.

Pour point depressants These aren't something that shuts off the spout of your bourbon bottle, but chemicals that permit the oil to flow freely in cold weather. Any oil with a "W" (winter) in its SAE viscosity number (10W-30) will have extra amounts of this additive.

Oxidation and bearing corrosion inhibitors Such inhibitors reduce the rate of oxidation (deterioration) of the oil and prevent corrosion in sensitive bearing materials.

Rust and corrosion inhibitors Just as baking soda will neutralize stomach acid, these additives will neutralize engine acids. The rust inhibitors also cover metal parts with a tough film that locks out water and moisture.

Detergent and dispersant additives Like dishwashing detergents, these dig out dirt and keep it suspended until it can be drained away.

Anti-foam agents These minimize formation of bubbles in the oil by causing them to burst quickly.

Anti-wear additives These prevent friction and wear under milder conditions of engine operation.

Extreme-pressure additives Similar to the anti-wear additives, these work best under high temperatures and heavy engine loads. They form an elastic film over metal parts that helps prevent metal-to-metal contact.

Viscosity index improvers These make possible the multigrade oils. They help the oil stay thick when hot and thin when cold.

Friction-reducing additives These do what their name implies—reduce internal engine friction. They are found in oil that bears "energy conserving," "fuel saving," or similar designations.

So oil isn't just oil, but a complete blending of the base oil with any number and amount of additives. The SG-rated oils will contain more additives when compared with lower-rated (SC, SD, SE, SF) oils, but two different brands of SG-rated oils can themselves vary dramatically in additive content, demonstrating again that no two oils are really alike.

The Right Oil for Your Engine

One of the most important decisions any car owner will make is choosing the correct viscosity oil for the engine, and there is a bewildering array of numbers to select from.

Low-viscosity numbers mean the car will have little protection under heat, high-speed, and high-engine loads. High-viscosity numbers could let the engine wear abnormally under cold-start and warm-up conditions.

Correct viscosity ensures better performance, fuel economy, and total engine life. How, then, does the motorist know which is the viscosity for his or her car?

All car owners' manuals contain the manufacturer's recommendations for the viscosity to use under various temperature conditions. These are important, and no two will be the same because no two engines are built the same. Dig that owner's manual out of the glove compartment, dust it off, and open it to the section that contains the "Recommended Viscosity Chart."

In the summer, look closely at the given viscosities for higher temperatures; in winter, check the colder end of the chart. One manufacturer might give only one or two viscosities as being suitable for use in temperatures around the 100°F mark, while another might give five or six choices. In the case of viscosity selection, what's good for Peter may not be good for Paul.

This is even more important if yours is a diesel engine because, in many instances, the manufacturer will recommend only one viscosity for all temperatures. Don't disregard this owner's-manual information; it is important when it comes to your engine. Don't try to outguess the manufacturer and use what your dad or granddad used. No one knows better what should be used in a car than the people who built it.

If you are using a single-grade-viscosity oil, make sure it also falls within the chart temperature recommendations. Many manufacturers don't even list single-grade oils among those recommended. And often, when they do, they drastically limit their use.

For instance, Porsche does not recommend using a single-grade, 30-weight oil if the temperature gets above 85°F. There is nothing wrong with single-grade oils, but their use demands continual monitoring of anticipated temperatures by the user.

In the winter, no matter where you live, always use an oil that has a "W" (winter) in its viscosity number: 5W-30, for instance. A good rule of thumb to follow is never to use the same viscosity in the winter as you use in the summer.

One point to keep in mind constantly when making the viscosity/temperature choice: The oil should be chosen to meet the requirements of the highest and lowest anticipated temperatures before the next oil change, and not for the temperature of the present moment.

The Best Cold Weather Oil

Old Man Winter is beginning to apply his car-defeating cold-weather grip to cars and trucks from coast to coast. Temperatures below freezing are now the norm in many areas of the country—and this is only November, only the beginning. The worst is yet to come.

Cold, colder, coldest. If you live in one of these three climates pay close attention to this column; it will help you get your car through what is one of the toughest—if not the toughest—and most automotive wear-intensive times of the year.

Winter and cold weather, snow and ice, drizzle and sleet: They all add up to misery for the car. I guess they don't make the car owners any too happy either. But get the vehicle "over the hump" and into spring, and you have won the wear war for another year.

If you want to get your car through the cold with minimum damage this is the perfect time to switch to a low-viscosity multigrade oil. An SAE 5W-30 is just about perfect for all but the warmest winter climates. You should not be using a single-weight 20 or 30 oil if you live in an area where temperatures fall below freezing on a regular basis.

Here's why a 5W-30 is best. As many of you know, a 5W-30 is one of a class of oils designated as "multigrade." The numbers simply indicate the range of viscosity the oil is capable of achieving when it is cold or warm. In our example, it is thin (5W) when cold, and thicker (30) when warm. It's the thin (or 5W) part we are interested in.

If you opened a can of 30-weight oil and a can of 5-weight oil (if they sold such a thing) and let them run at the mouth, it wouldn't take long to notice the 5W can was empty while the 30 was still pouring. Why? Simply because the 5W is thinner than the 30. Water pours faster than honey.

A 5W-30 lets you put both oils in your crankcase at the same time. The thin 5W gives your engine its best protection against premature wear of the cold start, especially on cold winter mornings. The 5W oil flows easily. Engineers would say it has superior pumpability when compared to a thicker, 30-weight oil. That simply means the oil pump can push and spread the oil around faster than the thick oil.

When you turn the key on a cold morning and the engine fires up, the oil-pressure light will go off or your oil-pressure gauge will show a normal reading. But that isn't proof positive that all parts of the engine are receiving lubricant. Most likely they are not. The "normal" reading indicates the oil pump is operating at correct pressure, but that doesn't ensure that all engine parts are being lubricated. It can take more than 30 seconds in some engines for oil to make its way through all the passages to the remotest parts of the engine. In the meantime, these parts are "dry running."

If you are using a heavier weight oil, especially a single grade, the problem is compounded. The heavier and thicker oil can't be moved as effectively by the oil pump; consequently, it takes longer for it to reach all engine areas. Once it does arrive, it is still on the gooey side and its immediate lubrication potential is questionable.

Not so with a 5W oil. It has good cold-weather pumpability. It is thin and can therefore move fast. And, once it gets to where it's going, it lubricates even minimal-clearance parts effectively. That's what you want for your car. And that's why you should be using a multigrade 5W-30 oil for winter driving.

In addition to its thinness and pumpability, the "W" designation right after the 5 stands for Winter. It means the oil has been specifically formulated with cold-weather driving in mind.

When your engine finally reaches normal operating temperature, the thin, 5W viscosity, through the magic of polymer chemistry, turns into a heavier, 30-weight, and that's just what the doctor ordered for protection against the higher internal heat of the warmed-up engine.

The period just after starting a cold engine car is probably the most wear-intensive of any. Couple it with cold weather and you have a double whammy operating against your car. Having a 5W-30 oil—be certain it's the latest API-SG rated—takes the edge off cold-weather, cold-start wear by ensuring the engine receives vital lubricant when and where it needs it.

What's Good For Peter . . . .

It's unfortunate that motor oils aren't covered by a truth-in-labeling law. Knowing exactly what is in the can would help each of us make an informed decision when choosing this important lubricant. But reading the labels as they now exist can help.

We know that all motor oils aren't created equal, that they aren't all the same. We know that some motor oils work better and are formulated to perform under more adverse driving conditions than we usually encounter on a daily basis. But what may be good for Peter may not be good for Paul and vice versa. Let me explain.

What most people don't know, and where many maintenance-conscious car owners make a mistake, is that oils formulated with additional additives to protect against severe driving conditions might not be good for your car when driven under everyday conditions.

What prompts this discussion is a conversation I overheard recently while having a cup of coffee at the counter of an interstate truck stop. A couple of guys were talking over the merits of different brands and types of oil. One of them mentioned that he uses nothing but racing oil in his daily driving, reasoning that if the oil is good enough to tough it out in a race-car environment, it must be double- or triple-good in an everyday car.

I wanted to chime in, but kept on drinking my coffee. Now the confusing part is that what the guy said does sound logical. So why don't we all use racing oil in our cars? After all, it's readily available at most auto-supply stores.

Most of us should not use it for the simple reason that we don't drive race cars. The formulation of a racing oil is different from that of an oil made for your to-work or to-the-store car. How's that? Because a race car doesn't have to contend with some of the most destructive forces acting on your engine: moisture, contaminant buildup from slow, stop-and-go traffic, acids, and unburned hydrocarbons, to name a few.

A quality everyday oil has plenty of additives to combat these common engine ills, while a racing oil might be devoid of these protectants.

Instead it has more protection against high-speed driving stresses and high heat, something you don't usually have to worry about. It sacrifices some important low-speed and cold-engine protection to get more top-speed protection. That's exactly what a high-speed car needs—but yours doesn't.

The same goes for other oils such as those formulated for use in big-rig diesel engines. You can apply the same reasoning and it sounds great: If it protects those big, bad diesel engines, think how well it must protect my smaller gasoline-fed one. Again, this kind of reasoning is misleading. The motor oil for diesels is formulated to combat the high sulfur content (and thus acid buildup) of diesel fuels the rigs burn, and cope with the much higher compression forces at work inside the diesel. But it might lack some of the specific protection you need at lower and colder driving speeds.

So unless you drive a car that has unique motor-oil requirements, leave the racing and diesel oils and the superhigh performance oils alone. They are meant to be used in those types of cars, not in the '79 Chevy you bought from Uncle Charlie.

"Energy Conserving": What Does it Mean?

Do you know what the words "Energy Conserving" or "Energy Conserving II" stand for on a can or bottle of motor oil? Are these words something a car owner should consider when trying to choose the best motor oil for his or her car? Should you consider an Energy Conserving (EC) or Energy Conserving II (ECII) oil instead of one that carries no such designation? Are these oils, as their names imply, really energy conserving and, if so, what exactly does that mean?

According to the American Petroleum Institute (API), "Engine oils categorized as energy conserving are formulated to improve the fuel economy of passenger cars, vans, and light-duty trucks. These oils have produced a fuel economy improvement of 1.5 percent or greater over a standard reference oil in a standard test procedure. Oils meeting this requirement display the Energy Conserving label in the lower portion of the donut-shaped API Service Symbol."

Oils that carry the Energy Conserving II label have been tested and show a fuel economy improvement of 2.7 percent or greater when tested the same way as the Energy Conserving oils. In other words, when these oils are tested and compared to a similar oil (standard reference oil) without an Energy Conserving designation, they will improve gas mileage by 2.7 percent or better.

So shouldn't everyone be using these energy-conserving oils? In my book, they should. For instance, if you are now averaging 20 mpg with a standard, non-energy-conserving oil, switching to one of like viscosity but with an energy-conserving designation will up your mileage to 20.3 mpg or greater. If you use an Energy Conserving II oil, the improvement is even more substantial: 20.54 mpg. OK, that might not sound like such a big deal, but if you have a 15-gallon tank, that means you will be able to travel an extra 8.1 miles free when you use the ECII oil. That's like getting an extra half gallon or more of gas free with every fill-up. And the best part is it doesn't cost you a big cash layout.

When the above API quote referred to the API Service Symbol "donut" it means the donut-shaped symbol found on all recently produced oil containers that shows the weight or SAE (Society of Automotive Engineers) viscosity number of the oil in the center, or hole of the donut, the API Service Classification at the top of the donut itself, and either "Energy Conserving," "Energy Conserving II," or a blank space on the bottom half of the donut. In other words, everything you need to know about the oil is displayed in that donut.

Although it has been proved that the energy-conserving oils will save you gasoline, what doesn't show up in these tests—or inside the donut symbol—is the fact that these oils will also help reduce engine wear. *And* less wear and more miles per gallon also mean fewer pollutants coming out the exhaust pipe. Sounds like a winner all around.

There's an unwritten rule, originally unwritten by me many years ago, that says: "Anything that helps save gasoline will reduce engine wear, and anything that reduces engine wear will save gasoline." Of course, as with any rule, there are exceptions, and this one is no different. But the exceptions are rare.

So by using an EC or ECII oil you also fight engine deterioration. Now that you know what Energy Conserving and Energy Conserving II mean, what say we all go out there and start saving some energy? It's about the most painless way to do it I know of.

Who said there's no gain without pain?

Synthetic Oil: What it Is, What it Does

Synthetic oils have intrigued drivers since their introduction a couple of decades ago, and there are still many misconceptions about them. Are they better than conventional mineral oils? Can you really keep them in the engine for 15,000 to 25,000 miles? Will they give you better gas mileage or help the engine last longer? These are but a few of the questions I get about synthetic oils. Here, then, are some answers.

What is synthetic oil? As its name implies, it's an oil made with some type of manmade base fluid, usually an ester or some similar synthetic. Conventional motor oils have a mineral-oil base; in other words, they are made from the black stuff that comes out of the ground.

"Can I really drive my car for 15,000 miles or 25,000 miles before I change the synthetic oil?" Yes and no, depending on the type of driving you do. One thing to remember: Those extended intervals promised by most synthetic oils are for what is considered "normal" driving. But no one drives "normally" anymore. Engineers usually define only one mode as normal: driving down a paved highway at 55 mph in a dust-free envi-

ronment on a sunny, 78-degree day. When was the last time you drove normally?

So look closely at the oil-drain intervals suggested by the manufacturer. Look for the more realistic "severe service" interval. You'll note that those high-mileage drain intervals are much, much shorter.

"Can synthetics hurt my engine?" Again, yes and no. If used properly in an engine in good shape (preferably one with less than 50,000 miles), no. But if the engine has a lot of miles on it or has been mistreated, switching from mineral-based oil to synthetic could cause the engine to start using more oil. Synthetics have a higher detergent factor than conventional mineral oils and can loosen sludge, dirt, and carbon deposits that might have kept the oil from leaking into the cylinders. Take these away and you have a cleaner engine, but it now uses oil.

"Will synthetics improve my gas mileage or help my engine last longer?" Providing the engine is in good condition when synthetic oil is first used, yes to both. Synthetics, in general, have a lower coefficient of friction than regular oil and thus generate less internal engine friction. That means the engine works easier and wears less.

"Can synthetics be used in a new car?" If it were my car, I would break it in using mineral oil. In fact, I would not begin using synthetics until after 5,000 or so miles. Why? Because the superslippery nature of synthetics could interfere with the proper breaking in of the engine. The parts might not be given the opportunity to wear and "mate" properly and grind their best working surfaces.

Another reason to wait: New-car manufacturers don't differentiate between synthetic and mineral oils when it comes to warranty requirements. Even though you are using synthetic oil, the car manufacturer says you must change it in accordance with its warranty requirements. Synthetics are up to four times more expensive than conventional oils, so that could mean pouring money down the drain, especially in new cars that require an oil change after only a thousand or so miles.

"Are synthetics compatible with mineral-based oils? In other words, can I mix them?" They are compatible, but why would you want to mix them? The best advice is to stick to one or the other. If you insist, you can get some benefits of a synthetic by adding a quart to your normal oil change.

"Are synthetics superior to conventional mineral oils?" They are superior in a couple of important areas, such as their added protection against high engine heat and the oxidation and engine-destroying contaminants associated with it. Second, their additive packages (the chemicals in the oil that protect against wear and tear) are less likely to be depleted by use.

"Are synthetics worth the extra cost?" Depends. If you live in a dusty area where frequent oil changes are the rule, using synthetic oil would be a waste of money. If you do a lot of highway driving or drive in high-heat areas, the extra price might be worth the added protection and miles you get.

Do I use synthetic oil? Not yet. With more than 350,000 trouble- and repair-free miles on one car and over 225,000 on the other, I see no value in switching at this time.

Super-Severe Service Requires Frequent Oil Changes

I have mentioned in several columns that changing oil according to the owner's manual severe-service change interval is the best way to guarantee a long-lived engine: You replace the old oil before it can do any harm. There are, however, a number of instances when you should take additional precautions and change the oil more often than even the stringent severe-service intervals.

If you do a lot of driving on dusty or dirty roads, more frequent oil changes should be the rule. An engine operating in "normal" air will draw in about .04 grams of dust per hour of operation. That same engine running over dusty roads will ingest about 87 grams of dust per hour—almost 2,200 times the amount it swallows when breathing normal air! That's a lot of abrasives. Much of this dust, dirt, grit, and sand finds its way into the engine oil, where it is circulated and wears on internal parts.

Remember that abrasive wear is one of the most prevalent causes of engine failure and take special safeguards against it. If you must drive over dirt roads, more frequent oil changes should be at the top of your car-maintenance list. How frequent? Depending on how "dirty" your driving is, at least 20 percent and up to 50 percent more frequently than the severe-service recommendations.

If you are caught in a dust storm and must drive any distance in it, be sure to have the oil flushed out at the first chance, even if you changed it just before encountering the storm.

Other super-severe-service conditions:

○ *Pulling a trailer.* If you plan to pull a trailer any distance (more than 1,000 miles), one of the best things you can do is change the oil immediately before and after the pull.

○ *City driving in the summer with the air-conditioner on.* Change oil according to the severe-service interval minus 20 percent. If your owner's manual recommends every 3,000 miles, it should be cut to every 2,400 miles.

High-heat operation with the air-conditioner on, trailer pulling, especially in the summer or in mountainous country, and dusty roads or dust-storm conditions—all call for super-severe-service provisions if you want maximum protection for your car.

Highway Driving Means Fewer Oil Changes

A while back I did a column on the proper time to change engine oil. It was followed by another column on special conditions that require even more frequent oil changes for maximum engine protection.

Since then, a number of readers have inquired if there are any circumstances when the oil can be left in longer than the severe-service interval given in the owner's manual. There are.

Highway driving in good weather at or near the speed limit is one condition that will safely allow extending the interval between oil changes. Most vacation driving falls in this category.

Another condition would be if your job entails a lot of highway driving (at least 75 percent of the total miles driven is on the highway) at or near the speed limit. In these cases, the oil-change interval can be extended by about 50 percent.

In other words, if your owner's manual recommends 3,000 miles as the severe-service oil-change interval, it can be extended to 4,500 miles, provided the above conditions are met. These are the only two conditions under which oil can be safely left in the engine for longer that the severe-service interval.

Quick Lube: Your Car Will Love You for It

A number of years ago car owners had a readily available excuse for neglecting the maintenance and servicing of their vehicles. It was a hassle to take the car to the corner service station, dealership service department, or repair shop; leave it while the work was done; and pick it up later, most likely after work or late Saturday afternoon. For those who didn't do their own oil and filter changes this was what you had to do. And it was usually a pain, or we just didn't have enough time, or we put it off—usually much longer than we should have—because we needed the use of the car.

But today's car owners have little excuse for ignoring the major mechanical components of their car and the required lubrication and/or fluid and lubricant changes or top-offs. It isn't because the cars don't require servicing anymore; they do, maybe even more so than older, more forgiving vehicles. And it isn't because everything is so simple now that we can do it ourselves, because it isn't and we don't. The reason we no longer have an excuse for neglect is the proliferation over the past few years of the 15-minute oil-and-lube centers—"quick lubes" as they are commonly called.

I don't want to sound like a commercial for these quick lubes, but I believe they do the average car owner a great service. Anyone can pop into one of these centers and, in about the 15 minutes they advertise, have his car serviced quickly and thoroughly.

A quality quick lube will not only change your oil and filter and lube the car, but it also includes a check of other important fluids and lubricants such as the brake fluid, coolant, transmission fluid, power-steering fluid, and battery electrolyte level—and they'll top them off if necessary.

And while your car is being serviced, trained personnel are keeping their eyes peeled for any obvious problems you should be aware of: a fluid leak, tires wearing improperly, a damaged muffler or catalytic converter. And because these outlets usually deal only in the lubrication and fluid-change aspects of car care, they have nothing to gain by telling you something is wrong with your car when it isn't, because someone else is going to do the repair work. This extra safety inspection might well be worth the price of the lube and oil change service alone.

Of course, as with any type of business, some quick lubes are better than others. I have personally done some work for one of the best, Chicago's Oil Express, which runs about 40 stores in the Chicago area and is now expanding nationally. If ever there was a company that put the customer first, this is it. But there are others in your area that provide excellent service.

How can you tell a good lube from a bad one? It won't take long. Look for:

- Professionalism in the way they treat you and your car
- The efficiency and time-saving service they advertise
- Cleanliness and employee neatness and courtesy
- A code of ethics
- A neat customer waiting area
- Quality, major brands of oil and replacement parts such as air and oil filters. (Many quick lubes stock oils other than their advertised major brand for those who desire a particular brand.)

What's particularly nice about quick-lube service is that you don't have to know a thing about a car to use one. Experienced personnel—the good shops will train their people thoroughly before turning them loose in the shop—should know every point on your car that needs servicing, so nothing should go lacking. To paraphrase an old Greyhound saying, you can just leave the servicing to them.

Typical prices for a complete lube, oil, and filter plus fluid check and top-off run from $14 to $24. That's a small price to pay for peace of mind. It's a small price to pay to know that your car is being given the attention it deserves at the intervals prescribed. And it's a small price to pay to keep your car in tip-top condition.

Going to a quick lube requires only a small investment in time on the part of the car owner. And for many, the time saved may be the most precious commodity of all.

So there's no excuse anymore for not having your car serviced at regular intervals. There's no excuse anymore for not having more "Drive It Forever" cars on the road. It doesn't take much time, it doesn't cost an arm and a leg, and your car will just love you for it.

Don't Wait to Add Oil

Ever since most of us were old enough to drive or were handed the keys to our very own first car, we probably were admonished by an authoritarian figure to never let the oil get more than a quart low. Many of us grew up hearing the familiar "You're almost a quart low" edict echoing from underneath the hood as a service-station attendant checked the oil.

Not letting the oil fall below the "add" or one-quart low mark on the dipstick was, and still is, an ironclad rule of automobile maintenance. Not a bad rule. However, never letting the oil fall below the half-quart-low mark would be a much better rule.

Many of the cars on the road today have small engines with correspondingly small crankcases; that is, the volume of oil the engine carries is small, as little as three quarts. If the oil level in these engines is allowed to drop to the add mark (one-quart low), the engine is running much of the time with a radically diminished oil supply, perhaps as little as two-thirds of what it could have available.

This shouldn't be allowed to happen, for the amount of oil in the crankcase directly affects how the engine runs and wears. Keep in mind that oil does more than just lubricate: It also must allow for easy starts, keep engine parts clean, reduce deposit buildup, provide a good cylinder seal for efficient combustion, reduce friction and wear, not foam when agitated by moving engine parts, and act as a primary coolant for many engine parts. Quite a list of chores.

When the engine oil level is allowed to drop into the range of the one-quart-low mark, a considerable amount of the oil's protective, anti-wear, and cooling properties is lost—pure folly in the summer heat, pure folly any time. More oil means better, efficient cooling for engine parts.

As the oil nears the add mark, less protective additives are at work in your engine. If you add before the oil level drops to the add mark, you greatly enhance the oil's protective and cooling capacity. Fresh additives and extra oil go to work immediately. Sure, it may be a bit of a bother deciding what to do with or where to put the other half quart of oil, but it shouldn't be too much trouble finding a storage place for it until it is needed. And don't worry if you don't put exactly a half quart in; you won't hurt anything. The important thing is to not let the level drop to the one-quart-low mark.

Adding oil before it reaches a quart low is a good prevention and preservation practice. I have often wondered if waiting until the oil is a quart low before adding is one of the contributing factors that have added up to making cars wear out long before their allotted time. Follow the "add when a half-quart low" rule, and you will add yet another valuable life-extension practice to your growing automobile anti-senility repertoire.

Important Facts about Oil Use

Engine oil consumption has always intrigued me. We tend to judge a car's worth and potential longevity by how much oil it uses. There isn't a used-car buyer worth his or her salt who hasn't asked the salesman, "Does it use oil?"

The amount of oil a car consumes is a fair indication of the internal condition of the engine. If the car doesn't use oil, it is assumed that the engine is tight, has good compression, and will serve its owner for many years.

But sometimes the source of oil consumption can be tough to put your finger on. Recent experiments by Ford Motor Co. have shed light on a few ways an engine in good condition can use oil. Testing was done using commercially available 10W-30 oils in a Ford 1.6-liter, 4-cylinder, overhead-cam engine.

Now remember, we're not talking about an engine blowing out oil because its rings or valve seals are shot. By consumption we're talking about oil used up by the engine, and this can happen in two ways:

1. The oil can be combusted in the engine (that is, burned along with the gasoline).
2. The oil becomes vaporized and passes out of the engine through the exhaust system as an oil aerosol.

But in the Ford experiments the loss of oil through oil-aerosol formation accounted for less than 0.1 percent of the total oil consumed, an insignificant amount. What other things did the experiments uncover?

Well, the amount of oil used was directly related to engine speed. At 1,750 rpm the test engine consumed a little more than half a quart of oil per 10,000 miles. But when the engine speed was upped to 3,500 rpm—equivalent to high-speed interstate cruising for many 4-cylinder cars—the consumption increased to about 1.5 quarts per 10,000 miles, about triple the amount used at slower speeds.

Another notable phenomenom was that the amount of oil consumed was related to the engine coolant temperature: The hotter the coolant, the higher the oil consumption. What this means is that the cooler the engine runs the less oil it will consume.

And when the oil was changed, the initial oil consumption proved to be quite high, stabilizing only after about five hours of engine running time. Most of the fresh oil used during this period went through the positive crankcase ventilation (PCV) system, which sucked the most volatile portion of the oil through the PCV apparatus into the combustion chamber where it was burned. The study suggested that this high initial burning of fresh oil is mostly a function of the brand of oil you use.

That's all fine and good, but how does this information affect us? Well, it tells us some ways oil is consumed and offers clues as to what we can do to avoid it. We know that lowering highway speeds will reduce oil consumption in two ways. Slower speed means the car runs cooler, and a cooler engine uses less oil. And because oil use is a direct function of engine speed, when you decrease your highway speed you will reduce oil consumption.

And we know that we can expect the first five hours of engine operation after an oil change to be the time of highest oil consumption, and that this is directly related to the type of oil we use. We can try switching brands to reduce the initial oil consumption.

But what the study doesn't tell us is that when we switch brands we should expect even more consumption after the first oil change, and that we should use the same oil for two consecutive changes to get an accurate reading on the amount we are using.

In everyday language, these technical probes into oil use can help us find the best oil, consumption-wise, for our cars and teach us ways to drive that not only reduce the amount of oil we use and pollutants we spew into the air, but will also, if we choose to run our cars at lower speeds, help make the highways a safer place.

The Mystery of the Missing Oil

You've got this mysterious problem with your car and can't figure out what's causing it. You've asked 10 people and received 10 different answers. It's really bugging you, so you drop me a line. A number of you, with exactly the same problem, have done just that. I can see why it has baffled both novice and mechanic alike.

Your car never uses oil. You change it regularly every 3,000 miles or so. The car is seldom driven at high speeds and is used almost exclusively for in-town chores. A lot of slow stop-and-go coupled with extensive periods of idling is typical.

So the new 65 mph limit comes into being and you decide to take the old buggy out for a spin. Blow some carbon out of the engine and give it a little run at the legal limit.

After an hour or two of highway driving you stop, get gas, and ask the attendant to check the oil. To your amazement it turns out to be 2 quarts low. That can't be, you think, this car doesn't use oil. You check it yourself. Yep, 2 quarts low and you've only gone about 100 miles.

You replace the missing oil and drive back to town, apprehensive about checking the oil level for fear it will be 2 quarts low again. Something must have happened to the engine during the trip to cause the car to use that much oil. But when you check, lo and behold, the oil is up to the full mark. What in the world is going on?

The answer lies in your suspicion that something during the trip caused the car to use oil. You're right, but for the wrong reasons. Although you never knew it, your car has always used oil, but its usage was never evident because the crankcase replenished itself with—no, not oil—unburned fuel and other combustion by-products. This not only diluted the oil in the crankcase, but also made it appear full.

Your city-only driving continued to produce lots of unburned fuel and never provided the opportunity for the contaminants to burn off. When you took the car out on the highway and got it going 65 mph for an extended period, the volatile contaminants were, for the first time, heated to a high enough temperature to allow them to boil off. What happened?

Bingo! The 2 quarts of "false oil" were gone before you could say Jack Robinson. The highly diluted oil, quite thin and low in viscosity, had little resistance to the rigors of high-speed driving and was rapidly used up.

Why didn't another 2 quarts boil off on the return trip? Because by then most of the volatile contaminants had boiled off, and the 2 fresh quarts you added were providing true protection. Fresh oil is not as easily burned off as the volatile hydrocarbons that had accumulated.

Add to this the fact that high-speed driving will burn oil much faster than slow driving and you have the reasons why your car suddenly began to use oil. Remember that a gasoline engine can use up to seven times the amount of engine oil at 70 mph as it uses at 40 mph.

Best advice here: Change the oil more frequently when doing in-town-only driving. Always change it before a trip. Try upping the viscosity by at least 10 numbers; if you are using 10W-30 for city driving, change it to 10W-40 for that highway trip.

Petroleum Distillates: Grisly Business for Your Car's Engine

Let's see now, how does one write about such a delicate subject? Hmmmm. Well, I guess you just go ahead and do it, so here goes.

When I was a little kid my mother would occasionally have to give me one. I hated 'em. And the few times I had to go to the hospital some gruff nurse would wake me up at an ungodly hour and give me one prior to going under the knife. Embarrassment city. Adulthood didn't diminish my dislike for them.

Sure, I'm talking about enemas—I told you it was a tough subject to broach.

Why a discussion of enemas in a car column? Because many car owners have been smitten with giving just that to their vehicle's engines. Car enemas? Don't laugh, it's true. That is exactly what these owners are doing. Sounds grisly and it is. And their cars, for the most part, feel the same way about them as I did—and still do. Let me explain.

A number of products on the market claim to purge engines of all impurities, thus making them run smoother, quieter, and longer. They have a variety of names, but all have one important thing in common: They contain *petroleum distillates*, chemicals that do the purging.

Petroleum distillates come in all forms and are, as their name implies, chemical compounds that are by-products distilled from the breaking up of petroleum during the gasoline-making process. When added to the oil they can rid the engine of gums, varnishes, grime, and even some carbon. After using these products the engine is clean as a whistle.

At first glance this doesn't seem all bad; in fact, it seems like a good thing. The powerful internal cleansing action of various types of petroleum distillates leaves an engine clean, but "clean" can be a two-edged sword. In older engines that have logged 60,000 miles or more, many "false seals" have been deposited. These seals (some type of postcombustion product) are usually deposited in the piston/cylinder area and prevent oil from entering the combustion chamber and burning off. In fact, one major car manufacturer has recently claimed that in some cases these deposits or false seals help the engine run better.

But many car owners have complained about excessive oil use after using one of these distillate-based engine enemas. What has happened is that the purgative action of the additive has cleaned away the false seals, and now oil flows freely and is burned in the combustion chamber along with the gasoline. There is also a general loosening of internal engine parts when the false seals are purged.

With newer engines, in which seals haven't had time to become established, the symptoms are not as obvious. But then, in a newer engine, you shouldn't use a strong cleanser in the first place. High-quality, high-detergent gasoline, coupled with frequent oil changes using high-quality detergent oil, is all you need to keep the engine sparkling clean.

In my opinion, these engine-cleaning treatments should never be used in older engines, and their use in newer engines should be limited to times when an experienced mechanic thinks their action might be beneficial to cleaning up premature carbon buildup on the cylinder heads. In these limited instances better engine performance can be obtained by their use. But as a general rule, if the label reads "Contains Petroleum Distillates," tread with caution.

Remember, your engine feels the same way you and I did when Mom said during one of those childhood crises, "OK, dear, it's time for your . . ." Boy, it *is* tough to write about those things!

Solid Lubricants for Trouble-Free Engines

I have always been a firm believer in adding some type of solid lubricant supplement every time I change my oil. For many years now I have added either a molybdenum disulfide (moly), graphite, or polytetrafluoroethylene (PTFE) supplement when changing oil. Perhaps the longevity of some of my vehicles and their trouble-free engine performance can be attributed largely to these solid lubricants that provide additional engine-wear protection while they reduce internal engine friction. My old Volvo now has over 350,000 miles without a single engine repair; my even older Volkswagen bus has over 200,000 miles on its little air-cooled engine—again, without any major repairs.

Solid lubricants are just what their names imply: nonliquid lubricants that are added to the oil (or transmission fluid or rear axle fluid) and enhance the fluid's lubricating and protective properties. These solid lubricants bond themselves to, and fill the microscopic cavities in, the metal surfaces inside the units to which they are added. The protective film reduces friction between sliding and rotating parts, enabling the mechanical unit to give better performance with less effort and wear. Picture someone stretching an impervious layer of Saran Wrap over each engine part. They work something like that.

But to do it properly, each of these solid lubricants must be colloidally suspended in the oil. If they are not, the particles of solid lubricant tend to agglomerate and settle out to the bottom of the container or, once in your motor oil, settle out in the crankcase. That's why I always caution against using any product that tells you to "shake well" before using. If you have to shake the can to mix the product before use, what's going to happen to it once it's inside the engine? You guessed it—a lot of it will settle out somewhere where it does little good and can do a lot of harm. Unless you are strong enough to shake your whole car before using it, stay away from these products, even if they do contain moly, graphite, or PTFE.

A colloidal suspension, on the other hand, means the particles of moly or graphite or PTFE are milled to super-small particle size, usually less than 5 microns, and preferably about 1 micron. (A *micron* is one-millionth of a meter.) These small particles are easily suspended in the carrier oil and will not migrate to the bottom of the container or the bottom of your engine.

Numerous lubrication and *tribology* (the study of the relationships of friction, lubrication, and wear) studies vividly demonstrate that all three of these products can increase fuel economy and reduce wear of the engine, transmission, and rear axle or transaxle. Unlike some oil additives, they are chemically inert and will not disturb the carefully blended additive package of the motor oil itself. On the contrary, they enhance it.

They are especially valuable during winter because they make dry lubrication-starved cold starts much easier. By placing a superslippery coating over and between moving metal parts, the engine cranks (turns over) much easier because it has less friction and drag to overcome. And the ravages of cold-start wear—during the exact time when lubrication efforts of the motor oil and the engine's oiling system are marginal—is greatly reduced.

Each of these solid lubricants has a very low coefficient of friction. They are much more slippery than motor oil and, when added to the oil, they add their low coefficient of friction to the new mixture. The lower the coefficient of friction, the less friction produced between the parts in question—in this case, the moving mechanical lubricated parts of your car.

So why don't oil companies add these solid lubricants to their oils at the processing plants? Economics. They are expensive. Of the three, moly and graphite are the least expensive; PTFE-type compounds are the most expensive.

The finished consumer-usable products range in price from about $6 to $35. Some are added with each oil change, others less frequently. Each can offer its own array of benefits to the car owner looking for economy of operation, extended engine, transmission and axle life, and money saved because of reduced operating and repair costs.

If you'd like a brief list of the brand names I have tested and personally used and feel offer a good payback, send me a self-addressed, stamped envelope in care of The Mileage Co., P.O. Box 40063, Tucson, AZ, 85717.

Solid Lubricants Encore

No column in recent years evoked as much reader reaction as the one I did about six weeks ago on solid lubricants. My offer to send a brief list of solid lubricants (molybdenum disulfide or moly, graphite, and PTFE or Teflon-type oil supplements) I have tested and used, in exchange for a SASE, brought many thousands of letters. I quit counting at 10,000. Move over, Dear Abby.

With those requests came hundreds of questions about the solid lubricants—so many and varied that I thought another column on the subject was in order.

Let's look at some of the most common questions you asked:

"Can I use a solid lubricant in my new car?" Any friction-modifying agent, and that's what solid lubricants are, should not be added to the oil while the car is breaking in, a process that takes 2,000 to 5,000 miles. After 5,000 miles they can be used.

"Can they be used in a diesel engine?" Yes, it makes no difference whether the engine is gasoline- or diesel-powered.

"I have a high-mileage car. Can I use these solid lubricants in it?" The amount of mileage on the car makes no difference; they can help prolong the life of already long-lived vehicles.

Remember, solid lubricants aren't panaceas, nor will they undo the effects of years of owner negligence. In some vehicles their effectiveness may be minimal. Before adding these products to your crankcase know exactly how many miles per gallon your car is getting, what its idle speed is, and if it is using oil. Run the car at least 1,000 miles before judging the merit of the lubricant. Although these products aren't formulated to cure oil burning, in some cases they may help reduce oil consumption.

"Can they be used in transmissions and axles also?" Yes, but there are different formulations for the engine, axle, and transmission. Be certain to use the right product in the right place. **Caution:** Do not use the axle supplements in limited-slip differentials. Check if your car has one before using one.

"Do STP or Marvel Mystery Oil contain solid lubricants?" No, they do not.

"Is Slick 50 a solid lubricant?" Yes, and, I might add, an excellent one.

"Can these products be used with synthetic oils?" Yes, they can. However, a little less improvement can be expected if you are already using a low-friction synthetic oil.

"Will the solid lubricant particles get caught in my oil filter?" Most modern oil filters trap particles in the 10- to 15-micron range. Quality

solid lubricant dispersions have particles from $1/2$ micron to 5 microns in size, small enough to pass through most oil filters. However, super-fine, specialty oil filters that claim to filter particles of 1 micron and larger are available. I would not use solid lubricants with one of these extra-fine oil filters.

"*Is it worthwhile to use a solid lubricant if I change the oil every 3,000 miles?*" I change oil every 2,000 miles or less and have used them continually for the past 15 years.

"*Do these lubricants foam when added to the respective mechanical units?*" No, they are mainly inert substances.

"*Can solid lubricants be used in 4-, 6- and 8-cylinder engines? Are they more effective in one than the other?*" They can be used in any size engine with equal effectiveness.

"*Can the axle lubricants quiet a whining in the rear end of my car?*" I'll speak from experience here. I used a moly gear supplement in a rear axle with a slight whine. That was four years ago, and the axle hasn't complained since. However, if gears are badly worn, nothing can help much.

"*Will they help free a sticky valve?*" No, they don't contain chemicals (usually petroleum distillates) needed to do internal engine cleaning or purging.

"*If I am already using a type of nonsolid oil supplement, can I change to a solid lubricant without doing any harm?*" Yes, there is no problem in switching.

"*Is there any reason you would not recommend using a solid lubricant supplement?*" None that I can think of.

"*Can I lengthen my oil-change interval when using solid lubricants?*" I wouldn't recommend it, but if you do, don't do it by more than 500 miles or so.

"*Will use of these supplements void the warranty on my new car?*" No, they don't affect new-car warranties.

Many of you were wowed by the high mileages I have achieved on two of my vehicles. Please remember, even though I have continuously used solid lubricants in these vehicles, other factors such as good driving habits, frequent oil changes, and a solid maintenance schedule played major roles in the long, trouble-free lives of my cars.

And last but not least, if you choose to use one of these solid lubricants, always follow the instructions on the product label.

4

Everything you need to know about gasoline

IT'S LATE AT NIGHT in a seldom-frequented area on the outskirts of town. The stillness is interrupted by the muffled sounds of the engines of large tanker trucks. They move slowly, one behind another, lights out, each stopping and taking its turn filling up with gasoline from a large, dimly lit storage tank.

Flashlight in hand, you wait, concealed by thick underbrush. You shine the light at the trucks, and the drivers cover their faces as they retreat lower into their seats. The light dances across lettering on the tankers. Shell, Texaco, Standard, independents; they're all there, the big boys and the little ones, all filling up from the same tank.

It's a scenario almost everyone has envisioned or heard about at one time or another. Is there any truth to it? Are all gasolines, in fact, the same?

Regardless of what you have heard to the contrary, no two gasolines are the same. Gasolines can and do vary because of differences in the source of the crude oil from which they are made, differences in the respective refining processes, and differences in the amount and kind of additives put into the finished product. Just as brands of food can vary in quality and our palates detect this difference, so do brands of gasoline vary—and the differences, in this case, are detected by an automobile.

Each oil company has its own formula for making gasoline. The discerning motorist will shop around and not just settle for the brand nearest to home or work, or buy a certain brand simply because he holds that particular credit card.

Try different brands of gasoline. Keep in mind that even though brands A and B might have the same octane, it doesn't necessarily mean that the gasolines are the same, and they can perform very differently in your car. Octane (the number you see posted on the pump) is not the sole criterion of the gasoline's quality and performance ability.

Give each brand a fair test. Be critical. Listen to your car; it will tell you if it likes the gasoline. Choose the brand that works best in your car.

Fast cold and warm starts, smooth idle, good road performance, and minimum knock, ping, and engine run-on are indications you have found the perfect mate for your car.

A car that is fed properly (the right gasoline) will live much longer than its malnourished counterpart. In addition, you might discover that something you originally mistook as an engine malfunction might have actually been the fault of the gasoline—which could save you the cost of an unnecessary tune-up. In the case of gasolines, it definitely pays to shop around.

Octane: Key to Engine Performance and Longevity

Octane is a familiar word to almost everyone who likes driving. We hear it a lot and see the ratings numbers every time we pull into a gasoline station. But do we really know what it means and how important it is to proper engine performance, longevity, and fuel economy?

Simply stated, the octane rating of a gasoline (the number you see posted on the pump) is a numerical expression of a particular gasoline's ability to resist engine knock, pinging, and run-on or *dieseling*.

Typically, the octane ratings of various leaded and unleaded gasolines run the gamut from about 87 to a high of 93.5 in some parts of the country.

How significant is the octane rating of the gasoline you use? Very! Octane is to your car what vitamins are to your body. Not enough vitamins and your body responds with poor performance and questionable durability. Take too many vitamins and your body uses only what it needs and discards much of the rest.

Octane is no different. Too little and the car becomes edgy, cranky and cantankerous. If you use more than necessary, the engine won't run any better—it just won't use what it doesn't need.

How do you know which octane rating is best for your car?

Start with the owner's manual. Check it and find what rating is recommended, then use it. If you don't have an owner's manual, experiment with different octane ratings and brands of gasoline.

Don't be afraid to mix different quantities of regular and premium gasoline to try to get the exact mix and rating you need. Mixing won't hurt a thing and can save you money over the long run.

And remember that as your car gets older, it will require additional octane to achieve performance comparable to when it was new.

After a few years, a car that ran great on regular unleaded gas may require almost a premium octane rating to maintain equivalent performance. This is when mixing can come in handy.

You should also keep in mind that no two gasoline brands are exactly the same. Two gasolines, each with identical octane ratings, can perform quite differently in your car.

So don't be influenced entirely by the number on the pump.

Before you change to a higher octane, try a different brand that has the same octane you are now using. In many cases, this simple switch will do the trick.

There is another reason why the numbers on the pumps can be misleading. A number of years ago, I took part in a TV special in which we tested the octane of gasoline samples taken from various stations.

We found that every sample had an octane rating less than the number posted on the pump. In one case, a pump that boasted 89 octane was, in fact, dispensing a paltry 86 octane, three points below the advertised rating.

The unwary consumer, filling his or her tank at this station, probably attributed poor engine performance to other factors, when in fact low octane was probably to blame.

Listen to your car. The engine will let you know if it is happy with the octane of the gasoline it is feeding on.

If it is knocking, clattering, pinging and running on, try a different brand and higher octane. Somewhere the ideal number is waiting.

And always keep in mind that in the case of the octane ratings posted on the pumps, what you see is not necessarily what you get.

High-quality Detergent Gas
Helps Clogged Fuel Injectors

Over the past year and a half many car owners (General Motors owners in particular) with port fuel-injected engines have been running their cars at less than full capacity. Poor performance—stalling, hesitation, bucking, loss of power, hard starting—was a common complaint flooding dealership service departments and independent repair shops.

The problem was easy to spot: clogged fuel injectors. Something was causing the fuel injectors to foul, which, in turn, affected the way the gasoline was injected into the engine's cylinders. Instead of a fine, even mist sprayed into the cylinders, it was as if someone had turned on a tiny dribbling hose. The small hole at the tip of the injectors was filling with deposits. Service centers could clean up the deposits, and the car would run fine for a short while. The deposits eventually returned and the cleaning had to be repeated. At best, it was a Band-Aid solution to a major ailment.

The problem sent the industry into a tizzy because more and more new cars were being made with fuel injection. In fact, it is accepted that fuel injection and not carburetion is the wave of the future.

So what was causing the fuel injectors to clog? Much industry research (General Motors was at the forefront here) showed that it was the poor quality of the gasoline. The fuel did not contain enough detergent additives and had too much olefin. When combined with typical American driving habits—a lot of stop-and-go and long periods when the engine is off—the injectors became fouled. It worked this way.

Port fuel injectors (located on the hot intake manifold) were subject to a phenomenon called *heat soak*. The gasoline remaining in the injector tip was baked by the high heat in the engine immediately after it was shut off. The heat caused the detergent-poor, high-olefin gasoline to break down and form deposits at the tip. The clogging never occurred when the engine was running because the moving gasoline acted as a coolant and lowered the injector tip's temperature.

So General Motors issued a challenge to the major oil companies. Could they make a gasoline with enough detergents that could safely and effectively be used with the heat-soak-susceptible, port fuel-injected engines? The answer turned out to be a resounding yes.

In no time at all most major oil companies and some independents came up with formulations that proved to be compatible with fuel-injected engines. The extra detergents and revised chemistry of the new blends kept injectors sparkling clean (and even cleaned out clogged ones). Cars everywhere began to breath a sigh of relief—and so did Detroit. These new-generation gasolines are now readily available throughout the country, and almost every station that sells them advertises the fact. It was a classic case of cooperation: Two giant segments of the automobile industry put their heads together and beat the problem.

Fouled fuel injectors should plague motorists no more. Using high-quality, high-detergent gasoline is the key. It's up to you, the car owner, to make certain you are not indulging in false economy by buying a cheap brand that contains no detergents.

What is that Awful Odor?

One of the most frequent questions people ask me concerns new cars and the foul odor that seems to accompany many of them. The question goes something like this:

"On occasion my new car emits a strong rotten-egg odor that is very annoying. What is causing it and how can I get rid of the smell?"

Many new cars are plagued by this foul odor. I've noticed it in almost every new car I have tested over the past two years or so (I test a new model each week). The condition seems to be most prevalent immediately after full-throttle accelerations.

According to John P. King, manager of the service engineering office at Ford Motor Co.'s parts and service division, sulfur is the cause of the odor. The strength of the smell depends on the amount of oxygen present in the catalytic converter at any given time. The catalytic converter, an integral part of the emissions-control system, converts harmful emissions into environmentally acceptable ones. Sulfur in the gasoline—all gasolines have some sulfur—undergoes a chemical reaction in the catalytic converter and is released as hydrogen sulfide (H_2S). Many engineers believe the problem is made even worse when gasoline refined from Alaskan high-sulfur crude oil is burned. Add to this the fact that the human nose is extremely sensitive to H_2S—remember when the entire high school knew rotten-egg gas was being made in chemistry class?—and can detect even the smallest amounts. A little can go a long way.

For the most part this nasty odor did not exist with older, two-way catalytic converters, but it became quite common with the introduction of three-way converters that treat hydrocarbon, carbon-monoxide, and nitrous-oxide emissions. The smell comes from the third stage when nitrous oxides are treated.

Can anything be done about it? Although many car owners may just have to grin and smell it, the following tips can help ease the burden:

○ Switch to another brand of gasoline. It may contain less sulfur and smell less offensive. Two tanks should let you know.

○ If switching brands of gasoline doesn't seem to help, try a commercial emissions-control-system cleaner. Some of these preparations claim to reduce rotten-egg odor. They are available at most auto-parts stores and service stations.

○ Go easy on the full-throttle accelerations. When gasoline is suddenly dumped into the engine, some of it escapes unburned and will come into direct contact with the hot catalytic converter. This intensifies the odor. Feed the accelerator gradually.

○ Have the ignition timing checked and set to factory specifications.

○ Ask your repair shop or dealer if recalibrating the engine computer or changing the air/fuel mixture will help.

What to Do about Lead

The one question my readers have asked most during the past 18 months concerns the Environmental Protection Agency's (EPA) order requiring refiners to reduce the amount of lead in gasoline. How will it affect the 30-odd million cars and engines that were designed to run on leaded gas and what, if any, precautions should be taken?

Since the EPA ordered a gradual phaseout of lead in gasoline for environmental and health reasons, the lead content has dropped from a high of about 2.5 grams per gallon (gpg) to the current maximum allowable 0.1 gpg. Leaded gas itself has become more difficult to find. For years tetraethyl lead (TEL) has been used by refiners as an economical way to boost octane. It also lubricated the upper cylinder area of the car's engine, and it is that lubrication that worries car owners.

During the combustion process, TEL in the form of lead salts is deposited on or around the valves, valve guides, and, most important, the valve seats. It acts as a buffer for metal-to-metal contact as the valves close against their seats. Gasoline exploding in the cylinders constantly replenishes the lead coating. Without lead, valve seats can wear rapidly and recede into the cylinder head. If this happens, engine compression and performance suffer and can only be restored with a costly engine rebuild.

Is the current 0.1 gpg enough to protect valve parts against premature wear? That depends on the vehicle and how it is driven. If used moderately in urban areas, a vehicle can do quite well with low-lead gasoline. But if the car is driven at higher speeds—the 65-mph limit didn't do any favors for cars that use leaded gas—or pulls trailers or climbs hills regularly or is operated at high engine rpm or in high-heat conditions, then 0.1 gpg is not adequate. Most farm vehicles, construction equipment, large trucks, buses, mobile homes, and even pickup trucks, along with passenger cars that are driven "hard," fall in this category.

But there is a catch: 0.1 gpg is the *maximum* allowed by law. Many refiners actually add less, as there is no minimum standard for what constitutes leaded gasoline. Indeed, the gas you are using now, although technically called leaded, may just barely be so. There is no way to tell at the pump. But will even that small amount be phased out?

James Caldwell, chief of the fuels section of the Office of Mobile Sources at the EPA, says that although the proposal for a total ban on leaded gasoline is still on the shelf, the EPA at this time has "no final plans to proceed with a ban on leaded gasoline." That is good news for older cars—some lead is better than none.

If your car was made prior to 1975, it does not have hardened valve parts and should use leaded gasoline. (Hardened valve parts are used in newer cars that burn unleaded gasoline and don't require lead for valve lubrication.) Ford Motor Co. echoes this, recommending leaded gasoline for all its cars with soft, metal valve parts built before 1975. General Motors says all its cars built before 1971 should use low-lead gasoline. (Owners of pickup trucks and other vehicles should consult their owner's manuals for fuel type.)

If your car does not have hardened valve parts:

o Continue using leaded gasoline as long as possible.

o Monitor driving habits closely. Keep speeds under 55 mph. Avoid driving in high heat for prolonged periods or overheating the engine. Don't pull trailers or carry heavy loads. Keep engine rpm to a maximum of 2,500. Don't gun the motor at idle or use full-throttle accelerations.

o Consider using a lead-substitute additive available at many service stations and auto-parts stores. They offer some protection against valve-seat wear. Recent testing by the EPA and Department of Agriculture showed that lead-substitute additives decreased valve wear when used according to the manufacturer's directions. However, they didn't halt wear completely. When another test was done using four times the recommended amount, valve wear was stopped completely

o If your engine must be rebuilt, hardened valve parts should be used. The parts may cost a bit more, but they will enable your car to run safely on unleaded gas.

Mothballs in your Gas?

When I was in school in western Pennsylvania and just becoming interested in cars, I was in awe of an older kid who drove a V-8 Mercury. He hailed from the rough part of town and had the reputation of owning the fastest car around. The inner circle of teenagers would look at each other, whisper, and shake their heads knowingly because Meatballs—yep, that was his name—it was rumored, made his car go fast by putting mothballs in the gas tank. Meatballs, with his Merc and the mothballs, was king of the hill.

What we never considered was that Meatballs was continually rebuilding or working on his engine.

What prompts this discourse on Meatballs and his mothballs is a letter I recently received from—no, not Meatballs—a lady, a "limited income senior citizen," who writes:

> "I dissolve 64 mothballs in 1 gallon of gasoline, filter it, shake it up, and add 1/4 cup of this solution to each 4 gallons of gas. This costs less than commercial octane boosters, which is important to me. My 1964 Buick seems to respond better. I feel it in the steering wheel and in the improved ride. Good or bad practice? Continue or not?"
>
> C.M.E.

Well, C.M.E., that is probably the same way old Meatballs used to do it. And if you continue to do it you'll be rebuilding your engine just like Meatballs used to. But I admire your gumption and your sense to ask if it is a good or bad practice.

For years mothballs have been a favorite "underground" quick fix for obtaining higher octane in gasoline. With today's low-octane stuff at the pump, I've often wondered when mothballs would make a reappearance.

Modern-day mothballs are made of naphthalene and, indeed, they will offer a temporary power and octane boost to any car, old or new. As you say, they are much cheaper than commercial octane boosters. But their cheapness is deceiving, because eventually you must pay the piper for those temporary thrills.

Mothballs are aromatics that are distilled from petroleum or coal and are what chemists call a "heavy-end distillate;" that is, in the fractional distillation process necessary to produce gasoline from oil, these heavy aromatics boil off at about $80-100$ degrees C. When added to gasoline, these heavy aromatics cause the flame in the combustion chamber of an engine to spread and burn slower. This in turn has the bottom-line effect of boosting octane and providing the engine with more power.

But there is an insidious side effect. Mothballs (naphthalene) are extremely corrosive to the upper-cylinder area of an automotive engine, the area where combustion—the actual exploding of gasoline—takes place. Serious and speeded-up wear takes place in the whole valve train, especially the intake-valve guides. Even in the concentration you are using, damage could be just a mothball away.

Bob Bowen of the Phillips Petroleum Research Division tells me that a number of years ago Phillips tested the mothball hypothesis and ruined an engine in about 1,000 miles, using a somewhat concentrated mothball solution. Your old Buick may go a bit farther than that, but eventually you will have to pay for a rebuilt engine, just like old Meatballs often did.

The best bet to get more octane to your Buick engine is to mix a half tank of regular leaded gasoline with a half tank of premium unleaded. Or you can alternate tanks of premium unleaded with tanks of regular leaded. In lieu of this, a commercial octane booster can be used. Even though it does cost a lot, it is much cheaper in the long run. Save the mothballs for that old trunk in the attic.

Say, C.M.E., you didn't happen to live in western Pennsylvania back in the early '50s and have a son named Meatballs, did you?

5

When you're hot, you're hot (& vice versa)

I WAS DRIVING THROUGH the Arizona desert trying out the new 65-mph speed limit, which, incidentally, I'm having a hard time adjusting to. Outside temperatures were tickling the 100-degree mark, while those nearer the road surface had to be much higher. After a couple of hours I spotted a small cafe and decided to stop for a bite to eat and something cool to drink.

I eased the car into the parking lot, turned off the engine, locked the doors, and headed for the restaurant. I hadn't taken more than 10 steps when I heard someone exclaim, "Hey, what about me?"

I looked around. There wasn't a soul in sight.

"Here, under the hood of your car. Me, did you forget about me, your faithful old engine?"

I couldn't believe my ears. I walked back to the car and opened the hood. A blast of searing heat greeted me.

"Lordy, that feels *soooo* good. It gets awful hot under here."

It was my engine. I knew the car had a talking instrument panel, but this was a surprise. A talking engine, what will they think of next? It really let me have it.

"Sure, you go in and have something cool, but how about me? I just had a couple of hours of high-speed, high-heat driving and what do you do for me? Just let me sit here and soak in the heat. A sauna I don't need. And I thought you were supposed to know something about cars."

The engine wouldn't ease up. "Of all people, you should know that we engines like to be idled for a minute or so after a long run in high temperatures. It helps alleviate hot spots and permits under-the-hood heat to dissipate and temperatures to normalize. Don't you know this is one of the few times when idling an engine can actually be beneficial to its health?"

I was embarrassed because I did know that. I restarted the engine and let it idle. All the cylinders chimed in, "Ahhh, that sure feels better."

The engine continued its stern lecture. "Haven't you watched a groom walking a thoroughbred after a hard race? Do they just put him in the barn after a race? No way! They walk 'em to cool 'em down first, gently, slowly. These horses under this hood are no different. Shame on you for forgetting about us, and in this summerlike heat, too."

What could I say? The engine was right. I had goofed. But the engine wasn't finished with me yet.

"What about the turbocharger right next to me? Sure, sure, I know the owner's manual says these new turbos don't have to be coddled or idled after heavy use, but do you think any of those Detroit engineers have lived under the hood of a car? In Arizona? In the summer? Hey, they may write about it, but we live it. I don't care if your car has a water-cooled turbo, it's a good idea to let the engine idle for a minute or so to benefit the turbo. Otherwise, it could be damaged by heat soak or oil starvation—this is especially true of older turbos—and can literally fry right there in the car." The turbo grunted its approval.

I had no argument with the engine; it knew what it was talking about. It was beginning to feel a bit better, because it had been idling for about a minute and a half and was beginning to shush up. It became quiet and content now that the under-the-hood temperatures were stabilizing and those bothersome hot spots were gone. In fact, its quiet hum convinced me that it was napping, so I slipped back into the car and turned the key off. This time, silence greeted me as I ambled toward the restaurant.

I can't be lax anymore, I mused as I sank my teeth into a burger and washed it down with a cool lemonade. This is one summer-driving technique I won't forget in the coming high-heat months.

I got back into the car and turned the key. The engine roared to life. Its quick response made me realize that this technique would also help eliminate vapor lock in the fuel lines, a malady that affects all too many cars in the summer.

As I gently guided the car out of the parking lot, I swear I heard a voice over the cacophonous digital chatter of the dash. It simply said, "Thanks, Bob."

Winterize Your Car Now

Sitting here in sunny Tucson, Arizona, watching the Penn State-Notre Dame football game, I suddenly became aware that much of the nation is already in the grip of some nasty winter weather. Reports from State College, Pa., told of temperatures in the 20s with a minus-6-degrees wind-chill factor. If you live in the Midwest or the East, I don't have to remind you that the cold has arrived. But I might have to remind you that your car feels the change in the weather, too. Only trouble is, your car can't go to the closet to get a heavy coat or sit down at the table and have a cup of hot chocolate. It depends on you to provide its cold-weather support system.

When a vehicle switches from warm-weather attire into cold-weather gear it does so without benefit of a change of clothes. The battery it is wearing, for example, must do the same job in winter as it did in summer. But doing the same job requires a quantum leap in the battery's output. No more nice warm-weather starts. It gets serious from now on.

When it is cold out, a battery loses much of its ability to supply a strong starting current. That loss is in direct proportion to how cold it is. If it's near zero, most batteries are only about 50 percent as effective as they are on a 78-degree day.

That's bad, but there's more: The battery must contend with thicker oil in the engine (due to the cold), which makes the engine harder to turn. Winter means shorter days and that means the car's lights are used more. Add to that the overtime work of the heater, defrosters, wipers and washers, and other electrical equipment. End result: more demands on the battery.

Even more important than the battery is the ignition system. If it isn't in good condition the best battery in the world won't start the car. Best way to make certain the ignition system is in top order is to have the car tuned to meet the demands of the cold months ahead. That tune-up should include a thorough check of the fuel system—especially any cold-start mechanisms such as the choke or cold-start injector, and in older cars the manifold heat riser.

It's also important to have a fresh charge of antifreeze and a correct thermostat in the cooling system. The thermostat is especially crucial because it forces the car to warm fast and keeps the engine at proper operating temperature.

Winter means snow and generally bad driving conditions. If you need a set of tires there's no time like the present to purchase them. All suspension components should be in top shape to ensure the car has maximum traction and steering control.

Check all exhaust-system components. Winter means driving with closed windows. Be absolutely certain the exhaust system is leak-free.

This is also the ideal time to switch to a low-viscosity winter-rated 5W-30 motor oil. It will help make those cold starts a little easier.

Where there is snow there is most likely to be salt on the roads. Remember that the corrosive action triggered by road salts is mainly active in the 32-to-40-degree Fahrenheit range. Those conditions are perfect for the salt to dissolve into solution, a prerequisite to attacking the metal. Below freezing, it's simply too cold; even road salt doesn't like to work when it's that cold outside. Above 40, the solution begins to evaporate and loses some of its sting. Rationale: Wash your car frequently if you are driving on salty roads and the temperature is in the "rust range."

As a former Boy Scout—maybe there are no former Scouts; once a Scout always a Scout—I know the value of being prepared. You should, too. Carry some type of winter emergency kit in your vehicle. Some suggestions: jumper cables, flashlight, tool kit, washer fluid, wiper blades, tire chains, shovel, window scraper, extra clothes, warning flags. If you live in an area where blizzards are possible, stock extra clothing, food, and water.

There is no reason to let winter catch your car with its guard down. Proper winter maintenance plays a major role in assuring that you and your car get through the cold trouble free.

Tune-up Is Indispensable for Cold-Weather Driving

I recently received a letter from a reader in Kansas City who commented on a column I did on the importance of keeping a battery in good condition, especially in the winter. He noted that although this is a must for winter driving, other components of the car's engine may play a more important role than the battery in ensuring fast, quick, cold-morning starts. He enclosed some literature from Champion Spark Plug Co. to back up his contention, and I am passing it along to you because very good points were made.

According to Champion, the condition of the ignition system, and not the battery, is the most important factor in starting your car in cold weather. When other engine components are not properly maintained, even a new or well-charged battery can be worn down quickly before the engine starts. This is because the voltage required to start a car increases when the engine has such maladies as broken or cracked ignition cables, worn spark plugs, or a worn or corroded distributor cap or rotor.

All these problems are compounded during wet or cold weather, and the components require even more current to perform basic operations. Electricity, like water, seeks the easiest path along which to flow. Faulty wiring or any deficiency in the ignition components interrupts or drains the flow of an already diminished electrical supply. For example, worn spark plugs require easily twice the electricity as new ones.

Cold temperatures also adversely affect the capacity of the battery to produce the necessary power for starting. For instance, at 80 degrees Fahrenheit, a battery has its maximum capacity. This drops to 60 percent when the temperature drops to 32 degrees, and tumbles to 46 percent at 0 degrees. Often during cold or wet weather the battery may not generate enough power to start the engine, but this is not necessarily the battery's fault. This condition is frequently caused by worn ignition parts requiring more voltage than they would if properly maintained.

Tests at Champion demonstrated the relationship between these voltage-required and voltage-available factors. In the tests engineers attempted to start cars at 0 degrees. Two cars were purchased as-is from used-car lots. One, a Chevrolet Camaro, had a conventional ignition system; the other, a Dodge, had electronic ignition. Before undergoing tests both cars were able to start in normal warm-weather conditions. Then they were "soaked" in zero-degree cold with the following results:

The Dodge, with its battery and engine in their original condition, did not start in four 30-second attempts. A new battery was installed, but another attempt at starting was unsuccessful.

Technicians then tuned the car, replacing old spark plugs with new ones, resetting the timing to factory specifications and replacing distributor components. Using the original battery, five new attempts averaged starts in 2.67 seconds.

In the tests on the Camaro, with the battery and engine still in as-is condition, there was one unsuccessful start, one start after 9.52 seconds and one start at 2.31 seconds. When a new battery was installed the average starting time was 9.87 seconds in eight attempts. With new spark plugs and the original battery, average starting time was 1.67 seconds. And with the engine tuned and still using the old battery, starting time averaged 1.75 seconds. All tests were conducted by remote control to make sure that driver habits did not affect the starts.

According to Champion, these test results should negate the long-held assumption that the battery is the cause of most trouble when starting a car in cold weather. A new battery could not help start these cars at zero degrees, yet once the engines were tuned even the old battery could provide sufficient voltage to fire the engine.

The conclusion wasn't surprising: Champion noted that a prewinter or, even mid-winter tune-up is indispensable for dependable starting. If your car hasn't had one, better late than never.

Gesundheit!

A-a-ahchoo!!! Welcome to fall weather. Cold mornings and, lately, cold days too. Colds, flu and other pesky ailments abound. Life is a lot harder in cold weather. But pity your poor car. Did you know that cars can catch colds too? Absolutely.

Ever hear your car sneeze? Ever hear it cough? Of course you have. These are but a few symptoms of the common car cold and, like human colds, they tend to be more prevalent during cold winter months.

One of the main reasons cars catch cold is that the choke mechanism in the engine is never readjusted to compensate for the difference in temperature when the weather begins to cool. Thus the car is operating in wintertime on a summertime choke setting. That is a lot like wearing a T-shirt in Detroit in January. No wonder so many cars catch cold! And how about that accompanying cough? Irritating, hacking, persistent. Makes the car buck and jerk when it is cold. Won't go away until the engine has warmed. Again, the culprit could be the choke, that silver-dollar-size gizmo that controls the air/fuel mixture when the engine is cold.

It is miserable, I know. The sneezing and wheezing and flulike symptoms. No pep, sluggishness, hard to get going in the morning, raw gasoline smell, post-exhaust drip. And it could all be because you didn't give your car that prewinter or mid-winter checkup/tune-up.

A malfunctioning choke that is either too "rich" (too much gas gets to the engine) or too "lean" (not enough gas gets to the engine) is a bad-news proposition.

A too-rich choke can waste copious amounts of fuel. In some cases up to 95 percent (that's no misprint) of the fuel supplied to the engine will go unburned during the interval when the choke remains closed (set too rich). That means that a car getting 20 miles per gallon (mpg) when completely warmed may be capable of only 1 or 2 mpg when running with a too-rich choke setting.

Much of this unburned fuel finds its way into the oil, where it dilutes and contaminates it and renders it less effective as a lubricant. It also washes away vital cylinder-area lubrication at the exact time when it is needed most—during the cold start. These combined factors greatly hasten engine wear.

A sticking or maladjusted automatic choke is a major cause of poor wintertime engine performance and fuel economy. If your car is exhibiting any of the above symptoms, it may be wise to take it to the doctor for a checkup. And if the doctor asks you to leave the car at his office for a while—perhaps even overnight—don't be alarmed. The best way to adjust the choke mechanism is to let the engine cool down to the approximate outside early-morning temperature. Then the adjustment can be made properly.

If you are lucky, this little service can get rid of your car's cold and put it back on the road to good health.

Emergency Driving Situations

The record-setting cold weather that gripped—and is still gripping—major portions of the nation during December no doubt has made many motorists aware of just how unprepared they and their cars were for driving under severe winter conditions. Engines that won't start, frozen gas lines, frozen engine blocks, ambient conditions that demand extra skills behind the wheel—all are part and parcel of the frosty-faced reality that has recently confronted drivers. If you have followed the advice in this column, I hope you were better prepared for the cold than other motorists.

But there is something else we must deal with when adverse weather conditions beset us. Most of us are woefully unprepared to cope with an emergency if one should arise due to or in bad weather. Emergency driving situations are bad enough when the weather is nonthreatening, but add severe cold and snow and ice and the wind chill factor on cold days and the situation becomes drastically worse. I'm not talking about things like not knowing how to drive out of a skid or getting your stuck car out of a snow bank. I'm talking about being properly prepared in case you become stranded or your car breaks down when weather conditions are at their worst.

Here are some suggestions on how to cope with severe winter emergencies and what emergency equipment and supplies a properly outfitted car should be carrying on these super-cold days.

○ If you become stuck or stranded in severe weather, especially extreme cold and snowy conditions, be certain you can reach help before leaving your car. If there is noticeable activity within easy walking distance (a house with lights, moving cars on another road), then leaving the car to get help is probably the best thing to do. In other cases most experts agree it is best to stay with the car.

○ If you must get out of the car, remember that with a wind-chill equivalent temperature below minus 25 degrees F (and so many cities have recently recorded such low temperatures), exposed skin can freeze within a minute.

○ Keep the gas tank full, especially if you will be driving in open country. This gives you the means to supply heat in case you become stranded. It also minimizes the chance of moisture—and possibly ice—building up in the gas tank.

○ Experts advise running the engine and heater about 10-15 minutes every hour. That will keep you warm and not allow the engine to cool enough so it may be hard to start or use extra fuel. Open a window a bit and be certain the tailpipe is free of obstructions.

○ Don't think you can outwit the weather. If conditions begin to worsen, don't push on. Take shelter at the first opportunity. Many drivers have lost their lives trying to beat the storm and make it to the next town.

○ Carry some type of emergency supplies in the car. Here are some suggestions gleaned from safety experts' recommendations:

> one or two blankets
> gloves
> a flashlight with good batteries
> spare fuses
> ice scraper
> pocket knife
> first-aid kit
> flares
> a tool kit with pliers
> screwdrivers
> adjustable wrench
> tape
> wire
> rags
> jumper cables
> sandpaper or steel wool (to clean battery terminals)
> extra engine oil and coolant
> a miniraincoat and/or umbrella
> tire chains
> small shovel
> small bag of sand
> a ''send help'' sign
> a CB radio
> coffee-can survival kit

A coffee-can survival kit? Here, courtesy of the Illinois State Police, is how to make a coffee-can survival kit. Fill a 3-pound coffee can with a couple of candles, a pocket knife, three pieces of bright cloth (tie to antenna to attract attention), several packets of instant soup, hot chocolate, tea, bouillon cubes, and similar fare. These can be mixed into melted snow gathered in the coffee can. The candles (or sterno cans) are used to heat the mixture. You can also cook on the engine. Raise the hood, place the can in a hot spot, close the hood to conserve the heat, and remove the mixture when it warms.

Other items to stash in the coffee can: packages of peanuts, hard candy, extra-heavy socks, matches or a butane lighter, and a couple of black plastic bags that can reflect and store body heat. The coffee can should be covered with its lid and a stocking cap placed over it. The cap can come in handy.

When we are snug and warm in our cars the furthest thing from our minds is trouble. But severe weather can have an unfunny way of turning secure circumstances into worrisome or even life-threatening situations when and where we least expect them, and with eye-blinking rapidity. My wife is from western Kansas where they tell frightening tales of motorists stranded by weather conditions. But western Kansas or western Pennsylvania, don't be caught unprepared this winter. Just taking the few simple precautions outlined here can ensure you will get to your destination safe and sound.

6

You hold the keys

WHEN WAS THE LAST TIME you got your hands dirty? That long, eh? When was the last time you took a short hike? Can't remember? OK, when was the last time you took a short hike and got your hands dirty at the same time?

If you are a car owner, these are good habits to cultivate. I'll explain. In a book of mine, *Drive it Forever,* I wrote the following:

"Want to know at a glance how your engine is doing without even raising the hood or lifting a tool? Walk to the back of your car and look at the inside of your exhaust pipe. What do you see there? Rub your finger around the inside and see if the deposit is wet. Is it oily? Is it dry? The color and condition of the deposit on the inside of the tail pipe are two of the best indicators of engine shape. Just as an automobile traveling over fresh snow will leave tire tracks, so will an engine leave its imprint on the tail pipe. By looking at the tire tracks in the snow, you can get a pretty fair idea of the condition of the tires; by the same token, looking at the imprint the engine leaves on the exhaust pipe gives you an idea of the condition of the engine."

Just make sure the exhaust pipe has had time to cool before you touch it. A light gray to light brown, fine, powdery deposit indicates that, most likely, all is well in the engine. Black, wet, oily, sooty, or gasoline-smelling deposits indicate something is amiss.

If the deposit is wet, black, sooty, or smells of gasoline, probably the carburetor is set too rich; that is, the air-fuel ratio is improper, or the automatic choke needs adjustment or the engine needs to be tuned. All these conditions rob you of miles per gallon and, if left unchecked, will accelerate engine wear. They could also mean that you don't get the car out on the highway enough; too much city driving will blacken any tail pipe. In this case, a little highway exercise will do wonders for the car.

Is the deposit oily and black? It could indicate worn piston rings or valve-associated problems. It could also signal a less serious condition, but for our purposes it means something is causing oil to get back to the tail pipe, and that's a no-no.

If the inside of the pipe is covered with a white glazed, glassy material, the engine might be running too hot, the timing is incorrect, or there is an intake manifold leak. Any of these conditions needs immediate attention.

So take that hike, bend down and look at your tail pipe. Get your hands dirty. The color and type of deposit in your tail pipe can furnish a wealth of free information about the state of your engine and carburetor. It also can tell you about the quality of gasoline and oil you are using, the kind of spark plugs you're using ("hot" plugs or "cold" plugs), your driving habits (too much city, not enough highway) and much more. It's not an infallible check, to be sure, but it will give you some idea of just how happy and healthy your car is.

Is Your Car Sending Smoke Signals?

Smoke signals were one of the earliest forms of long-distance communication. Puffs of smoke rising high in the sky helped American Indians convey messages that would have taken hours to deliver in person.

Your car can also send smoke signals. The color and amount of your car's exhaust smoke can help you discover that something in the engine may need attention.

Let's look at the most common causes of exhaust smoke and what these smoke signals mean.

There are basically three colors of exhaust smoke: white, black, and different shades of blue.

If the exhaust is white when you start your cold-engine car—especially in cold or damp weather—that's most likely normal. It is signaling that the condensation that collected inside the engine and exhaust system overnight is being burned off.

The resultant water vapor coming out of the exhaust shows itself as a white cloud, much like your hot breath does on a cold day. This white "smoke" or vapor will disappear as soon as the engine has burned off all the collected condensation.

If the white cloud persists, there is a good chance that coolant is leaking into the combustion chamber through a cracked head gasket or other route. In this case, the combusted coolant is causing the white cloud. That's definitely not normal and the car should be checked by a mechanic. You might have to have a head gasket replaced or the cylinder heads (if they are warped) milled.

Black smoke indicates that the fuel/air mixture is too rich. Because the engine can't burn all the fuel that's coming its way, it spews a lot of the unburned or partially unburned hydrocarbons (black smoke) out the exhaust.

Such a simple thing as a too-rich or stuck automatic choke can cause black smoke. Other times you might need a complete tuneup to correct the rich fuel mixture. Black smoke means that your car is wasting gas and polluting the atmosphere.

Bluish (blue, blue-gray, or blue-white) smoke is the result of oil being burned in the combustion chamber. How the oil gets into the combustion chamber is important because it could mean the difference between a major engine overhaul and a minor, less-expensive repair.

Of the three types of exhaust smoke blue is the worst because it can mean your car has a case of the wallet-thinning blues. Here's what to look for:

If blue exhaust comes out in a steady stream, that's usually an indication that the engine has had it—with one exception: Blue exhaust smoke can also come from an engine that is in excellent condition. A faulty vacuum diaphragm in a fuel pump can cause motor oil to be sucked out of the crankcase and routed to the combustion chamber where it is mixed with the fuel and burned.

Combination fuel/vacuum pumps are found most often on older vehicles (if you have an electric fuel pump, it is not vacuum-actuated). The resultant tail pipe signal is a constant plume of blue smoke that gives the impression of a more serious problem. In this case a new fuel pump can cure the blues.

If the blue is seen only on hard acceleration it could indicate worn piston rings and the specter of a major engine overhaul to cure it.

A slight puff of blue smoke when the car is started might indicate that oil is leaking past the valve seals or guides and finding its way into the combustion chamber. If blue smoke also appears when you decelerate (foot off gas, car in gear), it's another indication that valve seals or guides or both are faulty.

Ideally, exhaust should be colorless except for an occasional brief puff of white when the vehicle is cold-started or operated in very cold weather. If your car is sending you smoke signals, pay attention; it is trying to tell you something.

Keep Your Car's Exhaust System Clean

Back pressure can be nice. When my chiropractor applies pressure to my lower back it makes me feel good. I cry (laugh?) for more. But there are other times when back pressure can be a pain—for instance, if too much of it is applied to your car's exhaust system.

All engines and the exhaust systems attached to them are subject to varying amounts of back pressure, the resistance exerted by all exhaust-system components on the flow of exhaust gases to the outside air.

Mufflers, catalytic converters, heat-riser valves, the diameter of the exhaust pipe, and the number of turns in the pipe all influence how much and how fast exhaust gas is expelled from an engine. No two engines will expel gases the same way.

But all engines, big or small, must get rid of waste gases pronto or they will be in big trouble. And all engines are engineered to get rid of them efficiently, each with varying amounts of resistance (back pressure) from their respective exhaust systems.

If too much back pressure is in the exhaust system the gases can't escape and pressure is built up in the system. This will directly affect the way the car runs—most noticcably, through a loss of power and a drop in fuel economy.

What can cause excessive back pressure? A number of things—some so simple that we might ignore them, then pay the price for doing so. Let's start with the tail pipe. When was the last time you checked it closely? It should be nice and round with no obstructions or dents.

I once received a letter from a man who had backed into a dirt bank and rammed his tail pipe full of mud. He drove his car like that for a number of days, curious as to why it was losing power. The engine was checked, but no one looked at the tail pipe. Pity, it cost him a rebuilt engine.

No time like the present to check the tail pipe for obstructions. And while you're at it, inspect the entire exhaust system. Look for dents or crimps in the muffler, pipes, and catalytic converter. If the dent looks deep enough to block the free movement of gases, have the part in question replaced or the dents removed.

There are other, more insidious ways back pressure can play its engine-defeating game. By using dirty gasoline or leaded gas in a car meant to use unleaded, you will slowly but surely plug up the catalytic converter. Remember, the converter is a part of the exhaust system. All gases must pass through it on their way to freedom. If you have noticed a gradual loss of power, it's one of the things that should be checked.

Have the exhaust manifold heat-riser valve checked to make sure it opens and closes freely; it is the first restriction exhaust gases meet on their trip out. This valve closes when the engine is cold to keep the exhaust gases from escaping so they can help warm the engine. As the engine warms, the valve opens to allow the free flow of gases once again. If this valve is stuck closed, it limits the escape route, thus building up excessive back pressure on the engine.

And mufflers. If cars didn't have them, we'd all be wearing hearing aids. But engines pay a penalty for mufflers and catalytic converters. They are major restrictions in the exhaust system and because of them the engine is forced to run at less than maximum efficiency. But I have no quarrel with that, because the trade-off is a good one. In return for less engine efficiency, we get peace and quiet and cleaner air to breathe.

But don't just put any old muffler or catalytic converter on your car. Remember what I said earlier: These stock components are designed with a predetermined amount of back pressure built in and the entire exhaust system and engine are tuned to operate at those pressures. Install a "universal" or bargain "any brand" muffler in place of the factory-recommended one, and you're asking for trouble. Keeping the exhaust system clean is an important step in getting the most from your car.

Have Mercy on Your Engine: Never Clean the Air Filter

How many times since you've owned your car have you cleaned the air filter? Not changed it, but cleaned it.

A typical reply might be, "Oh, I have it cleaned about every 3,000 miles or so, sometimes more frequently." Unknowingly, each time you cleaned the paper-element air filter, you were raising the odds of engine failure.

"That can't be," you reply. "A clean air filter is a necessity if you want a long-lived engine. Any fool knows that. What's this drivel about it making my engine wear out?"

It's true. The common paper air filters have, for years, been cleaned by either tapping them on the ground to shake the dirt loose or by blowing compressed air through them. If you've owned a car for any length of time, you are probably familiar with the routine. For sure, these methods do remove dirt, and lots of it, and no one will argue that the filter isn't cleaner afterward.

"So what's the problem, then?" you ask. It's that the villain doesn't enter until the second act, when the filter is placed back on the engine. The instant the engine is started and it takes its first breath, it sucks in all the dirt, sand and grit that was loosened but not removed by the "cleaning."

This dirt was originally trapped in the filter and the cleaning shook it loose but didn't remove it. No matter how thoroughly the filter is cleaned, some dirt will remain and the strong suction of the engine will draw it in.

Abrasive wear is one of the four major causes of engine wear, and the main soldiers in its army are good old common dirt, dust, sand, and grit.

The moral here is clear: Let sleeping dogs lie. The rule is: If the filter looks dirty, change it. Do not attempt to clean it. If it looks clean, leave it as is, or carefully rotate it 180 degrees so a slightly cleaner area will be the first to greet the incoming air.

Recently, I saw a newspaper ad extolling the virtues of one of the new quick-lube franchises. The fee included "cleaning the air filter." Shame on you guys! You should know better.

If someone else services your car, insist that the filter either be changed or left alone. Volvo recognized this long ago when it advised its owners to change but never clean the air-filter element. A new filter is cheap insurance against one of the most serious and prevalent causes of engine wear: abrasives.

Remember: If it's dirty enough to be cleaned, it should be changed.

Take Care of Your Car's Air Cleaner

If you are a regular reader of this column, you know I often emphasize the importance of being careful when replacing an air filter. I have also recommended that you never try to clean paper-element-type air filters because it usually does more harm than good, dislodging trapped dirt particles that are sucked into the engine when the car is started. Sure, you may remove a lot of dirt, but you also disturb other particles and send them careening into the engine where they can do their dirty work. The rule is: Always change the air filter, don't try to clean it.

Even if you are careful and always replace the paper element, many car owners ignore another area of the air-cleaner housing. Five will get you 10 that there is an accumulation of debris in the bottom of the air-cleaner housing. When you remove the old filter be certain the bottom of the housing is cleaned. In fact, it is better to remove the entire air cleaner from the car and clean it. That way, no dirt can be accidentally swept into the carburetor or air passages.

If you replace an old filter with a new one and fail to clean the housing on which it fits, some of that debris (bug parts, silica, dirt) can find its way into the engine and sensitive parts of the carburetor. If junk becomes lodged there, reduced fuel economy and engine run-on can result.

In addition, dirt between the air filter's rubber gasket and the housing prevents a good, tight seal and could allow unfiltered air to find its way into the engine. These air leaks can upset the controlled balance of air and fuel coming into the engine. In computer-controlled engines, that excess air can cause the oxygen sensor to misread the amount of oxygen present in the fuel/air mixture and overcompensate when it adjusts the fuel mixture, possibly causing rough running and a drop in fuel efficiency.

Hang on; there's more. I've often wondered how many cars are operating without an air-filter or carburetor air-horn gasket. These rubber gaskets seal the juncture between the air cleaner and carburetor and/or fuel-injection apparatus. If the gasket is missing or frayed, a tight seal can't be made. That area becomes another point for unwanted and unfiltered air to gain entrance to the engine, carburetor, or fuel-injection system. Gaskets cost only a few dimes and provide protection you don't want to be without.

Keep in mind that plain, old, everyday dirt is very abrasive and the number-one cause of engine wear. And where does most of this Engine Enemy Number One gain entrance? You guessed it. Through unfiltered air leaks in and around the air-cleaner housing.

A couple of examples may drive home the importance of keeping this area in top-notch condition. Normal air contains a dust concentration of about 5 milligrams per 1,000 cubic feet of air. An engine breathing normal air will inhale about 40 milligrams of this dust each hour it operates. Not much, but it translates into about 5 milligrams of actual engine metal being devoured per hour.

If that same car were run over dusty roads, the dust concentration soars to 10,000 milligrams per 1,000 cubic feet of air. In this case the engine would draw in about 87,000 milligrams of dust each hour it operates. At this concentration of dust, the engine would lose metal at the rate of about 11,000 milligrams per hour of operation! In fact, there are stories about cars whose engines were literally scoured to death by ingesting large amounts of abrasive volcanic ash during the eruption of Mount St. Helens in 1980.

I hope these mind-boggling numbers drive home the importance of having an efficient air-filtering system and making sure that all gaskets and gasket surfaces are clean and in good repair. If you are doing the work yourself it will take only a few minutes to check these areas; if you are having the work done elsewhere, make certain they do it right.

Avoid a Hot Stop: Check Your Fan Belt Now

They begin appearing along our roadsides in late spring. In other parts of the country that aren't blessed with early heat, their appearance is delayed, but June and July will find them in profusion along the roadside.

Like grotesque creatures in a bad dream, their long, twisted, thin carcasses litter our highways and byways. All are dead now, put to the test just a little too long, the encroaching heat finally causing their demise. Almost exclusively summertime creatures, they are *prima facie* evidence of human neglect.

But many of these deaths could have been avoided, and the grief that accompanies them might have been unnecessary. The inconvenience, the extra cost to their owners could have been circumvented. If only the car owner had taken a minute or two to see how they were feeling and looking while they were still alive before summer's heat set in.

They never did like heat. They have it tough as it is, and more heat only makes matters worse. Some just can't handle it and call it quits. Our roadsides are their graveyards.

Snakes? The myriad animal types that are put into early graves by speeding iron? No, nothing like that.

How about fan belts? Or, if you wish to get technical, engine accessory drive belts.

Whatever you call them, they should be checked before the high-heat season. These belts run numerous under-the-hood accessories such as power steering, air conditioning, alternator, fan, water pump, and more. Some cars have only one belt, others a regiment. Each one should be checked closely for fraying, cracking, splitting and general deterioration. It is one of the more important summertime inspections any car owner can make or have made.

You can spot a lot in a simple visual inspection. Taking the belts in hand (engine off and cool) and twisting each so the underside can be seen is helpful in revealing hidden splits and cracks that otherwise would have gone unnoticed. If the belts are more than three years old it is a good idea to have them replaced, regardless of how they look. This is even more important in Sun Belt areas.

Check the belts' tightness and adjust them according to your owner's manual recommendation. Remember, belts always loosen with use; they never tighten. Be careful when adjusting tension: A too-tight belt will apply too much pressure to accessory bearings and can cause premature failure of the unit. Not enough tension can cause the alternator to work inefficiently, the engine to run hot and the air conditioner to work only so-so. Loud screeching noises when starting the engine are signs that one or more of the accessory belts—I still like "fan belts"—might be loose.

It is a good idea to carry an extra belt. The one that runs the water pump, fan, and alternator is the one you want to have with you. Have someone show you how to replace it. If your mechanical knowledge is limited, write the directions down and draw a sketch of what goes where and what comes off first, etc. Place these directions with the extra belt, and make sure you have the proper tools on hand to make the change. The belt won't be much good if you can't get it on.

Fan belts are relatively cheap, and the car absolutely depends on them. Check them now as summer lays its warm hand across the land, and rest comfortably knowing that you won't be bothered by a vision of twisted, snakelike creatures.

South-of-the-Border Trip is a Timely Reminder

A little while back I did a column on how various under-the-hood drive belts should be examined before the high-heat season. I advised checking them for proper tension and for signs of wear. A loose belt, I wrote, "can cause the alternator to work inefficiently, the engine to run hot, and the air conditioner to work only so-so." I should have taken my own advice, but in a way, I'm glad I didn't. Let me explain.

A few weeks before I wrote that article I had my car serviced. The belts were supposed to be checked along with a number of other engine items. When a couple of friends and I prepared for a trip to Mexico, I didn't think of checking them again.

My old '75 Volvo ran just fine, uncomplaining on the trip south, just as it has done for the past 300,000 miles. But as we neared Guaymas, a sleepy fishing town about 350 miles south of Tucson, Arizona, on the Gulf of California, I noticed the fuel gauge was near empty. Couldn't be, I thought, it was half full in Hermosillo, just 80-odd miles back. Taking no chances, we pulled into the first Pemex station and gassed up. The gauge went up, but not to where it should have. There is an electrical problem somewhere, I thought.

We noticed too that the AC wasn't working very well, the fan barely blowing. A little hot and a little cranky, the three of us and the car limped into our motel on the San Carlos strip, a beach community not far from the main town.

The next morning I went to start the car—nothing! Not even a moan from under the hood. I cleaned and tightened the battery terminals. No help. We started the car by pushing it and headed into town to look for a repair shop. Just outside Guaymas I spotted an "Auto Servicio Electrico." Just what the doctor ordered.

We wheeled the car into the small shop and I approached a man who was busily working on an alternator. In my broken Spanish I got the point across that something was making the car lose its charge or preventing it from charging. He dropped what he was doing and came to check our car.

Felipe pulled the hot terminal off the battery and declared that I needed a new one, sending a boy on a bike to a parts store to get it. He then checked the battery cells and jump-started the car to check the alternator. Both were OK. Then he checked the belts. I don't know how you say "loose as a goose" in Spanish, but that is what they were.

I took for granted that the belts had been checked when I had had the car serviced. They hadn't. With a big grin, Felipe said that the belts, along with the battery terminal (another item that should have been checked) were causing my no-charge situation. He tightened the belts and put on the new terminal. After jump-starting the car again, he assured me that by the time we got back to the motel, about 7 miles, the battery would be charged. He was right.

Loose belts and a dirty battery terminal—two inexcusable items to cause trouble, especially on a trip, especially in a foreign country, and especially for someone who should know better. But, in a way, I'm glad it happened. It reminded me not to take for granted any repair work and, if possible, to check to see if the work was done properly. It reinforced the fact that even the simplest items can disable a pile of iron just as efficiently as a blown engine or a dropped transmission. It underscored how important it is to check the little things.

And if it hadn't happened, I never would have had the chance to meet Felipe at his auto electric shop on the outskirts of Guaymas. I would not have been witness to what would be considered a phenomenon in the United States: a mechanic dropping his work to help a traveler in distress. I wouldn't have had the chance to be dumbfounded when he presented his bill for about $2.50 American money for 45 minutes' work and parts (you bet he got a tip!). And I wouldn't have an even warmer feeling for our neighbors south of the border.

Some things, it seems, are just meant to be.

Proper Oil Filter Service Could Save Your Car's Life

A service bulletin recently sent to me by the Pennzoil people reinforced some valuable rules about choosing and changing an oil filter. Whether you are a do-it-yourselfer or a have-it-doner, this information can be important to your car's life.

The do-it-yourselfer will benefit directly; the have-it-doner can also benefit by observing the oil change when possible and by yelling if the mechanic violates any of the following steps.

Make certain the old gasket is removed entirely when the old filter is taken off. The filter-mounting base should be checked thoroughly to see that no part of the old gasket remains. This is an all-too-frequent occurrence and, although it could go undetected and not cause problems for a number of oil changes, it could in some future cold-start situation cause overpressurization because of sluggish operation of the pressure-relief valve in the improperly mounted oil filter.

The filter-mounting base should be wiped clean of all contaminants. Feel it and visually inspect it. The new gasket on the new filter must also be perfectly clean. If you are doing the job yourself, it is a good idea to leave the filter in its package until the last moment. Remember, a small piece of grit in a new gasket can result in gasket failure.

Rub the new filter gasket with new, fresh motor oil, preferably the kind you will be putting in the crankcase. Do not, I repeat, *do not* use grease of any kind on the gasket. Use only fresh motor oil.

When placing the filter on its mount, take great care that it does not become cross-threaded on the mounting-base stud. If it does not go on easily, remove it and try again—gently. Never force it.

Screw on the filter until you feel light resistance, indicating that the gasket has made contact with the mounting base. Visually note a point on the filter and tighten it one full turn until that point comes back around to the same position. You'll need a filter wrench to get the full turn. Do not try to estimate proper filter torque by using only hand pressure. A hand-tightened filter is a major cause of leaks. Use a filter wrench or be certain your mechanic does.

After filling the crankcase with fresh oil, start the engine and observe the oil-pressure light or gauge while the engine idles. It should take no more than 9 or 10 seconds for the light to go out or the gauge to read normal. If this does not happen, stop the engine, loosen the oil filter to break a possible air lock inside, then retighten it and attempt another start.

If oil pressure is still not evident, take off the filter, fill it with fresh oil, and repeat the procedure. If oil pressure is still not evident, do not attempt to start your car again. Have it towed to a garage. Never drive a car without proper oil pressure, and never rev the engine in an attempt to gain oil pressure.

After the engine starts, oil pressure has been normal for at least two minutes, and no leaks are seen, the car is ready for the road. If you had someone else change the oil and filter, start the car and repeat the above procedure before driving it away from the mechanic's garage.

When choosing an oil filter for your car, make certain it is one that fits your car and is listed in an oil-filter application manual. Filters might look alike but can vary dramatically in the services they provide. They can have different strengths, flow characteristics, inside valve structures, and pressure-relief valve settings.

For instance, two look-alikes can differ by as much as 45 psi (pounds per square inch) in the bypass setting. This could result in no oil being filtered if a filter with a 7-9 psi bypass setting is used where a 45 psi is called for.

When it comes to filter choice and change, do not take chances—and do not buy from the guy at the swap meet with those super weekend filter specials. It could cost you your engine.

The Right Oil Filter

Most of us know motor oil is meant to lubricate an engine; not many know that it has other important functions. Three of the most important are to clean, cool, and seal.

Oil must be clean to accomplish these three goals. The main item in the oil system that keeps it clean is the oil filter. Filters remove contaminant particles from the motor oil. Most modern filters remove particles about 15 microns and larger.

A filter must be designed to permit oil to flow through, yet not be so compact that it will stop the flow of oil. However, this task is made more difficult when oil thickens due to cold weather or when it becomes supersaturated with contaminants.

A recent Pennzoil technical bulletin presented some good pointers about oil filters; I think they are worth repeating.

All oil filters aren't the same. Most modern oil filters include an interior valve that allows unfiltered oil to bypass the filter element and still reach engine components if the filter should become clogged. These bypass valves are typically located at either the dome end of the filter or near the threaded hole at the opposite end.

Although you can find both types of filters—those with the bypass on the dome end and those with the bypass on the engine side—filters with the bypass valve located near the oil inlet/outlet ports will not allow bypassed oil to recirculate around the filter element or through the collected residue found in the dome end of the filter.

When an oil filter of this type enters the bypass stage—and due to the thickening of oil, it can do so on cold mornings even though the filter is not clogged—it isn't as likely to pick up contaminants, because most of its oil flow doesn't get into the body or dome end of the filter. The filter operates in bypass mode with minimum reintroduction of contaminants.

On a filter with the bypass located at the dome end, the bypassed oil comes in contact with the element and residue collected in the dome end; a lot of old dirt and grit is then reintroduced into the engine.

There's an additional reason to be selective when choosing an oil filter: Modern motor oils have additive packages that hold contaminants in suspension. If a filter can remove and hold contaminants (without reintroducing them during the bypass stage) the additives will not become depleted as fast and the oil will remain effective longer.

Some car manufacturers consider the position of the filter bypass valve so crucial that one has designed the system of some of its engines to include a bypass in the oil pump, while another specifies that filters used in its cars should have the bypass valve located at the engine side (threaded side) of the filter.

You might want to consider these points the next time you shop for an oil filter or have your oil changed. If the person changing your oil doesn't know which side of the filter the bypass is located on, request that he find out. With the wrong type of filter on your car a little bit of your engine's life could be passing you by each day.

Filters: Good Defense Against Automotive Wear

OK, so we've seen worse winters. But that's no excuse to ignore preparing your car for spring and summer driving. A number of items should be checked or changed to ensure maximum performance and longevity for your car. These items tend to lose their effectiveness during the winter— yes, even a mild winter.

Your car has a number of filter systems; they are the first line of defense against contaminant wear. When any of these filters becomes clogged with dirt, water, and whatnot, they become useless. Just like the bag on your vacuum cleaner, they should be changed periodically. No better time than after cold-weather driving, the exact type of driving that makes filters work overtime.

Paper-element engine air filters should always be changed, never cleaned. If you haven't done this since last fall, chances are your car is craving a fresh one. Air filters are cheap insurance against abrasives, the number-one messenger of doom for automobile engines. Always change air filters in accordance with the car manufacturer's suggested interval for severe-service driving. These intervals vary from car to car, so check your owner's manual for the correct one for your car.

Always change the oil filter when changing the oil. Sounds logical, but many people try to save a buck by changing the filter at *every other* oil change. It's the height of false economy. Fresh oil filters are crucial for today's smaller, higher-revving engines. They need clean oil to function properly and achieve any semblance of longevity. Again, follow the manufacturer's recommendations for severe-service oil-and-filter-change intervals.

With more and more new cars using fuel injection, the fuel filter is key to your car's performance ability. Starting and engine-power problems can often be traced to a clogged fuel filter. A new one can work wonders.

If someone were to take his hands and slowly cut off the air supply at your throat, you wouldn't feel too good and your performance would suffer considerably. Dirt has the same effect on your car's fuel filter: It slowly cuts off the supply of gasoline to the engine. The filter is there to trap dirt, but it can hold only so much and must be changed periodically for top engine life and performance. Don't make it harder on your engine by ignoring this crucial item.

How about the positive crankcase-ventilation (PCV) filter system and the PCV valve itself? The filter and valve must be clean to guarantee filtered air to your engine's crankcase. Cold-weather driving tends to clog them quickly and can be a prime cause of rough engine running, poor fuel economy, and undue use of oil.

Ever hear of a transmission filter? A lot of drivers haven't. Automatic transmissions probably have more parts than an engine, and each one works under extremely close tolerances. This causes the transmission to shed metal much like a dog sheds hair. The metal-wear debris, much of it normal and acceptable, is trapped by the filter and kept out of the circulating lubricating fluid. If the filter becomes clogged, much of this abrasive debris is recirculated throughout the transmission where it will do its dirty work. If you haven't changed the filter, there's no better time than now.

Fresh air, oil, gas, PCV, and transmission filters: a defensive team effort against unnecessary automotive wear. Football pundits always say a good offense will beat a good defense. Automotive pundits know that the opposite is true: A good defense of fresh filters will always beat the offensive offense of engine and transmission contaminants.

Brakes: The Most Powerful System in Your Car

What is the most powerful system in your car? Before you answer, let me define what I mean by system. In this case a system is an individual working unit that contributes to the overall operation of your car. For instance, the engine, suspension, brakes, and transmission are some of the major systems in a car.

So which do you think is the most powerful? I hear some saying, "the stereo system in my kid's car," and I guess I'd have a hard time arguing with that. And I hear a resounding chorus of "ayes" for the engine as being the most powerful system. And indeed, that does sound like the answer. But it isn't.

The most powerful system in any car, no matter what its horsepower, is the braking system. Think about it. No matter how much power the engine has, the brakes always have the capacity to override the engine's power. Thank goodness for that. In the battle between brakes and accelerator, the brakes will win if they are in proper operating condition.

Note the proviso, "in proper operating condition." The brakes are one of those automotive systems that are often ignored until work is absolutely necessary. We wait to put on new brake shoes or pads until we hear metal-to-metal contact, which requires resurfacing or even replacing the drums or rotors. This is an unnecessary expense and can be dangerous.

As a rule, front brake linings wear faster than rear ones, and many times it is an acceptable and safe practice to redo only the front brakes the first time around. That saves you some money and doesn't compromise the efficiency of the braking system.

Or we ignore the hydraulic part of the system. When was the last time you changed the brake fluid in your car? Or checked the hoses? Hydraulic brake fluid has built-in protectants to disperse condensation, but these can be depleted and the moisture in the system can cause parts to corrode. Master cylinders and individual wheel cylinders are notorious for becoming pitted due to moisture buildup in old fluid. I suggest changing the brake fluid by completely flushing the system at least every two years, or at the interval recommended in your owner's manual.

You can improve the overall longevity of the braking system, especially the brake pads and linings, by observing a few simple driving practices. If you pump the brakes gently instead of applying continuous pressure each time you stop, you allow for brief intervals of cooling at the surface of the linings and wheels. Ever smell the noxious fumes emanating from a large truck after it has come down a long, steep hill? The heat generated at the brakes becomes excessive and causes the linings to burn and lose their braking ability. Overheated brakes sometimes fail. That's why you see those runaway truck ramps on steep hills.

So pump those brakes gently and evenly, and you'll increase their life dramatically. You should avoid hard or sudden stops when they aren't necessary; they are not only tough on the brakes, they play havoc with the entire suspension system, from the shock absorbers to the springs.

If you do need a new set of brakes, break them in properly. Press hard on the brake pedal while feeding enough gas to keep the car moving. Do this at five-second intervals every 20 or so miles for the first 200 miles to burn off any debris on the brake linings and to help the surfaces mate properly and efficiently. This simple procedure starts the brakes out right and allows them to be at their most efficient for the life of the linings.

Spot-Check Your Car for Fluid Leaks

I was perusing some information sent to me by the Automotive Information Council (AIC), and one item caught my eye. AIC has a little pamphlet that gives tips on how to check various under-the-hood components and make sure your car is in proper working order. AIC recommends a once-a-month inspection of this sort. A good idea.

But let's take it one step further by suggesting an inspection that can be done almost every day. It's an easy preventive-maintenance practice that anyone can do. All it takes is a glance at your driveway or garage floor. I call it the "spot check."

The area underneath your car should be inspected frequently for fluid leaks. The most common liquids that will "spot" a garage floor are motor oil, grease, transmission fluid, radiator coolant/antifreeze, brake fluid, and power-steering fluid. It will pay for the conscientious car owner to be aware of the look and smell of these various fluids, and under which part of the car they are likely to be found. If ignored, those little spots will turn into big ones, and big ones mean big problems.

It's best to start with a nice clean area in which to park your car, so any signs of fluid spotting will be easy to—forgive me—spot. If the floor is already stained, a large piece of clean cardboard or even newspapers will work nicely as a leak detector.

The color of the fluid should give you a clue as to which unit is leaking.

○ Green-yellow drops or puddles indicate radiator coolant.

○ Motor oil is, well, oil-colored, usually brown to blackish.

○ Transmission fluid will have a red tint.

○ Brake fluid is clear, has a slight peppermint odor, and is usually found near the wheels.

○ Rear-axle fluid/grease, like motor oil, will be brown and is found underneath the rear of the car.

○ Power-steering fluid, like brake fluid, is usually clear, although some cars may use automatic-transmission fluid in the power-steering unit.

Don't be alarmed if you find pools of water underneath the engine compartment. Most likely, it will be condensation from the air conditioner and is perfectly normal. The water will eventually evaporate; the other fluids will not.

Remember that all fluids—yes, even radiator coolant—are lubricants. Any decrease in the quantity cuts the unit's ability to function at maximum efficiency. Leaks on the garage floor are signs that one or more mechanical units are lacking proper amounts of fluid, and that means they will wear out faster.

Spotting leaks via the spot-check method is a valuable tool for catching a problem in its early stages, allowing you time to correct it before it becomes a wallet-sucking monster. So if you look at your garage or driveway floor and see spots before your eyes, don't run to the eye doctor. Check it out; try to find the source of those spots. Your car is trying to tell you that something is wrong.

Check That Battery Before Old Man Winter Does

Under summer- and fall-like temperatures batteries might work just fine, have plenty of power, crank the engine fast, and start the car quickly and efficiently. But, lo and behold, when the temperature drops, so does the willingness to perform. The lower the temperature, the crankier the battery.

Many times the battery is not at fault. Indeed, some may be worn out, shot, long past their warranty period, and these should be replaced. But with others, symptoms that appear to be terminal (no pun) might just be the battery's way of saying, "Hey, check me out. Structurally, I'm fine, but I can't work without proper nourishment and efficient support systems."

If your heater fan is running slow or your lights are a bit dim or your turn signals aren't blinking as fast as they used to, chances are the alternator belt needs to be tightened or replaced.

If this belt does not have the proper tension, the alternator will not supply an adequate charge to the battery and the battery will gradually lose its power to perform. (Even a new battery will not hold up long under a no-charge or insufficient-charge situation.) Make certain this belt is tight—It should give no more than 3/8 inch when moderate thumb pressure is applied. If the belt is worn, frayed, cracked, or glazed, replace it. Trying to make it through a severe weather with an old belt is false economy. Remember that an overglazed belt can slip even when it is tightened properly.

Next on the agenda is the condition of the battery connections. Corrosion, oil, and dirt buildup between the battery posts and battery-cable clamps aren't always visible to the naked eye. The connections can appear to be clean and tight, but dirty, unseen interfaces between the two can impede—sometimes even halt—current flow from the battery to the engine's starter motor and from the alternator to the battery. Never rely on a visual inspection for a prewinter battery checkup.

The battery cables should be removed (check your owner's manual for the sequence of removal). Bathe both the positive and negative battery terminals and the cable clamps in a mild solution of baking soda and water. Be careful not to drip any into the six holes found on the battery; it will neutralize the acid found there. If the cables look shaky or if the clamp ends can't be tightened properly, replace them.

Once clean and dry, the posts and clamps should be brushed with a battery-terminal cleaner or some coarse steel wool. I've even used sandpaper in a pinch. When the metal is shiny, dry, and clean, replace the clamps and tighten gently, making certain you don't bend the battery posts in the process.

Check the level of electrolyte and, if it is low, add distilled water to bring the fluid up to the required level. (Never smoke or bring a flame near an open battery. The gases can explode.)

Clean, tight battery connections, a full fill of electrolyte, and a properly charging alternator will ensure fast, easy starts if the battery is still in serviceable condition. A little foresight now can save a lot of mournful hindsight later. Check that battery and charging system before Old Man Winter does it for you.

The Big Three for Trouble-Free Driving

What do you think is the number 1 cause of a mechanical breakdown on the highway? OK, what do you think is the number 1 cause of any kind of breakdown, including mechanical, on the highway? Give up?

Hey, don't give up so easily, think about it. What things will most likely disable a vehicle on the road? OK, let's see how close you are to being right.

According to a U.S. Department of Transportation technical report, bad tires are the number 1 nonmechanical cause of breakdowns on the highway. Can you guess the number 2 nonmechanical cause? It is running out of gas, an old-fashioned but still potent way of putting your car out of commission.

Now, the number 1 cause of mechanical breakdowns on the highway: It is—ta da!—a cooling-system problem. The cooling system ranks number 3 after bad tires and running out of gas on the overall highway-problem profile.

The chances of having tire problems, running out of gas, or experiencing cooling-system malfunctions are three to five times greater than those of the next item on the list, engine trouble. This means problems with valves, bearings, or other major engine complications. In descending order after engine trouble are problems with the fuel system, electrical system, transmission, drive line, ignition, wheels, suspension, fire, brakes, other equipment, and cargo.

This study is telling us to be doubly sure that our tires are in good shape, that we have plenty of gas, and that our cooling system is operating at maximum efficiency before we hit the highway. Remember, hoses and belts that run the water pump and cooling fan are also vital parts of the cooling system, along with the coolant/antifreeze mixture and the radiator itself.

There is no good excuse for running out of gas, although I admit I've done it. Tires should undergo a routine safety inspection at least once a month, and the air should be checked even more frequently. The cooling system is the bugger. We tend to take it for granted and don't change the coolant every year or at least every other year. We seldom check the condition of the belts and hoses, other than glancing at them when the hood is open.

We pay for these slights, because the cooling system, as shown by the government study, has a way of getting even on the road at night when you are driving alone.

Even though this was a highway study, you can apply the results to everyday in-town driving, because it is likely that in-town problems will be similar.

Keep the big three under your thumb and both you and your car will have a more relaxed life, free of trouble and worry.

Non-Use Can Be Hard on Your Car

"When Rolls-Royce and Bentley automobiles break, it is often because they are not driven enough. Routine service needs are often overlooked because the ultra-expensive luxury cars are generally driven very little." Those were the two lead sentences in a recent *Automotive News* article, "Don't Let Rolls Sit Idle."

You don't have to own a Rolls-Royce or Bentley to know that your car can pay the piper for non-use. Think of it this way: If those very well-built, durable vehicles can suffer wear and tear just by sitting, your less well-built car will probably suffer more under similar circumstances.

Owners think that because the vehicle isn't being used, it isn't wearing and therefore doesn't need servicing. It sounds logical, but it is convoluted logic that's hard for many car owners to decipher. In reality, non-use can be as wear-intensive as driving the vehicle hard.

Remember the body/car analogy: If you don't use your body, it begins to atrophy, becomes weak and flabby, isn't as serviceable as it once was and is more susceptible to disease and wear and tear. Same with your car, be it a Rolls or a Yugo.

Wear from non-use is a double-edged sword. If you don't use the car you tend to forget about servicing it. That neglect then causes parts to wear more rapidly, both when the car is used and when it is idle. Here's an example of how non-use works:

Non- or limited use causes various lubricants—oil, transmission, power steering and brake fluids, coolant (you bet; coolant is also a lubricant), and differential fluids—to lose their protective qualities. Non-use breeds fluid deterioriation through condensation buildup, unburned hydrocarbon, and varnish and acid buildup. The acids and condensates are particularly harmful because they are working on the metal parts when the car sits idle, rusting and pitting them. The car must be used frequently—at least several times a week—to ensure that these contaminants are being boiled, burned, or heated away. The problem is intensified in cold weather.

To prevent wear and mechanical problems that can result from lack of maintenance, stick to a service schedule during times of non- or little use the same way you would if you were driving the car daily. Don't alter your fluid change or tune-up schedule because you aren't using the car. Remember, if a Rolls can break down because of non-use, so can your car.

Your Owner's Manual Is Good Reading

When things get a little slow around the Sikorsky household I turn to one of my favorite pastimes, reading a good book. Oh, I could pick up one of the current Top-10 novels my wife is usually engrossed in, or I could even massage my ego and read a graph or two from some of my own books. (It's amazing how one forgets what he wrote just a few years ago.)

But do I do any of these things? Nah. Instead, I pick up the owner's manual of whatever new car or cars I happen to be test-driving that week. In the course of a year I've read just about all of them. Talk about excitement! Talk about fascinating reading! Hey, this is *New York Times* bestseller-list stuff.

Of course, every car owner should be intimately familiar with his particular owner's manual; that's a given. But when I pore over the various manufacturer's manuals, I often come across helpful suggestions that are applicable to all cars.

The 1990 Hyundai Sonata with its new V6 engine is a nice car. It also has an information-packed owner's manual with one of the best do-it-yourself maintenance sections. Here are some points from Hyundai you can do no matter what kind of car you drive.

o "Under some conditions your parking brake can freeze in the engaged position. This is most likely to happen when there is an accumulation of snow or ice around or near the rear brakes or if the brakes are wet. If you think the parking brake may freeze, apply it only temporarily while you put the gear selector lever in P (park), and block the rear wheels so the car cannot roll. Then release the parking brake." I might add, don't try this if you are parked on a steep hill.

○ Here's a tip you'll find in all owner's manuals: Don't do any towing with a new car during its first 1,200 miles in order to allow the engine to properly break in. Hyundai adds: "Failure to heed this warning may result in serious engine or transaxle damage." This also applies to an older car with a freshly rebuilt engine or transmission.

○ Don't let one kind of trouble cause you more serious problems. Cars with transaxles (that's front-wheel drive) can suffer damage because of improper towing. Never tow a car with an automatic transaxle from the rear with the front wheels on the ground. It can seriously damage the transaxle. If the car must be towed from the rear, a towing dolly must be used under the front wheels. Otherwise, tow with the front end lifted off the ground and the rear wheels rolling, or place the entire car on the truck bed. Good towing companies should know this—you should too, just in case.

○ Do you know that it is important to service your air conditioner in winter too? It's easy to do and doesn't cost a penny. Savvy car owners have done this for years. Now you can join them. Hyundai: "To lubricate the compressor and the seals in the system, the air conditioner should be run for at least 10 minutes each week. This is particularly important during cool weather when the air-conditioning system is not otherwise in use." If you want your air conditioner to last and work at maximum efficiency there is no time like now to start. It may seem weird to run the AC when it's 10 degrees above zero outside, but it's worth it.

○ Many newer cars have electric engine-cooling fans that turn on and off according to engine temperature. If you are working under the hood—even checking the oil—stay away from the fan because it could kick on at any time.

○ Any time you replace an accessory belt on the engine—we used to call them fan belts—it should be readjusted for tension again in a few weeks to eliminate slack resulting from the initial stretching after use. Wonder why your AC or alternator or power steering isn't working too well? Could be that you didn't readjust tension after you put that new belt on.

○ "Grinding noise from power steering pump may be heard immediately after the engine is started in extremely cold conditions," says Hyundai. "In this case, if the noise stops during warm-up there is no abnormal function in the system. This is due to a power-steering fluid characteristic in extremely cold conditions." That's probably true no matter what car you are driving.

○ Do not push or pull a car with a catalytic converter to get it started. It can cause the converter to overload. Check your individual owner's manual for proper emergency starting procedures.

o Most newer cars use halogen headlamps. If you must replace a halogen bulb remember that it contains gas under pressure and if it shatters could produce flying fragments. Always wear eye protection when servicing halogen bulbs, and dispose of the old one in the protective cap and carton the new one came in.

o Brake fluid is unforgiving. If you add your own, remember that it can damage vision if it gets into an eye and it will also severely damage a vehicle's paint. Remove it immediately if it spills on a car's finish.

Oh yes, how do you say "Thanks, Hyundai" in Korean?

Treat Your Cooling System Right

Can you believe it? It's spring-cleaning time again for your car. One of the most overlooked items in the annual pilgrimage to the font of auto renovation is radiator coolant. People wax and wash and polish and tune and lube and change oil and clean interiors, but the poor old cooling system is neglected and alone under the hood doing one of the toughest jobs in all cardom. Never getting any credit, seldom getting any help.

Changing the radiator/cooling system antifreeze/coolant should be an annual event. The best time to do it is prior to either the cold weather or summer heat. In winter antifreeze protects the engine from freezing, while in summer it protects it against overheating. Pretty versatile stuff this antifreeze/coolant.

The main reason for changing coolant is that the additive package in it is used up over time. For instance, antifreeze/coolant contains rust and corrosion inhibitors that can protect new aluminum radiators as well as older ones. As the solution works to protect, the additives become used up. Also, additives and the solution itself can be lost by evaporation or through small, undetected leaks in the cooling system. Each time you add water to make up for the lost solution you weaken the power of the coolant to protect. Because of these processes, the coolant gradually becomes less potent.

Imagine, if you will, a bar of soap. It does its job washing hands time and time again, but eventually it wears down and can't do its work. The additive package is like that, taking anywhere from one to two years to become depleted, depending on how and under what conditions the car is driven.

The amount of additives in the coolant varies from manufacturer to manufacturer, with the cheaper brands containing less. Bargain brands may also contain less glycol (the main ingredient that protects against boiling and freezing) and more water than name brands. Quality antifreeze/coolant is made with approximately 97 percent glycol. An expert for an antifreeze maker tells me that some bargain brands contain as little as 50 percent glycol. So be careful—you get what you pay for.

Use the dilution factor recommended in the owner's manual when you change the coolant. Usually a mix of 50 percent antifreeze/coolant and 50 percent water is recommended. Adding more coolant in hope of getting more protection might have the opposite effect; the system becomes less and not more efficient. Both the coolant and the cooling system are designed to work with about a 50/50 mix or the mix recommended in the owner's manual.

Changing the coolant annually (I recommend this instead of every other year) can eliminate the need for power cooling-system flushes that might be necessary after the coolant is left in too long.

Problems with the cooling system, according to a U.S. Department of Transportation study, are the number 1 cause of mechanical breakdown on the road. And neglect is what causes those problems. Treat your cooling system right and it will return the favor.

And if you get stuck some place this summer with the radiator boiling over and kids crying and the wife mad, I hope I'm not near enough to hear you say, "Boy, I sure wish I had listened to ol' what'sizname."

Thermostats Keep Autos Cool—and Hot

If someone isn't feeling well, one of the first things a doctor does is take the patient's temperature. If the reading is more than 98.6 F, the doctor confirms what the patient knew all along: Something is wrong and is causing the body's reliable and accurate temperature-control system to overheat. Your car also has a temperature-control system, and if it gets out of whack, the car will complain that it doesn't feel well.

The cooling-system thermostat is an integral part of this temperature-control system. It works like the one that regulates the temperature inside your home, shutting off or turning on depending on the temperature of the environment. In the case of the car's thermostat, the environment is the engine.

The thermostat will open or close when the coolant in the cooling system reaches a designated temperature. When the engine is cold, the thermostat remains closed; when the engine is hot, it opens.

Most thermostats open, and thus permit coolant to flow through the engine's cooling system, when the coolant reaches a temperature between 170 degrees and 195 degrees. If the coolant temperature falls below this range, the thermostat closes, hindering the flow of coolant and allowing the engine to increase its temperature. It's like having a temperature-activated guard open and close a gate.

The thermostat must function properly for your car's engine to run with maximum efficiency. If the thermostat is stuck in a closed or partially closed position, the free flow of coolant is blocked, and the engine is likely to run hot or overheat, especially during summer driving.

If the thermostat is stuck in the open position, the amount of time needed to warm up the engine is greatly extended. In this case, fuel economy and engine longevity take a nosedive.

The cooling-system thermostat plays a very important part in your car's economy and engine-wear equation. Anything you can do to get the engine out of its cold operation mode as fast as possible improves gas mileage and boosts longevity.

The thermostat is a basic consideration in this quest. By staying closed when the engine is cold, it accelerates engine warm-up time and reduces the amount of time the car must spend in high wear and low fuel-economy operation.

The temperature designation of a thermostat (195 degrees, for instance) doesn't indicate that this is the temperature at which your engine will operate. It is the temperature at which the thermostat will open and permit coolant to start flowing through the engine's cooling system. Your engine, especially on a hot day, will probably run hotter than the thermostat's designated temperature. In most cases this is perfectly normal, just as long as the engine temperature doesn't reach the red or danger range on your temperature gauge, or as long as the "hot" light doesn't come on.

Once the thermostat is completely open, it is up to the car's cooling system to guarantee that the vehicle runs within factory-set engine-temperature parameters.

If your car takes forever to warm up, or if it runs hot as a matter of course, you might need to replace the thermostat. There's no better time to have it checked than before the onset of high summer or low winter temperatures.

Now Is the Time to Cool it

This is the time of the year when all good car owners should come to the aid of their cooling systems. "Oh no," I hear you say, "not another column on changing the coolant." Hang on, this one's different.

After a long, hard winter of fending off cold weather, cooling systems should be readied for the summer heat ahead. Of course, cooling systems were made to keep the engine cool, but with a little understanding of how the system works and what makes it deteriorate, you can feel more confident that yours will last longer and give trouble-free service. Here are some things you didn't know about your cooling system.

For years I have recommended changing the antifreeze/coolant on a yearly basis or at the most every two years. As more information on cooling-system maintenance becomes available, it turns out that I have been right; it's folly to ignore the coolant. So that's rule number 1: Be certain your coolant is changed each year.

Any air leak in the cooling system should be fixed immediately. Carbon dioxide in the air, when it mixes with coolant, will form carbonic acid. It will pit cooling-system parts and play havoc with the water pump. Oxygen in the air will deplete the coolant's built-in corrosion inhibitors.

Loss of pressure in the cooling system due to air leaks (usually from a bad radiator cap or pressure relief valve failure) allows coolant to boil. In extreme cases this can lead to engine failure. Outside air infiltrating the coolant can also cause salt buildup on parts.

When you mix the coolant/antifreeze with water to the specified owner's-manual recommended mix (usually 50 percent water/50 percent coolant/antifreeze) be sure you don't agitate the mixture and get air bubbles in it. That's another way air can infiltrate the system—and air just isn't welcome there.

Pour the mixture slowly into the radiator and allow time for trapped air to escape. Don't let the radiator chugalug the mixture; that will trap air inside.

As the coolant cools it contracts. This action in itself draws air into the system (it's unavoidable). That's one of the reasons it should be changed yearly—to guard against any damage air infiltration may have done to the coolant.

If you have any kind of electrical-system grounding problems, correct them at once. Electricity always seeks out coolant or motor oil to ground through, and that can destroy an engine.

According to James E. O'Neil of LOCC Corp., who provides cooling-system corrosion-inhibition programs for large fleets, as little as one-half volt in the cooling system can destroy an engine in time. In large diesel rigs, only 2 volts can destroy an engine in 24,000 miles, while 24 volts in the coolant due to a starter ground problem will put the engine to rest in a mere 6,000 miles. You're not driving a big rig, but electrical ground problems affect automobiles, too.

The hotter the operating temperature of the engine, the more likely is its cooling system to pit. Today's engines run hotter, mainly so they can minimize emissions and get better fuel economy. But the higher heat is also a bugaboo for engine cooling systems.

If a cooling system isn't maintained properly it will become acidic as the engine reaches operating temperature. The hotter the engine runs, the more acidic the coolant will become. In essence, the engine becomes a huge wet-cell battery: The coolant is the electrolyte between the two dissimilar metals used in the engine and cooling system.

The type of water you use is very important. Big fleets chemically test the water before they mix it with antifreeze. Water that might be suitable for engines operating at 180 degrees Fahrenheit to 190-degrees Fahrenheit can actually be bad for those operating at higher temperatures.

Cooling-system water should not contain hard minerals or be contaminated with by-products. Distilled water is great, but because it can be some of the most corrosive water there is, don't allow it to come in contact with metal or concrete before mixing it with the coolant. Contamination from plumbing or lime in concrete can cause engine damage. Keep the water in a plastic or glass container until you are ready to use it.

If you live or drive in an elevation above 5,000 feet, use 60 percent antifreeze in the mixture. This raises the boiling temperature of the antifreeze to compensate for the approximate 3-degree Fahrenheit drop in boiling point for each 1,000-foot rise in elevation. In other words, the higher you go, the easier it is for the cooling system to boil over. That's why you see cars pulled over on mountain grades with their radiators steaming.

Never let your coolant mixture fall below the "add" level. Too little antifreeze is as bad as any cheap brand or an incorrect mixture. And never, *never* use water alone in modern cooling systems.

Now that you know all this stuff you never heard about before, you have no excuse not to start taking better care of your cooling system. It's easy, not really expensive and cool.

Pure Antifreeze Can Harm Your Car's Cooling System

I receive a lot of letters asking about antifreeze/coolants. Maybe it's the current high price of the liquid that prompts these inquiries, but most of them are similar to the following letter. The question and my answer offer some little-known insights into this all-important fluid almost every car must use.

Dear Bob:
Why can't the consumer use pure, 100-percent antifreeze in the car's cooling system? A lot of us think it would be preferable to trying to mix the proper proportion of this and that.

In searching for an answer, I have heard numerous opinions from various "experts." Some mechanics/technicians say it's just fine—do it! Others claim that pure antifreeze will damage the car's cooling system. Manufacturers recommend not using more than 70 percent, but they don't say why and won't respond to a consumer's question.

Maybe it's a silly question. Perhaps we should instinctively know the answer. At any rate I would be grateful if you could shed some light on this mystery.

J.H., Fayetteville, N.C.

Dear J.H.: There are three main reasons why pure antifreeze (ethylene glycol) shouldn't be used at full concentration in a car's cooling system. The first and perhaps most important reason is that pure ethylene glycol freezes between 0 degrees and minus 5 degrees F. It is only when pure antifreeze/coolant is mixed with water that its freezing point is lowered. So if you need protection below the zero mark, you had best mix the antifreeze with water in the proportions suggested by either the car or antifreeze manufacturer. Playing guessing games or trying to alter the manufacturer's suggested proportions will only do your car harm.

The second reason is the flip side of the first one. Pure antifreeze/coolant doesn't have the heat-transfer abilities that an antifreeze/coolant-and-water mixture does. In fact, if pure antifreeze/coolant is used in a car's cooling system, the system loses about 35 percent of the heat-transfer capabilities it would otherwise have when antifreeze is mixed with the proper amount of water.

Now this might not seem too important in winter, but it is crucial in summer driving, especially in our power-accessory-laden vehicles where engine temperatures can soar. The cooling fluid must have the ability to absorb heat and carry it away from the engine—the faster, the better. Pure antifreeze/coolant isn't nearly as efficient at getting the heat out of the engine as is antifreeze/coolant and water. Running on pure antifreeze/coolant is pure folly and will only hasten the demise of your engine.

Reason Number 3 is that water must be mixed with the antifreeze/coolant in order to keep the performance additives (silicates, phosphates, and nitrates) suspended. Without water these important additives have a tendency to settle. If they do that, you lose anti-corrosion and other additive protection.

That's also why—although you won't find it stated on a container—it's a good idea to turn over the container of fresh antifreeze and shake it a time or two before adding it to the cooling system. The little extra shake is insurance that the additives are fully suspended in the container and haven't migrated to the bottom.

What all this is telling us is that the manufacturers know more about their products than the man in the street does. Second-guessing can have disastrous consequences—no matter how logical it seems at the time. As for the mechanics who told you to "do it!" they have a lot to learn, don't they? It's a shame people like that are telling us how to care for our cars.

7

Earth-friendly driving & maintenance

EARTH IS A VERY FORGIVING AND FLEXIBLE PLANET. It's a lot like the big old cast-iron automobile engines of yesteryear. You could abuse them again and again, but because of their innate capacity to recover, they kept running. But even those old behemoths, when taxed repeatedly, would finally give up the ghost. Earth could suffer the same fate if abuses against it don't stop. As grand as it is, the sphere is quite fragile and completely dependent on the interworkings of all its parts. The abuses I'm talking about are the innumerable toxic wastes disgorged by man into the biosphere.

One of the biggest abusers is car exhaust. This seemingly inconsequential polluting by drivers, who don't understand or care that car exhaust can affect something so large, is one of the main ingredients of planet degradation.

It's those bits and pieces, when coupled with the millions of others, that will ultimately spell disaster. We don't need a nuclear war or a nuclear winter to disarm the planet. We can, and are, doing it with our cars, trucks, and buses spewing millions of tons of toxins into the atmosphere. Unchecked, this poison will ultimately tax the recovery capabilities of Earth to such a degree that it will no longer be able to reverse the damage we inflict upon it.

Consider for a moment, if you will, automotive maintenance and the role it plays in the preceding scenario. Every vehicle owner must realize that a vehicle carries with it an unwritten mandate to maintain it at its most efficient so as not to add more waste to the already overburdened atmosphere. Indeed, maintenance, once the option of the car owner, should become a sacred responsibility.

We have made admirable strides because of some who have cared about what is happening. Cars burn fuel more effectively, emissions have been greatly reduced, fuels are cleaner, oils more efficient. But these improvements are only as good as the owner's commitment to keep the car in the shape it was meant to be in.

Maintenance should not be avoided, for example, if you are selling your car in a year and know it can run that long without any care. On the contrary, the main responsibility should be for the owner to ensure that his or her car is polluting as little as possible.

Maybe we need a whole new way of looking at automobile maintenance. Maybe we should consider not only what the improvements will do for our pocketbooks, but what they will do for the environment, for Earth itself and, ultimately, for the well-being of all who live here.

There is no question about it—it comes down to individual responsibility for our actions. How we treat our vehicles will impact directly on how planet Earth treats us. The responsibility is not only to ourselves but to those who will come after us. We are the caretakers of the globe for such a brief period, surely we can leave it in better condition than it is now.

Each owner must make the decision but, unfortunately, unless bold evidence is placed smack-dab in front of us, we can be lazy and avoid responsible action until we see how it affects us directly, and if there are immediate rewards. We don't have time for that nonsense anymore.

A new view of automotive maintenance is needed—one that says that taking care of a car is not only good for the car but is essential succor for mankind and the planet it inhabits. And if that doesn't have an immediate impact upon us, nothing will.

Controlling Evaporative Emissions

Rich Sommerville is the chairman of the committee created by the California Legislature to monitor the effectiveness of California's smog-check program and recommend to the Air Resources Board (ARB) and the Bureau of Automotive Repair (BAR) ways to improve the program.

Writing in a recent issue of *The California Independent*, a newspaper published by the Automotive Service Councils of California, Sommerville makes some important observations that have an impact on your car's operation, fuel economy, and longevity and directly and profoundly affect the quality of the air we breathe. And you don't have to live in California to follow these suggestions because they apply anywhere, anytime.

Most vehicles that go through state emission-control testing are checked by inserting into the vehicle's exhaust pipe a probe that reads the amount of pollutants and unburned hydrocarbons (HC) in the exhaust stream. But according to Sommerville, "The tail-pipe emission test is totally useless in finding problems with evaporative emissions. Exhaust emissions account for only about half the total hydrocarbon emissions from a vehicle with no emissions-control system. The combination of crankcase and evaporative emissions is almost a large as the exhaust emissions."

But on a car with a properly functioning evaporative-control system

(ECS), evaporative emissions are almost nil. Disconnect or tamper with the system—as some mechanics and car owners do—and fuel-vapor emissions can be "10 times higher than the exhaust HC emissions standard new cars are required to meet!"

According to Sommerville, several sources of evaporative emissions must be controlled. Fuel vapors that boil off a carburetor when a warm engine is turned off are vented from the carburetor to a charcoal canister. The vapors are stored there until the car is started. When the engine is restarted, fresh air purges them from the canister where they are drawn into the engine and burned. Other cars store these "hot soak" vapors in the air cleaner. Fuel-injected cars do not have this problem because injectors, unlike carburetors, are not vented.

Another source—perhaps the major one—of evaporative emissions is the gas tank. When it is warmed due to changes in outside temperatures or heat transfer to the tank from exhaust-system components or a hot road surface, vapors fill the tank. In cars equipped with ECS, these fumes are supposed to be vented to a charcoal canister. But if no gas cap is on the filler pipe, or if a vented gas cap is being used, these vapors escape directly into the outside air.

A recent survey by the California Highway Patrol found that 6 percent of all evaporative-emissions-control systems were disconnected, missing, or defective. Sommerville estimates that if these vehicles were all in compliance with law, the HC emissions reductions achieved by the California smog-check program would be over 30 percent greater. "The number of missing canisters and disconnected or broken vacuum hoses is large enough to be creating a serious emissions problem."

And this is happening in the state with the nation's most stringent emissions-control program. What must it be like in other states? Worse, no doubt.

But this is where individual car owners and the mechanics and technicians who service their cars come into play. The evaporative-emissions-control portion of a car's emissions-control system should not be ignored or tampered with because of the major role it plays in reducing overall HC emissions.

What can you do to ensure your car is not polluting unnecessarily?

o Be certain your vehicle has a gas cap.

o If your car is equipped with an evaporative-emissions-control system, be sure it is an unvented or sealed cap.

o If your car has a charcoal canister, be certain it is working and that vacuum lines are connected.

o Remember, canisters do need to be changed periodically. When was the last time yours was checked?

o If a mechanic suggests you will get better performance with the system unhooked, tell him no. Besides, it's against the law in most states.

○ Many studies show that tampering with or voiding any portion of the emissions-control system hurts overall engine performance. Cars with computer engine controls are especially vulnerable.

Perhaps John Goodman, state executive director of the Automotive Service Councils of California (ASC), says it best: "No matter how you slice it, the buck stops with us. Whatever they do in Detroit to reduce car emissions, the problem won't get solved if we continue to have a high level of tampering in the hands of the car owner."

Tampering, yes, but don't forget pure and simple neglect on the part of the car owner. It's just plain smart to make sure every part of the emissions-control system is working properly—both for your car's sake and for that of the air we breathe.

Don't "Duct" the Issue

Car been acting up lately? Does it exhibit any of the following symptoms: poor starting, loss of power, rough running, excessive emissions? And you say you had a tune-up not too long ago? Don't know what could be causing it? And to top it off, your gas mileage has dropped too?

Before you give the beast two aspirin, cross your fingers, and send it to bed, perhaps you should check one of the most ignored under-the-hood items. In fact, these parts feel so neglected that they go to bed many evenings with tears coming out of their ducts.

Oops! Gave it away. Yep, I'm talking about the carburetor and fuel-injection air ducts. Air ducts come in many sizes and shapes, but they all perform the same function. They route air to your car's engine.

There are two types of air ducts: fresh-air inlet ducts and preheater ducts. Fresh-air ducts supply outside air to the engine when it is warm, and preheater ducts supply preheated air to the engine during the cold-start and cold-engine warm-ups and operation.

Just as all roads once led to Rome, all air ducts lead to the engine air cleaner. The fresh-air duct provides air from some point near the front grill, and preheater ducts get warm air from some point on the intake manifold of the engine.

Both types of ducts look like overgrown hoses that have a corrugated, crinkly skin. The fresh-air duct is usually made of some type of fibrous material, and the preheater duct is typically fabric-covered aluminum. If these ducts are missing, have loose connections, or have been damaged by punctures or by being squeezed shut, they could be causing your engine's poor performance.

The amount and temperature of the air fed to an engine is of extreme importance to its performance, economy, and durability. If a fresh-air duct is missing or damaged, the engine must rely on under-the-hood air to keep it going. Most engines don't like that, especially if it is a hot day and the resultant fuel and hot air mixture causes it to perform erratically.

Same thing with the preheater duct. If it is damaged in any way, the engine can't receive correct amounts of preheated air under cold operating conditions. And that's important now during cold weather. Without preheated air, the engine gets confused, cantankerous. It doesn't like running on cold air when it, too, is cold. It should have its fix of preheated air when it is warming up, and the preheater duct provides it.

Once the engine has warmed to the correct operating temperature, a thermostatically controlled valve in the air cleaner closes. This shuts off the supply of preheated air and allows fresh air to enter by way of the fresh-air duct.

So take a few minutes and check those air ducts on your engine. If loose, they should be tightened; if damaged, they should be replaced. Give your engine what it craves—hot air when it is cold and cool air when it is hot. It will repay you with more miles per gallon, better performance, reduced emissions, easier starting, less stalling, and no carburetor icing.

Air ducts are easy to replace and relatively inexpensive. They can be found at most auto-parts stores. Don't duct the issue, check your ducts now.

Special note: Many older cars do not have carburetor air ducts. Look for special openings on your air cleaner to determine if it is one that should be fitted with ducts.

PCV: An Integral Part of All Newer Cars

Since its California introduction in 1961, the positive crankcase ventilation (PCV) system—most of us know it as the PCV valve—has become an integral part of all new cars and a major player in helping cars vent their frustrations and their contaminants back into the engine rather than the atmosphere. Crankcase (that's the area of an engine where the oil is kept) ventilation systems do what their name implies: They vent the crankcase with fresh air and that helps keep the contaminants from polluting the oil. Without these ventilation systems, oil and engine life would be appreciably shortened.

Older cars had a simple draft tube underneath the engine that only vented the crankcase when the car was moving. The motion of the car created a venturi effect at the road-directed tube opening, which sucked the fumes out of the crankcase. Unfortunately, these fumes were vented directly into the atmosphere. When the car wasn't moving, the nastiness just stayed in the engine. Either way, moving or not, somebody lost—the car, or Mother Nature, or both.

But PCV valves changed all that for the better. This simple check system vented crankcase fumes back into the engine where they underwent the combustion process again. After this additional test by fire—some of the foul air may even go around more than once—the pollutants become shadows of their former nasty selves. If the system is working properly, that is.

Most cars today use a closed (vs. open) PCV system. After it has passed through the air cleaner, fresh filtered air is routed through the crankcase where it mixes with the crankcase fumes and is then metered back into the engine via the carburetor or intake manifold where, along with the contaminated air it picks up in the crankcase, it is burned.

These systems usually work wonderfully well. But they do need care because if they are not operating properly, they can cause rough engine performance, a drop in fuel economy, hastened crankcase oil deterioration, and accelerated deposit formation in critical areas of the system.

There isn't really much to do to ensure the system works properly: periodic cleaning of system components, especially the PCV valve itself, replacement of the valve at manufacturer's suggested intervals, and—one most car owners think has nothing to do with keeping the system clean— use of a high-quality detergent/dispersant oil along with a detergent-fortified gasoline.

Good, fresh oil helps reduce deposit formation in the PCV system and keeps it cleaner and working as it was meant to. Detergent gasoline contributes to the same cleanliness. But even a high-quality oil will lose its effectiveness and cleaning abilities if left in the crankcase too long. So it must be changed at regular intervals. This very important function of motor oil demonstrates that oil, although primarily a lubricant, directly affects how efficiently the engine runs.

Any tune-up, major or minor, should include a complete check, cleaning, and replacement (if necessary) of all parts of the PCV system. Insist that your tune-up person includes it.

Inspection Reports Are
Good Clues to Your Engine's Health

Almost all states require that registered automobiles pass a vehicle-emission test once a year. Most of us are familiar with the procedure: You take your car to one of the test centers, wait in line, pull it into the garage, have the test done, and cross your fingers while the computer decides if your car passes or fails.

If you pass, you utter a sigh of relief and send the compliance slip and the required bucks to the motor-vehicle division. In time, you receive the new registration and the license-plate tags. All set for another year.

Seldom, if ever, does anyone glance at the vehicle-inspection report, and it usually hits the trash with the first glove-compartment cleaning. Too bad, because it contains valuable information about your car and its present and past state of health. Let me explain.

A number of years ago I bought a used 1975 car with more than 100,000 miles. I wanted to see how far it could go, even though I had no hint of what the car had already been through. Prior to taking in the car for emissions inspection, I changed the oil and tuned it to manufacturer's specifications.

It passed inspection with readings of 29 parts per million (ppm) hydrocarbons (allowable limit is 250 ppm) and 0.53 percent carbon monoxide (allowable limit is 2.2 percent). Not bad for a high-miler.

A year and 35,000 miles later, the car's readings had dropped to 21 ppm hydrocarbons and 0.16 percent carbon monoxide. After another 32,000 miles, it showed further drops in both emissions. Hydrocarbons were cut in half and now read 11 ppm, while carbon monoxide dropped to 0.13 percent.

Fine and dandy, you say, but so what? The point is that these vehicle-inspection reports give an overall profile of how your engine is doing. In my case, the car continued to improve as it aged, showing that I was, and am, doing something right.

Frequent oil changes using high-quality oil and fill-ups with quality gasoline contribute. Driving habits and techniques are important. Minimum cold and hot idling, keeping emission-control devices clean and functioning properly, and tune-ups to factory specifications at proper intervals were factors in reducing the vehicle's emissions.

Save those inspection reports. You are paying for that information, so why not use it? Compare the figures for one year with the next. You don't have to be an automotive engineer or a mathematician to do it. A consistent drop or holding pattern from year to year indicates that you are following maintenance and driving practices that will help extend the life of the vehicle.

High or erratic emission results, even if they are within the "pass" range, can be early warning signals that something is amiss and should be corrected if you want your car to last.

Emissions can be reduced through conscientious maintenance and consistent good driving habits. Low emissions mean a more efficient and longer-lasting vehicle. Watching those numbers on your inspection reports can be one key in helping you achieve that goal.

Think of your car as a cask of fine wine: It can continue to improve with age.

Minimize Harmful Auto Emissions

I have always been concerned about the amount of damage motor vehicles inflict on the environment and on living things, human or otherwise. Even though great progress has been made in reducing automotive pollutants—thanks to the Clean Air Act—motor vehicles are still the number 1 violators of American air. It's a classic Catch 22: We can't get along without our vehicles, yet each time we drive them we make the problem worse.

But if we are aware of the times cars produce most of their emissions we can take appropriate steps to limit their environmental impact. One of the worst times of all is the first few minutes after a cold-engine car is started. It doesn't matter if it's an older model or one with a full range of emissions controls and a three-way catalytic converter; this is a time of high emissions for all cars.

While more gasoline is needed to start a cold car, much of it remains unburned and finds its way into the air as unburned hydrocarbons (HCs). This waste and pollution continues until the engine has reached a normal operating temperature.

On newer cars, the catalytic converter is cold. Most catalytic converters must be heated to the 400- to 500-degree F range before they operate efficiently. Catalytic converters chemically convert the unburned portions of the exhaust into carbon dioxide and water. When warm, they operate at about 98 percent efficiency; but until then emissions get a free ride into the atmosphere.

The oxygen sensor on modern cars must also be warm. The O_2 sensor relays exhaust-richness information to the engine's computer, which then adjusts the air-fuel ratio accordingly. Until the oxygen sensor is warm enough to work, nitrogen oxide emissions are very high.

To understand how emissions-intense the first few minutes after a cold start are, consider what General Motors discovered while conducting a standard EPA 26-cycle cold-start emission test. This industry test is conducted over a 7-and-1/2-mile course starting with a cold car. GM reported that during the first cycle of the test—the first minute to minute and a half after the test car was cold-started—about 90 percent of the emissions of hydrocarbons and carbon monoxide produced during the entire 26-cycle test were generated.

The Swedish car maker Saab chimes in by saying, "Those first couple of minutes after you have started your car in the morning and begun that daily trek to work can be pretty rough, both on you and your car—and even on the environment. The heater has not yet started and your seat is cold; the car is not really up to it yet and tells you so by running somewhat unevenly.

"What you don't notice is that your car's exhaust is literally full of pollutants—unburned hydrocarbons, carbon monoxide and nitrogen oxides. . . . The first couple of minutes of driving with a cold engine are responsible for a great portion of all the pollutants a car emits during its entire driving cycle."

If you are a regular reader of my column, you know how I have emphasized time and again how important it is to get an engine to warm up fast. The quicker we can get the engine to warm, the less wear it experiences, the better its fuel economy and, as we have now seen, the less pollution it will produce.

A warm engine does little environmental harm compared with a cold one. You can help ensure a quick warmup with much less pollution by following these hints:

○ Don't warm the engine by idling. This creates a pollution cesspool. Start the car and get moving as soon as possible. Use slow-to-moderate speeds for the first mile or two.

○ Make sure your thermostat is working properly. If you have an older car, check the operation of the mainfold heat-riser valve.

o Consider purchasing an engine warmer or oil warmer for your vehicle. They will help eliminate much of the pollution associated with a cold engine.

o If you have a garage, use it to conserve any residual engine heat.

o Be certain the choke is adjusted properly on your carbureted car.

o Don't put the pedal to the metal while the car is cold. This pours raw gasoline into the air. Gentle is the key when the car is cold.

By taking these precautions you will contribute greatly to clean air, not to mention better gas mileage and longer car life. I don't see why anyone would want to do it any other way.

What I Learned from Aunt Stella

I never like it when people preach to me. When someone gets on a soapbox and starts shoving his views down my craw, I usually retreat to some safe corner where I can effectively ignore his or her persuasions. The act of preaching in itself is enough to counteract any positive feeling I might have on the subject, no matter how worthy it may be. I hope this column doesn't fall into the preaching category for it does attempt to persuade us to do something we all know we should be doing but for some reason don't. I'll cross my fingers and hope you make it through to the end and, if you do, actually begin to implement some of my suggestions.

She would never think of herself as a conservationist or an environmentalist, but when one looks at the way she has lived she would indeed fill those shoes perfectly. Nor would she think that her mode of transportation throughout her 80 years had anything to do with helping keep our air clean or, for that matter, that it was anything out of the ordinary. It was what people like her did, out of choice rather than necessity, and never thought much about it. It was how one got from point A to point B. You see, my Aunt Stella was, and still is, the quintessential public transportation user.

Aunt Stella only owned one or two cars in her lifetime. I vaguely remember standing on the running board of her old Chevy when I was about 5 years old. A bit clearer in my memory is a 1951 Dodge. But since the Dodge, buses and trolleys, with an occasional train sprinkled here and there, have provided transportation. Whether across town (Pittsburgh), or south to Florida in the winter, or east to Atlantic City in the summer, public transportation has provided the way.

I do recall an exception when a friend of hers, although she couldn't drive, bought a new car. She looked to my aunt to chauffeur her around. As a bonus, Aunt Stella got to use the car when her friend didn't require her chauffeuring services. That car was the exception and not the rule, and anyway, Aunt Stella still preferred the bus.

But why this diatribe on my favorite aunt? Because if each of us driving a car had a little bit of Aunt Stella in us, the air would be a lot cleaner, our oil import quotas would drop significantly, and our roads would be a lot less congested. When they dole out the awards for conservation or environmentalism my Aunt Stella and the many like her should be at the front of the line. Indeed, if the big oil and tire companies had to depend on Aunt Stella they would have long since become dinosaurs.

The time is right for each of us to make a serious effort to try car or van pooling or to use some form of public transportation on a regular basis. I know everyone agrees this is a good idea. Most everyone I talk to says so. Public transportation officials have expounded the merits of alternate means of transportation for years and have made it easy for anyone wishing to participate. Car-pool matching, van pools, and public transportation are at anyone's fingertips in large cities. And walking—horror of horrors—is free to anyone.

Motor vehicles are the number 1 violator of our nation's air. We could start weaning ourselves by leaving our vehicles at home just one day a week and using public transportation instead. Or, if we can match up with just one more person instead of driving to work alone, we will cut in half the amount of gas we use and the pollution our vehicles spew into the air. A large payoff for a small effort. So let's try to imitate my Aunt Stella—at least once a week, anyhow, for starters.

For those of you who are asking what all this has to do with preventive maintenance, I can only answer that using public transportation or car or van pooling might well be the ultimate preventive maintenance practice. For every time you don't drive, your vehicle can't pollute; in addition, you save gasoline and money, ease traffic congestion, add miles to the other end of your odometer reading by preserving your car, and, most importantly, you practice preventive maintenance on the planet itself. End of sermon; end of preaching.

Be Kind to the Pedaler

When was the last time you rode a bicycle? That long ago? OK, how long has it been since you owned one? Even longer, you say.

What brings all this to mind is an incident that occurred recently when I was driving to work. A bicyclist was going in the same direction as I was, keeping as far to the right as possible, hugging the curb as best he could. A driver a few car lengths ahead of me wasn't satisfied with the bicyclist's demeanor, however, obviously feeling that the bike had no right to slow him down (these roads are for cars, you know!).

The driver took out his pent-up aggression on the slow-moving bicycle, literally running the pedaler off the road, sending him careening over the curb and almost crashing into a nearby wall. The bicyclist raised a clenched fist as the car whizzed on. The driver of the car, grinning, countered with a raised finger.

Bicycling friends of mine say incidents like this are fairly common, and those who rely on a bicycle as their main means of transportation say they look at every driver as a potential assassin, an adversary in a battle they can't possibly win. All have had close calls; caution is the byword at all times. On streets where there is no bike path, they must join the main-stream of traffic, and most do so with great trepidation. Many use side streets whenever possible to avoid heavy traffic. They are all keenly aware that in a one-on-one confrontation with a car, they don't stand a chance.

Why all this talk about bicycles in an automotive column? Mainly because the number of bicycles increases each year, and more and more of them are sharing the roads with cars and trucks. Although most bicyclists use designated bike paths whenever possible, the paucity of these pro-tected areas forces them to use main traffic arteries at times. These are times when we, the pilots of those moving boxes of plastic and steel, should go out of our way to be extra careful when approaching a bicyclist.

I think every driver on the road owes something to every bicyclist. Why is that? Because bicycles aren't using any of the finite supply of gaso-line. Because bicycles aren't polluting the atmosphere with carbon mon-oxide, particulate matter, unburned hydrocarbons, lead, nitrous oxides, poisons, ad nauseum. Because they aren't adding to our tax burden by beating up on our roads; because each one on the road makes your town a much better place to live and breathe.

Bicycles are the ultimate mileage machines: unlimited mileage, on zero gallons of gasoline, zero quarts of oil; quiet, clean, relatively fast, nonpolluting, good for you and me. And if you own both a car and a bike, each time you use your bike you extend the effective life of your car. Why would anyone want to be aggressive with such a benign creature?

Oh, sure, occasionally you might become a bit irritated when a bike is in front of you and you have to slow down, but that is a small price to pay for what we are getting in return. A bicycle benefits everyone; a car, just its owner.

The next time you encounter a bicycle, slow down, smile, be extra careful, extra courteous. Remember, the gas it's saving could be yours.

Ensure Clean Air for Tomorrow

I was recently in Los Angeles on a business-related driving trip and had the opportunity to spend a few days there. It had been a number of years since I had been in the area and I immediately noticed that the smog problem had not changed. If anything, it was worse. A couple of days in the damp murkiness was enough for me.

My suspicion was confirmed as I began to drive to Tucson, Arizona, on Interstate 10. Years ago when you drove east of Los Angeles, you could bet your boots that once you got to the Banning area between San Bernar-dino and Palm Springs the smog would abate. It was as if someone had put up a wall at the point where lush vegetation began to turn into high desert and would not permit the smog to go any farther.

Palm Springs, which was just another 20 miles or so from this mythi-cal wall, was always pristine, as was the valley that stretched ahead toward Indio. The contrast was stunning: You could see forever. The San Jacinto

Mountains, with Palm Springs snuggled at the base, were always an impressive sight.

But the wall wasn't there this time. The smog bore on, invading the desert canyons and washes. Like a brown blanket, it had moved into the once-inviolable desert. Palm Springs? Not visible from the highway. Mt. San Jacinto? Like a giant iceberg whose tip was barely visible through a thick fog.

I found it hard to believe that the wall was no more, and that the dirt and pollution covered the desert floor and surrounding mountains all the way to Indio and beyond. The desert was scarred, the clarity gone, the air foul. Even the tough California anti-pollution laws had not been enough to stem the onslaught of obnoxious messages that poured from the exhausts of ever-increasing numbers of cars.

I thought to myself, if that can happen in California in just a few short years, it can happen anywhere. And it is happening, but we still have time to do something about it.

California has been the sacrificial lamb; no need for other states to follow suit. We *know* what happens when there are too many cars and not enough emission controls, and we will have only ourselves to blame if we let the same thing happen in other cities and towns.

Each day when I drive into town from the Tucson Mountains, I cringe when I see what our vehicles are doing. Visible layers of brown smog are now the rule rather than the exception.

But we can stop it in its tracks with tougher laws. We can't let some vehicles escape while others comply with emissions testing.

Can we place a price on pure air and quality of life? Can we be inconvenienced too much?

Cheaters who rig their cars so they pass the emissions test, then unrig them as soon as they get around the corner from the testing station, should be fined. We should be concerned about the condition of our cars at all times, not just before the emissions test.

We should limit our driving whenever possible and use public transportation, car pools, or van pools. And don't think your one car won't matter: It won't matter like one vote doesn't matter.

Look around you and envision a day in the not-too-distant future when your favorite vistas won't be visible except for times when the inversion layer is on vacation.

Is that what you want? What your children deserve? But if we continue—even at the pace we have now set—that is what we will get. The time is now; the choice is ours. What we do now will be irrevocable proof of how we feel about the people who inherit the land from us.

And, I hope, 20 years or so from today mothers will still be able to say to their kids as they shoo them off to school: "Don't forget your lunch, dear," instead of "Don't forget your mask, dear."

8

Keep the "power" in your powertrain

I WAS IN AN AUTOMOTIVE-PARTS store recently, checking out some of the offerings available to motorists. Of special interest were items that could help a car last longer, get better mileage and command a higher resale price. Because the high heat of summer is upon us, I was particularly curious about anything that would help offset the wearing effects heat can have on every part of a car.

I came to an aisle that had transmission coolers on sale. Ah, here is something quite useful, I thought to myself. Excessive internal temperatures, i.e., overheating, is the main cause of transmission failure. More problems can be traced to high heat than to old, dirty transmission fluid, which ranks a strong second in the destruction derby. An automatic transmission, if put under undue stress and heat, can break down in a matter of minutes. Keeping the transmission cool and clean is a definite prerequisite to long life for your car.

Add-on transmission coolers are about $35 and up, plus installation. They look like, and in essence are, tiny versions of your radiator. Transmission fluid usually passes through a separate section at the bottom of the radiator where it is cooled. But during high heat, the cooling effort can be marginal at best.

That's when an add-on transmission cooler—in reality, an extra cooler for the transmission fluid—comes into play. It's insurance that cool fluid will be circulating through the innards of that expensive automatic transmission. These coolers are an excellent add-on for those interested in helping the automatic transmission remain trouble-free. They are of special value to Sun Belt motorists.

But something was wrong. The sign said "SALE," but when I looked, the regular price was crossed out and a higher, not lower, price was marked in its place. The $39.95 cooler was now on sale for $99.95! Other units were similarly marked. Something weird here, I thought.

Then I saw them! Those two little grimy adversaries of mine, marker pens in hand, frolicking up and down the aisles, raising prices on any item they thought might prolong the life of a car. Yep, it was those demons of automobile destruction, those mechanics of malaise, the gremlins Wear and Tear—and they were having a ball!

My first reaction was to call the manager, but a greater urge overcame me. I stole up behind them and grabbed both by the necks.

They gurgled and turned their greasy faces toward me.

"Oh no, it's Bob," yelled Tear.

"So you guys are responsible for these sale items being marked up," I screamed. I held them upside down and shook hard. More marker pens fell to the floor.

"Raising prices on every helpful item! Why, you little . . . !"

Wear wriggled and bit down hard on my hand. I cursed out loud and dropped both of them.

"Nyaah, nyaah, Bobby," taunted Wear as the two scampered beneath the transmission-cooler shelves. "There are plenty of other stores around. We'll make sure no one buys a transmission cooler. Let's go, Tear, here comes someone."

Before I could say Wear and Tear, I felt a hand on my shoulder. It was the manager. I was standing there, four marker pens in hand, talking to the display of transmission coolers and licking my hand. I knew I was a dead duck.

"So you're the one who has been changing our signs," said the manager. "I knew we'd get you sooner or later."

Before I could reply, a store assistant grabbed my arm and confiscated the markers as evidence. They were going to hold me until the cops arrived. I knew it was useless to argue. Who in his right mind would believe the true story? It wasn't the first time those two had gotten the drop on me.

I couldn't believe it. There I was trying to help the consumer and I fell victim to those scoundrels Wear and Tear. Well, I consoled myself, I'll be able to write this column in jail and still tell readers about transmission coolers. And just wait until I get my hands on those two &%$!!.

Blotter Test Keeps Transmission Trouble-Free

An article in a recent issue of *Automotive Engineering* magazine, the official publication of the Society of Automotive Engineers, has brought to light much valuable information about automatic transmission fluids.

Some of this information can be removed from the narrow realm of automotive and lubrication engineers and placed before typical automotive consumers who can put it to good use. Let's take a look at some points the article makes.

Automatic transmission fluids are probably the most complex of all automotive lubricants, including even the most sophisticated synthetic motor oils. They can be made from as many as 15 elements. A typical motor oil may contain seven.

According to Automotive Engineering's article, transmission fluids are subjected to severe oxidizing conditions that can cause:

1. Deposits of sludge and varnish in the transmission
2. An increase in corrosion of copper-alloy bearings
3. Hardening of various elastomeric (rubberlike) seals
4. Glazing, flaking, and wear of clutch plates and bands.

Any one of these conditions is bad news for your transmission and wallet, but all can be avoided by changing to a high-quality transmission fluid before oxidation can alter its protective characteristics. But the big question is how to know when that time has arrived.

A good rule of thumb is to follow the change interval given in your owner's manual. For most transmissions in most areas of the country this will do just fine. If you want to be more precise, just use the time-proved paper towel test. Here's what to do:

Place a drop or two of transmission fluid from your car (you can get the drops by removing the transmission dipstick) on a clean piece of common paper towel.

Next to this drop, place another one or two drops of equal size of fresh, unused transmission fluid. (If you don't have a can of it handy, a service station will probably give you a few drops.)

You will now have two separate spots on the paper towel, one from the fresh fluid, the other from the fluid in your transmission. Now wait one hour, then observe the spots.

The fresh fluid spot is your reference point. It will be large and have a reddish or light-brown color. Compare your transmission fluid's spot to the one made by the fresh fluid. Is it about as large as the fresh fluid spot, and does it have some red or light-brown coloration? Or is it a small dark spot?

Automatic transmission fluid that does not exhibit good spreadability and coloration is probably suffering from oxidation and should be replaced. A spot that approximates the color and size of the fresh fluid indicates that the fluid is still fine and should be left in the transmission.

This fairly foolproof test is easy to perform once you get the hang of it. It should be done about every two months. As soon as you notice the fluid getting darker and the spot getting smaller and more concentrated, you will know it is nearing time to get the old stuff out and the fresh stuff in.

The paper towel test is a simple, inexpensive way of keeping that complicated, expensive automatic transmission trouble-free for a long, long time.

To Change or Not to Change? That is the Question

One of the toughest decisions a car owner can make is whether or not to change the fluids for the first time after a number of miles have accumulated. At first, this doesn't seem to be a problem—fluids should be changed periodically. While that is true and the rule applies to all fluids in the car—power steering, brake, coolant, oil, rear axle, transmission—there are times when an owner is caught in a Catch 22.

How's that? Well, here is a typical scenario. A car owner who has never changed the automatic-transmission fluid decides, after looking at the price of new cars, that he should take better care of his present buggy and make up for past transgressions. So, he thinks, I'm going to do it a favor and start by changing the transmission fluid because that would be the most expensive unit to replace.

He does; but, to his dismay, in a few days he finds the car dripping transmission fluid from both front and rear seals. The car had never leaked with the old fluid, why should it leak now? Isn't fresh fluid supposed to be good for the transmission?

It's leaking because the owner's neglect allowed crud to build up inside the transmission, causing the viscosity of the fluid to thicken and become a "false" seal. The crud locked in the old fluid and kept it from leaking past the seals, which in the interim had become damaged. The damage was masked because the thick goo blocked any escape routes for the fluid.

When fresh fluid was added to the transmission, the new additives attacked the false seals and opened a path through the bad seals so the fluid could escape. Result? A leaking transmission. Don't call a plumber, because he can't help. Only new seals and/or gaskets will do the trick.

To change or not to change, that is the question. Is an owner better off with old fluid and a nonleaking unit or with fresh fluid and a leaking unit? Talk about tough decisions, but the answer depends on how long you intend to keep the car. If you plan to keep the vehicle, you're better off with fresh fluid. New seals or gaskets, if required, are an extra cost, but not as expensive as a new car. If you are going to get rid of the car, why ask for trouble?

To add to the confusion, sometimes when fresh fluid is added to a high-mileage vehicle for the first time it might not cause the unit to leak. That could be the case with your car, but there is no guarantee. If you decide to change any fluid for the first time in a car that has more than 70,000 miles on it—there is really no way to set an exact number of miles—you are, in essence, rolling the dice.

I wish I could offer something better than that, but by being aware of what can and cannot happen, you won't be surprised if or when your car starts leaking.

Be on the Watch for Overheated Transmission

There's a warning printed inside the cabin of the new 1988 Subaru XT6 that reads: "Avoid hard driving when AT (automatic transmission) oil temperature warning light goes on." Subaru, aware that hot transmission oil means a hot transmission, advises its car owners to take it easy, thus allowing the transmission fluid and the transmission to cool.

It would be nice if all cars with automatic transmissions gave a similar warning for transmission oil temperature. Unfortunately, most don't. And that leaves it up to you, the car owner, to decide when and if the transmission oil is getting too hot.

Why is Subaru concerned about transmission oil reaching a certain temperature? Why do they advise the car owner to "avoid hard driving" under those conditions? It's simple, really. They know—and now you do, too—that high internal temperature is the number 1 enemy of long transmission life and good performance. Not dirt, not jackrabbit starts, not nasty old transmission fluid, but excessively high temperatures inside the transmission. Driving the car hard when the transmission oil and transmission are in the danger zone will only expedite the car's demise.

Although you might not have a temperature gauge or a warning light to indicate when your transmission is overheating, you can use a good dose of common sense to help you fight this wear and tear. Obviously, automatics are more susceptible to heat in the summer than in the winter, so now is the time to be cautious. A good gauge of transmission temperature is the engine temperature. Although they are two different units, high engine temperatures usually mean high automatic-transmission temperatures.

Stop-and-go rush-hour traffic is a prime candidate for spawning high automatic-transmission temperatures. Placing the transmission in neutral during long stops will help dissipate some of that internal heat, because the clutches and other components aren't generating the necessary friction to keep the car at the ready. This helps considerably in cooling the unit. Idling the car a bit faster than normal also helps. Transmission fluid, like engine coolant, circulates through its own little "radiator" at the front of the car, and better circulation and more cooling are the results of increased engine idle speed.

If you are driving at a speed at which the transmission is constantly shifting between first and second, you should choose the one gear you think is best and keep the transmission in manual mode. The less shifting, the less friction and heat generated and the better off your transmission will be during those slow, crawling conditions.

Although you can't change the fluid while you are caught in a rush-hour jam, you can have it changed this weekend. Fresh fluid, with its fresh oxidation (high heat) inhibitors, is another first-line defense against premature aging of automatic transmissions. And if you live in the Sun Belt, you might consider adding a transmission-fluid cooler to your vehicle—an excellent investment that can be had for as little as 39 clams plus installation.

Oh yes, I almost forgot, you could pray for rain or cooler weather, too. It worked for me one time.

Your Transmission: A Heartbreaking Tale

Automatic transmissions are a part of our cars that almost everyone takes for granted. When we start up, we put the car in gear; when we park, we put it in another gear. Other than that, the automatic transmission, that many-splendored marvel of automobile technology, does the rest. If automatic transmissions had a club, the motto would undoubtedly be: "Leave the shifting to us."

Most transmissions require only minimal servicing on the part of owners, but most owners balk at doing anything at all and literally drive the car until the transmission fails. Because of this neglect, most automatic transmissions fail long before their appointed time.

I stopped in at a transmission repair shop the other day to ask the owner a few questions about automatic transmissions. Although he was more than willing to field my queries, he suggested I go out back and direct them to the real experts—the old, abused and worn-out automatics themselves.

The transmission I talked to had only 75,000 miles on it, but looked as if it had gone 375,000 miles. Felt like it, too, the transmission said. I asked it what had caused it to wear so prematurely and look and act years older than it really was. What it told me brought tears to my eyes and wrenched my heart. In order to save you some tears and money, here are some tips given to me straight from the transmission's mouth.

The transmission said it really doesn't ask for too much in return for all the work it does, but that most owners are unwilling to even admit that it exists, let alone give it a treat now and then. The transmission told me that one of the most important things you can do is to have the fluid changed periodically, say every 30,000 miles. If you haven't done this lately, or at all, there is no better time than the present, just as we are entering the high heat part of summer. Fresh fluids make a transmission much better prepared to fend off the onslaught of high temperatures. Heat, this aged youngster told me, is the number 1 enemy of all automatic transmissions.

Most automatic transmissions are cooled by passing their fluid through a cooler contained within the vehicle's regular radiator cooling system. Under high heat, this stock cooling system works marginally at best. If the fluid is dirty, additive-depleted and old, it just won't work as well or cool as efficiently.

While its hundreds of worn-out friends chorused agreement, the transmission rambled on: "Have an extra transmission cooler installed," it said. "It doesn't cost much and is the very best insurance against wear due to high heat." No better time to have this done than now.

It advised all car owners to check the transmission fluid level frequently, at least as often as the oil is checked. The more fluid present, the better the transmission will run. More fluid also means better cooling capacity. Never let the fluid level fall below the 1-pint-low mark. Always try to add fluid before it reaches that mark. Fifty dry, parched transmissions yelled approval.

And if you are idling for a long time at a stoplight, please take the car out of gear and place it in neutral. This simple act will help the transmission run cooler and will ease the burden on both the over-worked engine and the transmission. This is a very valuable practice in hot summer afternoon rush-hour heat.

I looked at the pitiful sight before me. Hundreds of transmissions struck down in their prime, now useless, all due to owner neglect. As I said farewell, I could hear the transmissions talking among themselves.

"Who was that man?" one asked.

"I don't know," replied another, "but I sure wish he had been my owner."

The Axles' Tale of Woe

It was a beautiful Saturday morning, the kind of day that calls for activity. My wife wanted to go to the mountains; my kid begged me to take him fishing, but the day was too nice for any of those things. Instead, I took them along on one of my favorite pastimes—strolling through the local automobile wrecking/salvage yards. Talk about quality time.

Amid protest, I packed them into the car and away we went. I stopped at the first yard I spotted. We checked with the owner and, after being assured that we could browse and the guard dogs were tied up, I eagerly began my trip through the rows of wrecked and abused unfortunates. My wife and kid found a nice tree and decided to camp there while I shopped. I couldn't convince them they were missing a treat.

As I strolled down the aisle of doomed vehicles, I heard a voice haltingly call my name.

"Bob, is that you?"

I looked around but couldn't tell where the sound was coming from. I heard it again. "Bob, over here, by the big ragweed bush."

I glanced at the area and spotted a couple of old rear axles lying on the ground and, sure enough, one was trying to get my attention. They were a pitiful sight, rusted, mud-covered, weed-infested. To be kind I said hello, inquiring how the axle knew my name.

Al, the larger of the two, replied that one day a strong wind blew part of the newspaper into his face and it just happened to be the page with the "Drive it Forever" column. "I knew one day you'd come, I just felt it in my gears," he said.

He introduced me to the other axle, a smaller one named Virginia.

"Bob, please do me a favor," Al begged. "Tell car owners that even though we are one of the least troublesome parts of any car, we still crave some attention. We don't ask for much—a periodic change of our fluid and taking it easy on those pedal-to-the-metal accelerations.

"Tell your readers that they should change our fluid in accordance with the car manufacturer's severe-service driving fluid-change recommendations. If they do that I can almost guarantee that we will give trouble-free service for as long as they own the car. Fresh fluid with its revitalizing extreme-pressure additives works wonders for us.

94

"But most owners do nothing. They forget how hard we work between the two driving wheels. They don't realize that we, too, need a minimum of attention. Don't you agree Bob?"

"I couldn't agree with you more, Al. But tell me, what happened to you and Virginia?"

As Al related the story about their owner's neglect and how hard they both were driven, Virginia began to cry. I started to sniffle.

"Take it easy," I said, trying to console them. "I promise to tell car owners your story."

Al managed a weak, rusty smile, and Virginia's tears stopped. I felt a lot better, too.

Just then I heard voices and saw my family heading my way.

"Got to run now, or they'll have me locked up. But remember, I will tell car owners what you advised."

As we headed to our car, I could hear Al talking softly and reassuringly to Virginia. "See Virginia, there really is a Bob."

9

Inside,
outside

IT'S HAPPENED TO MOST OF US at least once. You know, uh, well, there is no delicate way to say it—getting bombed by one of our fine-feathered friends. It's not the world's best feeling.

It happened to me many years ago in San Blas, Nayarit, Mexico.

It was early evening and the Mexicans were just beginning their *paseo,* that delightful, once-traditional promenade around the plaza in which the males walk in one direction and the females in the other, stopping to chat when the right person comes along. Most of the older people sat on benches enjoying the spectacle.

At the time there was only one empty bench in the plaza, and I hurriedly claimed it, not aware that I was the target of muffled laughter and curious glances from other bench residents and promenaders.

It didn't take long to find out why the bench had been empty as numerous birds began using me for target practice.

I have nothing against birds, but after the San Blas experience, I always look up before I sit down. Pity your poor car. It can't look up, and it has no control over where it goes or where it is parked.

Bird droppings—there has to be a better expression—contain acid; some also contain strong red and purple dyes. The combination makes bird droppings a deadly enemy of your car's finish and, if left unattended for any length of time, they can etch mirror images of themselves in the car's paint. Buckets of water, soap, polish, or elbow grease can't remove them.

If your car has a finish worth preserving, remove any bird droppings at the first opportunity. You don't have to wash the entire car. A wet sponge or towel will remove the droppings before they can ruin the paint.

If the car is left in the sun after acquiring its "badges"—hey, that's it; bird badges—it makes matters worse. It's akin to pouring acid on the finish, then baking it to make certain it etches well.

New or freshly painted cars are particularly susceptible to bird spotting because the paint has not had sufficient time to dry. It takes a good six months for any new paint to acquire a proper set and hardness. Until that time, its protective qualities are a fraction of what they will be.

Be careful where you park your car. If you have a garage or carport, use it. Make sure your favorite shade tree is not the bird's favorite, too.

Taking Care of Clear-Coat Finishes

One departure from tradition in the past few years has been the way some new-car manufacturers paint their cars. I'm talking about cars that have a base-coat/clear-coat finish. Many General Motors (GM) cars are prominent members of that fraternity.

The customary method is to use a layer or layers of prepigmented enamel or lacquer paint. Clear coat uses at least two layers, but each is different. The first or base layer gives the car its color; the finish or clear coat is then applied over the base coat. It is usually some type of clear acrylic polymer (a variation of the clear stuff you put on your kitchen floor). Many car makers believe it gives the finish more luster and a deeper, mirrorlike look.

There is another reason for clear coating: The clear acrylic polymer seals the pigment layer from the elements, thus making it less susceptible to deterioriation and oxidation. With ordinary paint, the pigment is exposed to the sun, wind, and water. But clear coat protects and seals the pigment and acts like a good wax job on an enamel- or lacquer-finished car.

Here are some tips, courtesy of GM, on how to care for a car with a clear-coat finish. As you will see, they aren't too different from those used when washing and waxing enamel or lacquer finishes.

Take care not to scratch the surface. Clear coats tend to haze up when scratched and get a cloudy look. Use a gentle car-wash soap, and hose off any grit and grime before applying a sponge or cloth to the finish. The more dirt you can remove before you apply hand pressure, the better. When you begin washing the car be certain to rinse the sponge or cloth often. If you take your car to a commercial car wash, make sure it has soft brushes.

Although base-coat/clear-coat finishes don't need waxing as frequently as other types (once or twice a year is suggested by GM) a number of precautions are in order.

Don't use any type of power-polishing unit. I test-drive new cars daily, and many of these brand-new cars bear the scars of the most dastardly paint torture device ever invented by man: the electric polisher. The finishes are replete with swirl marks, *prima facie* evidence of an electric rotating polisher. Clear coat or not, don't use them.

Use a mild, non-abrasive cleaning wax/polish. Always apply the polish by hand. If you have aluminum mag wheels on the car check with your dealer to see if they are protected by a clear-coat finish; many are. If so, do not use—and so many of us do this—a brush to scrub the aluminum wheels. This will scratch the clear coat and give the wheels a fuzzy look instead of the brilliant one you desire. This is a little-known fact that should be tucked away in your automotive memory bank.

All nicks and chips in a clear-coat finish are treated a bit differently from those in enamel or lacquer paints. In the latter, a touch-up bottle of the same color paint is used to dab on the spot. With clear coat, the pigment must be applied first, then the clear coat. Kits containing both are available at auto-parts stores.

As with any type of paint, clear coat requires that you make some occasional effort to protect and enhance its beauty. I hope the above tips will help your finish live a long and beautiful life.

Keep Your Car's Paint in the Pink

Probably the most sensitive part of any car is its "skin." All cars have skin; just like the one on you and me, it is stretched over the entire body surface. Our skin is flexible and, to a degree, so is your car's.

Our skin can get sunburned; your car's can too. Our skin needs protection and care to keep it looking good; again, so does your car's.

Your car's skin—its paint—just as our skin does, reflects the care given the entire mechanism. Good-looking skin probably means a well-tuned body overall; good-looking paint probably indicates a well-tuned, good-running car. If you care for one part, you are most likely to care for the others.

Once a new car leaves the factory it is at the mercy of the environment. Its paint begins to lose luster from day one. Paint's worst enemy is sunlight. A pristine finish continually exposed to strong sunlight will deteriorate rapidly and take on a dull, weathered, chalky, oxidized look.

The Chemical Specialties Manufacturing Association, a Washington, D.C.-based group, has a few words of advice on how to keep your car's paint looking good.

According to the association, the best protection against sunlight and other environmental agents such as acid rain, smelter smoke, bug smears, and bird droppings is one or two coats of one of the better polymer waxes. The association says these waxes, if applied properly, offer long-lasting protection for the car's finish.

The association says to always wash your car before waxing it, but wait until the finish has cooled if the car has been out in the sun. Always wash the car in a shaded area. First run a stream of cool water over the finish to help carry away any fine dust that might be in residence there. Then proceed to wash the vehicle with a wet Turkish towel or a natural sponge.

If the car is especially dirty, a mild car-wash solution, available at all auto-parts stores, should be used. Never use a strong laundry-type detergent on the car's finish. Remember, you can never use too much water to wash the car. Once washed and thoroughly rinsed, the finish should be dried with another towel or chamois.

Bug or tar remover should be used on spots. Work it in lightly until the offending particle is removed. Go over the area with a clean, dry cloth when finished.

If the paint shows signs of dullness or oxidation, the association recommends that the finish first be treated with a mild polishing compound (usually white in color) before wax is applied. If the finish is severely oxidized, a stronger rubbing compound (orange in color and more abrasive than polishing compound) might be necessary.

Once the car has been washed, dried, and, treated with a polishing or rubbing compound, the polymer wax should be applied according to instructions. Never apply wax to a hot surface, and never wax the car in direct sunlight. Always do the job in the shade.

Try to avoid using any type of soap or cleaner once the wax has been applied. A good wax job should last about a year. Frequent rinsing with cool, clear water should keep the finish looking good in the meantime.

Don't Let Trees Make a Sap of Your Car

I don't like it when a tree attacks my car and I'm sure you don't either. Tree attacks can come in many forms: bird bombings from high or low branches, needles or leaves that find their way into vents and radiator pores, insects who make their homes in the trees deciding to do their thing on the car's finish, and the trees that simply play your car for a sap.

I've received a number of inquiries concerning the best way to safely remove tree sap from car finishes. Tree sap can be nasty and every area of the country has trees that freely ooze the stuff. Out West we have smoke trees that bombast cars with sap and needles; pine trees do their stuff in other areas, while maple and elm trees and their ilk can't wait for you to park under them. Stand under one of these offenders and sometimes you can even feel the sap falling like drizzle on a cloudy day.

There are a number of ways to remove tree sap; which one you use depends on how long the sap has been on the car. Before you rush out to buy a specially formulated sap-removal product, try these methods.

Let the car's finish cool. Then, while the vehicle is parked in a shady spot, wash it thoroughly with a non-abrasive car-wash preparation. Let the finish dry completely. Then, with the car still in the shade, use a car paste wax—not car cleaner—on the sap. Almost all modern wax formulations have cleaning agents in them and, although they are not aggressive cleaners, they will remove grease and grime and even tree sap, providing the sap hasn't had time to harden thoroughly.

Rub the wax on and let it sit awhile, but not as long as you normally would. Then buff it off while it is still a bit wet. You might have to repeat the process. If the sap hasn't hardened too much the wax will usually take it off and add a protective coating to the finish.

The bugger that causes sap to harden and become so tenacious is good old sunlight, more specifically ultraviolet light. The longer the sap is exposed to sunlight, the harder it gets and the more difficult it is to remove. So the less exposure the car gets to direct sunlight while you are contemplating removing the offending sap, the better.

If the wax treatment fails to get the sap off, try a commercial bug and tar remover. It will usually do the trick and, although it will also remove any protective wax that is on the finish, it won't harm the finish if used according to instructions.

If the bug and tar remover doesn't do the trick, zap the sap with a No. 7 polishing compound, available in all auto-parts stores. It is more abrasive than either wax or bug and tar remover and should be able to remove even the most stubborn sap buildup.

Cleaning solvents are rated by their KB or Kauri-Butonal value. This is a chemical measure of the ability of the solvents to dissolve paint. Auto-paint-surface-safe solvents have a KB value of about 33 to 35. Commercial bug and tar removers are in this range. Paint thinner—not the same as bug and tar remover—has a KB value of 65, making it far too aggressive for use on auto finishes and sap. Although I have recommended it in the past for taking marks off metal parts of the car, it is probably better not to use it at all. Any solvent or cleaner with a KB value of 45 or over can damage the finish and should be avoided.

Don't use household cleaners like Tide on the sap because they are caustic. Although they are excellent and cost-effective ways to clean clothes, they aren't good for car paint because paint is more sensitive to the caustic nature of the cleaners than your dirty clothes are. The high pH of caustic detergents will strip the car of wax and can encourage corrosion anywhere bare metal may be exposed.

A word about the cloth, sponge, or scrubber you use to apply these products: Don't use plastic-type dish scrubbers on the finish because they will mar it. A finish hardness of a car is somewhere between 3 and 5 on Moh's Scale of hardness. That's a scale—remember your geology?—that rates talc at 0 and a diamond at 10. These scrubbers can be harder than the paint's finish.

Your best bet is a 100-percent-cotton cloth. Closed cell sponges are good, but cotton is better. A 100-percent-cotton flannel is about as good as you can get for both applying and removing the products.

So don't let trees make a sap of your car. And if you really think of it, the best way to keep your car from being sapped is to not park under the tree in the first place. Hmmm, why didn't I think of that sooner? It would have saved me writing all this stuff.

Car Cover is Best Defense Against the Elements

You don't need to own an expensive sports car to have an incentive to keep your car's exterior and interior in excellent shape. With the price of cars today, it makes good sense to protect your investment. But too many times the exterior and interior are ignored in deference to the car's mechanical components. That's unfortunate, because these areas probably have the most influence on the trade-in or sale price when the time comes to get rid of the old buggy.

One of the best ways to protect the finish and interior of the car is what I call the lazy man's way. That is, you let something else do the work, and that something else is a car cover. Have you ever considered one? If your car is worth saving, a car cover will make an important contribution to its preservation.

Jim DeFrank, co-owner of Beverly Hills Motoring Accessories, the largest custom car-cover supplier in the United States, says a car cover is one of the best defenses a car has against the elements. "A cover will keep the paint from fading and the interior from discoloring and cracking," says DeFrank. Car covers can be especially valuable in the Sunbelt or coastal areas. Old Sol and salt spray aren't your car's bosom buddies.

The best car covers are made from natural 100 percent cotton. They are softer, and they breathe and protect better than those made from polyester or polyester blend. Of course, they cost more, too. The bottom line, however, is that any cover is better than no cover.

Chances are, a custom-fit cover is already available for your car. Shop around: Auto-parts stores and the Yellow Pages under "Automobile Seat Covers, Tops and Upholstery" are good places to start. If you can't find a cover to fit your make and model you might have to have one custom-made. But don't worry, it's a good investment even if it does cost a few more bucks.

If you keep your car inside a garage and out of direct sunlight, a good cover should last as long as you do. If the car is stored or parked outside, cover life will be shortened considerably. From two to five years is average, depending on how much and how strong the sunlight is.

Take care if you live in a windy area. If your covered car must be parked outside, try to park it where it is not subject to the blowing wind. Be certain the cover fits snugly and doesn't flap.

Always transport a car uncovered, because a cover blowing in the wind generates friction and can cause extensive damage to the finish. DeFrank says a cover can rub the paint off your car.

A car cover does just as good a job protecting the interior dash and upholstery from heat and sun damage. Indeed, it might be worth owning one even if you only use it occasionally.

Another car-finish protector—I'm not crazy about the name—is an auto bra. It's a vinyl device that fits over the front end of the car and guards the finish and parts against flying pebbles and other abrasive road dirt. And although you see many cars in town with a bra in place, its main use is for on-the-highway driving.

A car cover and auto bra—two protective accessories every car owner should consider. Cost? Either can be purchased for as little as $49, but a good cotton cover can cost as much as $200.

Rust is a Four-Letter Word

One area of great improvement in new cars is the protection they offer against that old bugaboo, rust. New cars give rust a hard time—such a hard time, in fact, that manufacturers have come up with some blockbuster warranties against what they call "outer-body rust-through."

Chrysler, for example, offers a seven-year, 100,000-mile anti-corrosion damage warranty on its '88 models. The warranty is even transferable to a second owner for a fee of $100. Stuff like that impresses me; it doesn't seem as if it will be too long before new-car engineers have relegated rust to that great museum of automotive afflictions of bygone days.

Ah, but what if you are not driving a new car? In that case, can anything be done to keep rust from eating away at your investment? (If you live in a Sunbelt state where rust isn't a problem, please read on. I will tell you how you can use the advice given here.) Yes, and one of the first is to be aware of when rust does its dirty work. An example is in order.

You bring your car off the salt-encrusted streets and park it in the garage, glad to be home out of the snow and cold. You figure your car is happy to be inside too. You feel sorry for old Joe across the street who doesn't have a garage and must leave his vehicle parked overnight on the street. What you don't realize is that by pulling your car into the garage you might have placed it in the perfect climate for rust to start a celebration. You see, there is one very important but little-known fact about rust: The chemical process that activates rusting is usually active in only a small temperature range from about 32 degrees F to 40 degrees F. Think about that.

Below freezing, it's too darn cold for road salt to react with the car's metal. At temperatures below 32 F, no rusting takes place. What happens when temperatures rise above 40 F? At that point, although rust is still active, much of the road-salt solution begins to evaporate and a lot of the oomph is taken out of the rusting process. It just doesn't have the zing it has between 32 F and 40 F.

What happens in the above scenario? The conscientious car owner, thinking he or she is protecting the car, unwittingly pulls it into an unheated garage where the temperature is probably—yep, you guessed it!—somewhere in the rust danger zone, and the rusting process is greatly encouraged. Joe, on the other hand, parks his car outside where the overnight temperatures drop into the 20s. That makes rust shiver and get too cold to even think about eating.

We all know that washing road salt off the car is one way to protect against rust. But there is no need to wash off the salt if the temperature stays below freezing. Who wants to wash a car when it is below freezing anyway? However, if you park your car in an environment where the temperature is above 32 F, frequent washing should be the order of the day. You want to get the stuff off the outside and underside of the car.

Remember the rust-zone temperatures, 32 F to 40 F. In this temperature range, whether you park the car inside or outside, it should be washed frequently and thoroughly. Below 32 F, no action is the best action.

Now for you Sunbelters who read along: Cut out this column and mail it to Uncle Jack or Cousin Emily back in Chicago or Pittsburgh or wherever there is a lot of snow, which is just about anywhere this winter. Smugly tell them, "I bet you didn't know about this." And while you're at it, tell them the temperature in your backyard. They will love you for it—and so will their cars.

Low-Cost Windshield Repair Now Possible with Resin

It used to be that if you damaged the windshield on your car you would pray that the crack didn't spread. More often than not, given time and weathering, it would, and the entire windshield would have to be replaced. Well, for certain types of windshield cracks, pits, chips, and abrasions, that need not be the case anymore.

I recently witnessed a demonstration of a quick-fix permanent windshield repair. I first became aware of this method about 10 years ago at a trade show, and I thought then it had promise. Time and research have turned promise into reality.

Many motorists aren't aware that windshield damage from flying rocks, pebbles, and whatnot can be repaired without removing the windshield. In many cases replacement is unnecessary.

Almost 5 million windshields are replaced annually at a cost of more than $1 billion. You can see how this method would appeal to both consumer and insurance company alike. But does it really work?

Novus, a leader in this type of repair, says the method won't work on all types of windshield damage, but can effectively repair the following:

o Cracks up to 8 inches long

o Bull's eyes: conical cracks where the tip of the cone is at the point of impact on the outside of the window

o Partial bull's eyes or half-moons: one-half of a bull's eye

o Stars: an impacted area with small radial cracks spreading from it

o Combination breaks: a bull's eye with cracks radiating from it

The repair I witnessed was to a bull's eye about the size of a half dollar. After checking the strength of the glass surrounding the crack and removing any loose material, the technician attached a device to the windshield directly over the cracked area. A clear resin was then forced into the crack under pressure, while air was simultaneously sucked out of the crack. Once the resin completely penetrated all portions of the damaged area, it was fast-dried or cured using ultraviolet light. The area was then polished and buffed. Elapsed time: about 30 minutes.

The results? The half-dollar-size abrasion with small radiating cracks was as clear as the surrounding glass; only a slight hint of the former trauma was noticeable. If I had not known that a crack had been there, I would never have noticed anything. Cost of this particular cure: about $45. Cost of replacing the windshield: well over $300.

It's no wonder many insurance companies are waiving any deductible you might have to pay for this repair. It's much cheaper for the insurance company to cough up $45 than it would be for you to kick in your $50 or $100 deductible. The company would still have to come up with the remaining $200 or more for a new windshield. Seems to be a good deal for both parties.

Is the cure permanent? Yes, according to the company that did the repair I watched. Yes and no, according to car owners I talked to whose windshields have had similar repairs. Some say the resin is affected by rainy weather and car washes and, over time, will begin to wash away and the crack will begin to reappear. The company says this will happen only if the repair is not done properly or is attempted on a crack with too much contamination in the form of road tars, wiper rubber bits, and the like.

If you incur windshield damage from a flying stone (the most common form of windshield damage) place a piece of tape over the area to help block any contamination from the crack. Also remember that the more time that passes between when the crack occurred and the repair is attempted, the more likely the crack will extend itself beyond the range of what can be repaired. This is especially true for today's cars with flush-mounted glass. When the car's body twists, so does the glass (they work as one unit, unlike older cars in which the glass was separated by a movable rubber buffer). And when a windshield with a crack does the twist, you can almost be sure the crack will spread.

Vinyl and Rubber Protectants: Regular Use for Maximum Benefit

A few weeks ago in one of my columns I answered a question about Armor All, a popular vinyl and rubber protectant. A reader had been advised by a new-car dealer's service manager not to use the product because it could cause stitching on a vinyl roof to deteriorate. My answer was basically "bunk;" no product that does the opposite of what it is supposed to do would last in today's competitive marketplace.

Well, I received a number of letters from readers seemingly confirming the service manager's position. Each had complained about the product. So I called Armor All, hoping to set the matter straight, and talked to Michael Caron, vice president of marketing, and James Lattey, vice president of operations, research and development.

"Armor All sells about 40 million bottles a year of the product," says Caron, "and we receive about 300 letters each year and only 100 to 150 are negative. That's not many considering the number of bottles sold. And 90 percent of those complaints involve people who don't take routine care of their vehicles. When their dash cracks they blame it on our product."

Lattey, who holds a doctorate in chemical engineering, is emphatic. "There is no ingredient in Armor All that could be detrimental to the car's vinyl dash or vinyl top or any of its rubber parts."

All vinyls contain plasticizers, liquid ingredients added by the manufacturer that give the vinyl flexibility. As plasticizers are lost through evaporation and chemical reactions with heat, the vinyl becomes brittle; the backing between the vinyl and the roof begins to separate and cracks begin to appear. Variations in temperature accelerate the deterioration and the vinyl starts to crack along its seams.

When a product such as Armor All is put on a vinyl roof it does a number of things: Silicon additives lubricate the vinyl, while another ingredient impedes the progress of cracks and blisters. Ultraviolet absorbers protect against sun damage, while other ingredients resist attack from ozone, which will cause vinyl to oxidize. In addition, another inhibitor prevents the formation of fungus, mildew, and mold.

Lattey said it is curious that the service manager recommended using paste wax on the vinyl roof, because it is usually made by combining silicon, water, mild abrasives, and a hydrocarbon-based solvent. The solvent, according to Lattey, would tend to remove the plasticizers from the vinyl, while the abrasives in the wax could chew up the stitching.

A vinyl dash is a different story. Its main enemy is heat, although the direct rays from the sun also help speed up its aging. Heat attacks the interface between the vinyl and the foam backing (usually urethane foam). As plasticizers escape, the vinyl eventually blisters and begins to crack.

Lattey believes that the few complaints they receive—and possibly the basis for the letters I received—are from people who have ignored their vinyl tops or dashes, then applied Armor All and expected it to rejuvenate those areas. When they used the product, they pressed down on the already brittle dash, which, in turn caused it to crack. The product is then blamed for the owner's negligence.

Lattey and Caron stress that their product—or any product for that matter—won't stop the aging and deterioration of rubber and vinyl. All vinyl and rubber will eventually meet their maker, no matter what precautions you take. But the product will help delay that process—and this is important—if it is applied periodically.

How to Store Your Car for the Long Term

About four years ago I wrote a column on the proper way to store a car for the long term, say six months to three years or more. Since then I have acquired many new readers and a question I often get concerns the right way to store a car. So here's the best way to do it.

A car is always better off stored indoors, preferably in a cool, dark, dry environment. Ideally, the temperature should never drop below freezing.

The battery should be removed. If you're going away for a few years give it to a friend—unless it has a lifetime guarantee.

Drain the fuel system. Any gasoline left in the bottom of the tank should be siphoned out.

After the tank is drained, the engine should be run until all the gas in the fuel lines, carburetor, fuel pump, injectors, and other system parts is used up. If the car uses leaded gas run it with a gallon or so of unleaded before draining and drying the system. Unleaded gas left in the fuel system is less likely to form deposits when it evaporates.

Now the engine. Have the oil and filter changed as close as possible to the time of mothballing. Don't store a car with old oil in it. The contaminants in that nasty stuff will wreak havoc while you are gone.

Ideally, a can of molybdenum disulfide (MoS_2) or Slick 50 should be added when you change the oil. The car should run with the new oil and engine treatment for about two hours, if possible, before the final shutdown. The MoS_2 or Slick 50 will coat the engine parts and make them almost impervious to moisture.

Pull the spark plugs and pour about a teaspoon of fresh engine oil into each cylinder. Then replace the plugs. This helps coat the cylinders with protective oil.

All engine openings, particularly the air cleaner and oil-breather cap, should be packed with absorbent cloth. The same applies to the exhaust pipe, but wait until it has cooled. Cotton towels will work.

With the exception of packing the exhaust pipe these engine procedures should be done when the engine is warm, not cold, because you will be sealing in moisture instead of keeping it out.

Ideally, the engine should be started once or twice a year and run for at least 30 minutes. If this isn't possible, the above procedures offer maximum protection.

Release the tension on all the drive belts in the engine. Top off the transmission and rear-axle fluids. If your automatic-transmission fluid hasn't been changed in the last 30,000 miles it would be a good idea to replace it.

Radiator coolant should not be drained. The cooling system should be left wet to help preserve the various seals and gaskets inside. If the coolant is more than two years old now would be a good time to replace it. But here's an exception to the radiator rule: If any part of the engine is aluminum, drain the cooling system. The electrolysis set up by the aluminum and coolant combination can corrode and ruin an engine.

Brake systems should also be left wet. If the fluid is old, change it. Old brake fluid will corrode and pit metal brake-system parts given enough time.

If the car will be in storage for a year or more put it on blocks or jack stands. This takes the pressure off the wheel bearings, shock absorbers and other suspension parts.

Remove the tires if they are in good condition. Leave them mounted on the wheels with the air pressure slightly reduced and store them on their sides out of the sunlight. If the car can't be put up on blocks, add another 10 to 15 pounds of air to the tires.

If the car is stored indoors it is best left uncovered. If stored outside a good-quality car cover is recommended. A frame should hold it above the finish so it won't rub the paint.

The car should be washed and waxed, and you should rub silicone preservative on all rubber door gaskets and other rubber parts. The interior should be cleaned and the vinyl coated with a vinyl protectant.

If the car is stored outside, cover the dash, rear deck, and upholstery with clean white sheets or towels. Cover all the windows so the sunlight doesn't penetrate, but leave one of them open just a bit.

Keep a list of the things you have done and place it in the car. When you return you'll know exactly what to do to get the car moving again (retighten belts, take out the engine packing, etc.).

Make Your Car Hard to Steal

I was browsing in my favorite hardware store recently and came across a number of brochures that dealt with preventing theft. Several caught my eye because they concerned car theft.

When it comes to car theft many of us are lulled into complacency by the "it happens to someone else, not me" attitude. With that kind of thinking "someone else" will eventually be you. But it doesn't have to be. Taking precautionary measures now—and every day—helps ensure that your car will be there the next time you want to use it.

According to the Crime Prevention League, a nonprofit organization in Tucson, Arizona, dedicated to crime prevention in the community, a car is stolen in the United States every 26 seconds. Four out of five thefts occur when the owner leaves the car unlocked; one out of five occurs because the keys are left in the car. Protecting your car takes only a few seconds—surely you can't be in that much of a hurry! Like burglars, most car thieves are opportunists; they look for an easy target. The following car-theft prevention tips will help you slam the door on would-be second owners.

○ Take your keys. So simple it hurts, yet many of us don't.

○ Lock your car. So simple it hurts even more. Just doing this will discourage most car thefts.

○ Close the windows.

○ Avoid leaving your car unattended in public parking lots for extended periods. You are five times more likely to have your car stolen from an unattended lot than from the street or an attended lot.

○ Park in well-lighted areas, preferably where there is pedestrian traffic.

○ Make it difficult for your vehicle to be towed away. Park with your wheels turned sharply toward the curb and pull on the emergency brake. Place automatic-transmission cars in park and manual-shift vehicles in first or reverse.

- Use your steering-wheel lock.
- Replace all door-lock buttons with the slim, tapered type. Try hooking a coat hanger around one of those!
- Don't hide a second set of keys on the car.
- Never attach a tag with your name or address to a key ring. It could lead a thief not only to your car, but to your home.
- Never leave your car running and unoccupied.
- If you have a garage, use it.
- Lock your garage door; lock your car even inside the garage.
- If you have an alarm, activate it.
- Don't let a prospective buyer test-drive your car alone. I have personal verification of this one. When I was in college I let a man and his "wife" test-drive a car I had for sale without going with them. About a month later I got a call from the FBI saying my abandoned car had been located in Needles, California. I had to hitchhike 300 miles to retrieve it. Later, I received another report that the man and woman had been apprehended; both were wanted by the FBI for other crimes. And they seemed like such nice people!

The following take more time and/or money, but could be worth it:

- Install a car alarm, secondary ignition switch or fuel shut-off device.
- Install an armored collar around the steering column.
- Remove the rotor and/or coil wire from the distributor cap.

Don't tempt thieves:

- Remove packages from view.
- Hide stereos and citizens-band radios from view.

In the event your car is stolen, make sure it can be identified:

- Etch an identifying mark on your car.
- Squeeze one of your business cards or other piece of identification between the door window and rubber frame.
- Keep a record of the car's vehicle identification number.

The first thing that might strike you after reading this is that tips are easy enough to follow. And they are easy. But you must follow them not just once, but all the time. Following these steps will make it much harder for both the professional and the amateur to take your car for a ride to Needles or anywhere else.

10

Break it in right

I WAS STROLLING THROUGH THE STACKS at the university science library while doing some research on engine wear in automobiles. As I entered one of the reading rooms I noticed two small kids buried deep in a large volume. I wondered what kids were doing in a university library, but dismissed it and became involved in a search for a particular book.

But when I came back to the reading room, I got a good look at the two: Those were no kids, they were my old antagonists, the demons of automotive destruction, Wear and Tear.

"What are you two doing here, and what are you reading?" I shouted.

"It's Bob," gasped the startled Wear, trying to hide the book from me.

Over their protests I grabbed the book from their grubby hands. I couldn't believe the title: "Effects of Automotive Tribological Methods on Reducing Wear and Tear."

I was dumbfounded. Here were two of the most irresponsible rascals in the automotive world reading a much-acclaimed and authoritative tome on tribology, the relatively new study of the interrelationships of friction, lubrication, and wear. What is going on here? I pondered.

Then it struck me. If these two knew the best methods for avoiding automotive wear and tear, they would know exactly what to do to combat those methods. So that's why they were here. I had to give them credit; they never rest but, then again, neither do I.

"How did you guys get into a university library?" I asked.

"None of your business, big boy," Tear taunted, while tossing a handful of his ever-ready, engine-destroying dirt in my face. By the time I recovered, they were gone and so was the book.

I checked at the desk. Sure enough, both had valid library cards and had checked out the book on tribology. I looked at the mailing address on their card application form: "Nearest automobile," it read.

Wear and Tear reading up on tribology—I couldn't believe it. American car manufacturers have, for the most part, ignored this blossoming science. But not those dudes. Talk about keeping abreast of technology.

But it made me think. The study of tribology has proved very valuable in helping motorists keep their cars for longer periods. European manufacturers have used tribological principles for years, and the use of these principles is one reason why most European cars require a thorough, detailed break-in when new. The manufacturers know—and tribology enforces their contention—that this crucial time in a new car's life must be accompanied by special, one-time-only, break-in procedures. Most have outlined these in their owner's manuals. American car manufacturers have ignored break-in recommendations, saying that their cars don't need special procedures during the initial miles. That's too bad for the consumer.

I believe ignoring these procedures is one of the main reasons American iron has trouble living up to standards set by some European models in the longevity race. And with the proliferation of smaller cylinder engines, which aren't as forgiving as their large V-8 ancestors, the gap could widen.

There is much that can be done to break in a new car properly. The same goes for a rebuilt engine or transmission; they, too, should be broken in properly, with tribological methods in the forefront. In future columns I will touch on many of these special break-in methods, all of which I have described in my book, *Break It In Right!* and to a lesser extent in *Drive It Forever*. (Incidentally, these books were missing from the library—I wonder why?)

Until then, be aware that there are many things that can and should be done during the initial 2,000 or so miles of new-car ownership that will ensure a long-lived car. In the meantime, I'm going to do my darndest to see that Wear and Tear aren't issued any more library cards.

Break-in Techniques Guarantee Tiptop Performance

A few weeks ago, after a near fight with my gremlin adversaries Wear and Tear, I promised some information on the correct way to break in a new car's engine. Contrary to what most manufacturers say in their owner's manuals—"This car needs no formal break-in"—a new car (or a rebuilt engine) should be subjected to special break-in techniques if the owner wants it to attain top performance, mileage, and long life.

Any new-car owner should be aware of a number of things, but varying speeds and pressure-sealing are two of the most important. These are simple break-in techniques anyone can master, and they should be done during the first 1,000 miles or so of vehicle ownership.

Varying speeds allows the engine and other mechanical components to wear evenly and ensures that all parts get broken in. On the highway, don't spend a lot of time at 55 miles per hour (mph). Travel at the limit for 10 or 15 minutes, drop to 50 mph for awhile, then back to 55 or 45. In the city, increase and decrease your speed from 0 to 35; you want to spend some time at each speed.

New engines have fine cross-hatching that resembles mesh screen on the cylinder walls. This cross-hatching is there for a purpose: It permits oil to flow more freely and thus lubricate better. The marks should wear off as the car breaks in.

If broken in properly at varying speeds the cross-hatching will wear off evenly. But if most of the break-in is done at one speed, the marks may wear off in one area and be untouched in another. This nonuniform wearing of the cylinder area is one reason a new car may use oil prematurely. Uneven wearing-in of both moving and stationary parts will cause the piston rings to seal improperly and can also affect engine compression. This, in turn, can allow oil to creep by the unsealed rings and be burned in the combustion chamber. Varying speeds during a break-in is one helpful method of ensuring proper mating of *all* engine parts.

Another helpful procedure is pressure-sealing, a variation of the changing-speeds gambit. Every 25 miles or so, with the car moving at moderate speed (20-30 mph), quickly press the accelerator to the floor and hold it there until the car reaches the legal limit (about 5 to 8 seconds), then gradually ease off. This sudden increase in internal engine pressure forces the pistons against the cylinder walls and helps seal the combustion chamber. Pick a safe driving area to practice this, and do it only while the car is moving. Do not attempt it from a standing start.

If you have a manual transmission, follow the owner's manual suggested break-in gearshift speeds or engine rpms. Try to shift the gears in the given range and never lug the engine in a higher gear when it should be shifted to a lower one.

Keep an eye on the temperature gauge. The break-in is a time of high friction and heat. If the car begins to overheat, pull over, let the engine cool, and get to a dealer or mechanic as soon as possible.

Monitor all the gauges. If you detect any abnormality, don't drive the vehicle; have it checked promptly.

These techniques take a little extra time. They might be a bit of a bother, but remember, you just laid a lot of bucks on the line. Why not give your car its best chance of serving you in tiptop fashion? A little help during those crucial break-in miles will be greatly appreciated by your new machine; it will be more than happy to repay you for your effort in the years to come.

Your New Car Needs Early Lubricant Changes

As the new car models are introduced across the land, a good many of us will find ourselves in new-car showrooms, looking, dreaming, and sometimes even buying that super-sleek temptress whose lure proved too strong to resist. There is no question that the new iron coming off both foreign and domestic lines is some of the best we have seen, both in looks and performance. This futuristic stuff is ready for your garage now.

But after you lay down over $15,000—the average price of a 1991 model was somewhere around that figure—for your new car are you going to treat it as if it's worth that much or are you just going to get in it and drive hell-bent-for-leather and forget about how much of your hard-earned money you have just put to work?

I'm amazed at how many new-car buyers do just that: lay heavy bucks on the line for some new iron, then go out and treat it as if it's some kind of tramp. And then, 50,000 miles later, they wonder why their car isn't giving them the service they think it should or why it seems to go into a repair mode just after the warranty has expired.

One of the main reasons cars act up sooner than expected is that their owners don't take the little bit of time and spend the few additional bucks to break the car in correctly. We're not talking big money or lots of owner inconvenience, just some simple maintenance procedures that will ensure you are doing it right.

Remember, even though the car's engine or transmission might be computer controlled, the mechanical makeup beneath all those electronic sensors is basically the same as it has always been. In other words, an engine is still an engine, a transmission still a transmission.

Here are three break-in maintenance tips that will help your car get off on the right track—better make that road.

If you study the owner's manuals of some of the most expensive import cars you will notice that they require the new-car owner to take the vehicle back to the service department after it has logged 1,000-1,500 miles. The reason? It's time to have some of the lubricating fluids changed. This is not an option with these expensive cars; it is a warranty requirement. Why? Because the manufacturers know that this break-in service will help set the groundwork for subsequent good performance and longevity of the vehicle. What are these three services?

The oil and filter are changed, the transmission fluid is changed and the rear axle—if the car has one—fluid is changed. But, I hear you complain, the car is brand new and has only a thousand miles on it. Why should I change these lubricating fluids?

Because the car has just gone through the most wear-intensive period of its life. The wear and tear on these major mechanical components is extremely high as their parts mesh and grind and find the best and most efficient mating surfaces, the surfaces that produce the least amount of friction.

This high rate of wear is actually desirable. You want the parts of your new car to wear in properly. When they do, a tremendous amount of wear debris, minuscule particles of metal that are shaved off during the wearing in process, is generated. This debris makes its new home in the lubricating fluids, and it isn't good to keep this junk circulating with the lubricants after the break-in mating surfaces have been honed. So how do you get rid of it? You guessed it: Change the fluids and put some new stuff in. This simple act of flushing away all of the break-in debris will have a profound effect on how efficiently the car will operate thereafter.

Remember, car manufacturers who have a reputation for longevity (Volvo, Mercedes, Saab to name a few) require these services. If these expensive cars mandate it, don't you think it's smart for your car to do the same? Believe me, it is.

So after your car has gone about 1,500 miles or so take it to a servicing agency and have these fluids changed. It's smart, it doesn't cost that much and it will help the car perform better and last a lot longer. Starting out right is as easy as 1, 2, 3: three fluid changes, that is.

Of course, there is more to the break-in than just changing these fluids, but it is one of the most important procedures.

Fuel Economy Will Improve after Break-in Period

When you buy a new car you expect it to get the gas mileage printed on the car's Environmental Protection Agency sticker. Many new car-owners are disappointed when they check the car's mileage and find that it is not what the sticker says it should be.

Well, not to worry—not too much, anyway—because in most cases this is normal. Let me explain, or better yet, Steve Rossi, Director, Public Relations for Saab Cars USA, will explain.

Saab recently did engine laboratory tests on some of its new 9000S Turbos and came up with information that, although not new, is something every new car buyer should be aware of.

"Many car buyers are disappointed when they trade in their car for a new one of the same model, only to find that it uses more gas," says Rossi. According to Rossi, the fuel mileage of a car built to tight specifications does not stabilize until it has traveled at least 6,000 miles.

"The reason is that the drivetrain's wear surfaces—bearings, for instance—are rough. The roughness is microscopic, of course, and disappears after the initial break-in period," Rossi says. "That's enough to make a 10-percent difference in gas mileage."

He points out that the rolling resistance of new tires is also higher than that of used tires. Rolling resistance is the friction or resistance generated by a tire as it moves. More rolling resistance means lower miles per gallon.

Using factory-fresh Saabs under simulated urban-driving conditions, Saab found that fuel economy climbed from 19.6 miles per gallon (mpg) to 21.6 mpg after the first 6,000 miles were logged. After 9,000 miles the average fuel economy climbed to 21.8 mpg, an 11-percent improvement.

Because manufacturing tolerances are extremely close, modern engines are very tight. They run more quietly, but because internal frictions are high when new, they use more fuel during the break-in period. The engine, however, becomes more efficient and runs quieter after it has been broken in.

There is another, less technical reason why the fuel economy of a new car can be less than that for the same used-car model: People often trade in their cars when the new model year begins at the end of the summer. Drivers are then comparing apples and oranges; that is, they are comparing the fuel economy of a well-broken-in older car that has been driven in summer with that of a new one running in colder weather.

Cold temperatures add up to lower fuel economy. When weather factors are considered, the fuel-economy difference between a new and used car of the same model can be quite a bit more than the 10 percent, the tests turned up.

The quality of the break-in is another factor affecting the fuel economy of a new car. It does make a difference—sometimes a dramatic one—in how the car runs, how efficient it is, and how long it will last.

In my book *Break It In Right!*, I noted that a new car has two break-in stages. The first, covering the initial 2,000 miles, accomplishes most of the actual breaking-in of the major mechanical parts; the second stage refines the honing of the first and continues well into the five-figure mileage mark. How you treat your car during those break-in miles will be seen in how it treats you in the following years.

The increased fuel economy demonstrated by Saab, although quite important, is but one benefit of a thorough and proper break-in. Remember, too, that all break-in advice applies to rebuilt engines as well. They should be broken in properly and given time to achieve their maximum mileage, wear, and performance potential.

11

New stuff
for a new age

TURBO, TURBO, TURBO. Talk about new cars and you're sure to hear that word come up. It's "in" in today's performance-oriented market, and turbos are frequently offered either as a high-priced option or as part of a standard package. But what is a turbo, what does it do, and should you consider one when shopping for a new or used car?

A turbo (short for turbocharger), a device affixed to the car's engine, uses waste exhaust gases to drive a turbine wheel(s) that forces fresh outside air into the engine and dramatically increases its horsepower output. It's a method of taking a smaller engine (usually four cylinder) and forcing it to act like the big ones of yore. It's like eating your cake and having it, too: You don't need a big engine, but you can have the power of one when and if you need or want it. At first glance this might not seem bad, but let's put a turbo under closer scrutiny.

First off, a turbo can add anywhere from $1,300 to more than $3,000 to the cost of your new car. That alone will eliminate a lot of prospective turbo-power enthusiasts. But if you get over that first hurdle the question now becomes: Are you aware of the hidden costs (and are they worth it)? There is only one valid reason to buy a turbo: performance. Although many turbocharged cars do have respectable gas-mileage ratings, remember that these ratings are hard enough to achieve in non-turbocharged cars and are almost impossible to achieve in a turbo, especially if one is inclined to use the turbo frequently. You don't buy a turbo for gas mileage.

If the turbo is there, you will undoubtedly use it, and if you're a performance fan, that is fine. But a prospective shopper should be aware that extra care—no matter what the manufacturer says—should be taken with a turbocharged engine. This additional care adds up to more dollars spent after the purchase.

Oil changes with a turbo should be more frequent than with a naturally aspirated engine. Why? The turbo, revolving at speeds in the 100,000 rpm range, creates great amounts of heat and places extreme demands on the oil. There is a whole new product line of more expensive motor oils specifically formulated for use in turbocharged engines. In a turbocharged environment, any oil is more likely to break down before its time. Frequent changes, at extra cost, are another price one must pay for having the power. Add to that the cost of gasoline that otherwise would be saved in a non-turbo engine, and one has a number of reasons to be on guard before making a decision to go turbo.

Turbos have been popular for about five years, and some of the older ones are now finding their way into used-car lots. Be extra careful before buying a used turbocharged car. If a car has a turbo, the previous driver no doubt used it and, because he used it, the whole car—not just the turbo—pays the piper. It's almost guaranteed that an engine in a turbocharged car will be more worn than the same engine in a non-turbo, given that they both have been driven the same number of miles.

Don't get me wrong. Turbos are a marvel of modern-day technology. They can make a small engine act like a large one. The price of the movie ticket can be expensive—just don't forget about the candy, drinks, and popcorn.

The Performance and Power Game

With Ford's introduction of a supercharged, 3.8-liter, V6 engine on both its Mercury Cougar XR7 and Thunderbird SC (Super Coupe), new car manufacturers have now come full circle playing the performance and power game.

There's no question that for the last five years or so, turbocharging small 4-cylinder engines has been the rage among auto manufacturers. It's a method of getting more power from a small engine at no cost in the way of lost horsepower for the effort. In essence, a turbo provides no-cost (meaning no extra engine work) horsepower to an engine upon demand.

Turbos are activated by the force of waste exhaust gases. The gases turn a turbinelike wheel or wheels and these, in turn, compress incoming air, making it denser and more palatable to the engine. When compressing the fresh air, turbos can spin upward of 100,000 revolutions per minute. The air is then force-fed to the engine, which milks the most out of, and takes advantage of, the more dense air/fuel charge to give the engine more power. It's an ingenious way of using the discarded remnants of burnt fuel, the exhaust gases.

But then comes Ford, which, right in the middle of all the turbo mania, reintroduces an old power-producing product, the supercharger. Superchargers were around long before turbos, but fell out of favor during the energy crunch when the emphasis was on small and economical. Turbos jumped in and filled the power gap because they were just what the doctor ordered for improving performance—and even economy, in some cases—of small-displacement and power-lacking engines.

Now superchargers are back. How do they differ from turbos? A supercharger—Ford's current one, for example—operates directly off the rotational force of the engine's crankshaft via a belt/pulley arrangement. For each single revolution of the crankshaft, Ford's supercharger revolves 2.6 times. Others have different ratios. Maximum rpm for the Ford unit is about 15,000, significantly less than the 100,000-plus of some turbo-chargers.

But whereas a turbo gets a free ride energywise (in other words, it doesn't cost gasoline to run it), a supercharger must use a portion of the engine's power to run itself. Ford's, at maximum power output, draws around 50 horsepower from the engine. But this borrowing from the engine isn't noticeable because the amount of power produced more than makes up for what it takes to run the unit. For the 50 horsepower it might draw from the engine at maximum output, the supercharger gives back much more than those 50 horsepower.

Turbochargers and superchargers have the same objective: to supply dense, cooled (for those units with intercoolers), and compressed air to the engine when they are called upon to do so, such as during full-throttle accelerations. This, in turn, produces more power. Because a supercharger's power is governed by the engine's rpm and its response to throttle position is instantaneous, it doesn't suffer from what turbo detractors term "turbo lag," the second or so it takes for a turbo to kick in after the accelerator has been pushed. A supercharger has no lag, its response is immediate. For that reason many power enthusiasts prefer the super-charger over the turbocharger.

But one thing is certain: Supercharger or turbocharger, the power game seems to be here to stay. At least until the next gasoline crisis.

Fuel Injection: What It Is, What It Does

One of the automotive buzzwords of the '80s, and one that has become a household word in the '90s, is fuel injection. To be more specific, let's make that electronic fuel injection. We hear or read about it almost every day in new-car ads extolling the virtues of their electronic fuel-injected engines. Let's look at the facts behind fuel injection: what it is, what is does, and how to keep it operating at peak efficiency.

Just 10 years ago fuel injection was found exclusively on slick, imported sports sedans; today the majority of all new vehicles are fuel-injected. Fuel injection is simply a method of supplying fuel to an engine so it will run. It is rapidly replacing the faithful old carburetor as the main fuel-supply device. Why? Because it is more efficient and economical and allows the engine to perform closer to its designed potential.

Typically, an electronic fuel-injection system must have an electronic fuel pump that is located either near or in the gas tank. Its job is to deliver pressurized fuel to the engine. Before getting there, however, it must first pass through some type of fuel filter just as in a carbureted car. It is crucial that the filter be clean and changed according to the manufacturer's instructions. Dirty fuel can immobilize an injection system—and the car—very quickly. Fuel injection is much more sensitive to fuel quality and cleanliness than a carburetor.

Once the fuel, still under pressure, passes the filter, it goes into a long tubular affair called the distributor pipe. Its job is to distribute fuel through smaller connecting tubes to each engine cylinder. As the fuel is fed through these individual tubes it comes in touch with the fuel injector, the final point of the journey from the gas tank. In other systems the fuel passes directly from the fuel filter into a throttle-body arrangement where it is mixed with air and passed into the intake manifold.

The fuel injector electronically injects fuel into the engine. This can be done in a variety of ways, depending on the type of system installed in the car. The current systems are single point, throttle body, and multiport or multipoint injection. Hang on, it's not as complicated as it sounds.

Single point means there is just one point where the fuel is injected into the engine. Throttle body means that the point of injection is on the throttle body, a unit that sits on top of the intake manifold. In both systems fuel is injected either through one or two injectors into the throttle body where it is mixed with air and fed into the intake manifold which delivers it to the engine's cylinders.

Multipoint means there is more than one point where the fuel is injected. Typically, an injector is located directly above each engine-intake valve where it feeds fuel into each cylinder. Multiport means the same thing as multipoint, that is, there are individual ports (or points), usually above the intake valves, where fuel is injected.

A variation of the multiport and multipoint systems is the sequential-port fuel-injection system. Instead of all cylinders receiving a shot of fuel at the same time, this system synchronizes the delivery with each intake stroke. It is usually considered the best and most precise fuel-injection system.

Fuel-injection systems are quite dependable but must be kept sparkling clean to perform properly. This is where the car owner comes in. If you live in a dusty area, change fuel filters more frequently. And no matter where you live, use nothing but high-quality, high-detergent gasoline to keep the injectors clean. I also recommend occasional use of fuel-injector cleaner as an extra safeguard.

Making Sense of Sensors

With today's electronic-controlled cars, what you feel when your engine isn't performing properly might not be what is really bothering it. Let me clarify a bit. On older, precomputer cars an engine problem could usually be traced to the ignition system, the fuel system, the electrical system, the cooling system, or the intake manifold system. The problem was isolated within one of those systems and a cure could be properly effected. An engine miss, for example, might be traced to faulty spark plugs. Change the spark plugs and—bingo!—the car runs like a champ.

Anyone trying to diagnose engine problems on today's cars must take into account another entire system, the engine-sensor system, an array of electronic sensors and sentries that control and watch various engine functions. An engine miss, for example, might be caused by a faulty sensor, not the spark plugs or carburetor or ignition timing.

Allparts, Inc. has a handy little chart that isolates some common problems related to engine-control components, and I have revised that chart here. Although it should not be viewed as the final answer to your electronic-controlled engine blues, the following suggestions can be helpful when you're trying to figure out what's causing that drivability problem. Here are some of the most common problems encountered by many present-day vehicles and a list of the possible faulty sensors that could be causing them:

○ ENGINE STALLING: coolant temperature sensor; temperature sensor/ switch; throttle position sensor; IAC (idle air control) valve and ISC (idle speed control) actuator; EGR (exhaust gas recirculation) valve.

○ ENGINE HESITATION OR STUMBLE: coolant temperature sensor; temperature sensor/switch; throttle position sensor; EGR position sensor; ported vacuum switch; EGR valve.

○ HARD STARTING: coolant temperature sensor; EGR valve.

○ ROUGH IDLE OR SURGING: coolant temperature sensor; IAC valve and ISC actuator; ported vacuum switch; EGR valve.

○ ERRATIC IDLE SPEEDS: throttle position sensor; IAC valve and ISC actuator; ported vacuum switch.

○ PINGING OR KNOCKING: throttle position sensor; EGR position sensor; ported vacuum switch; EGR valve.

○ POOR PERFORMANCE AND ECONOMY: coolant temperature sensor; temperature sensor/switch; throttle position sensor; EGR position sensor; oxygen (02) sensor; ported vacuum switch; EGR valve.

○ ERRATIC OR SUDDEN ACCELERATION: EGR position sensor.

○ COLD ENGINE WARM-UP PROBLEMS: coolant temperature sensor; temperature sensor/switch; IAC valve and ISC actuator; ported vacuum switch; EGR valve.

○ DIESELING (Run On): IAC valve and ISC actuator.

○ BLACK SMOKE FROM EXHAUST: coolant temperature sensor.

○ STRONG EXHAUST ODOR: temperature sensor/switch.

○ NO TORQUE CONVERTER "LOCK-UP": EGR position sensor.

○ HIGH HYDROCARBON EMISSION: oxygen sensor.

○ SURGING AT HIGHWAY SPEEDS: coolant temperature sensor; EGR valve.

○ "CHECK ENGINE" LIGHT AT HIGHWAY SPEEDS: oxygen sensor.

○ EXHAUST LEAK NOISE: exhaust check valve.

○ AIR PUMP FAILURE: exhaust check valve.

○ DIVERTER/AIR MANAGEMENT VALVE FAILURE: exhaust check valve.

The above list is not provided to make you an instant diagnostic expert of modern computer-controlled engine ills. It is offered as a guide, something that might help you isolate the system where the problem lies or at least give you some idea of where to look.

Nor is the list provided as a means for you to outsmart your mechanic or technician. Leave the final diagnosis up to them. But with some of the aforementioned sensors now becoming available to the general public at various auto-parts stores, some of you do-it-yourself fans may want to test the waters of electronic-sensor replacement yourself. In that case the list can also prove helpful.

Although this sampling might seem an oversimplification of what can sometimes be very hairy diagnostic dilemmas, it can help you make more sense of sensors, and that's something every car owner should be trying to do as we wind our way into the age and decade of sensors.

Old-Time Basics for Your New-Time Car

Over the past few years the following theme has turned up frequently in questions from my readers: "My car tends to surge or buck for no reason at all when it is sitting and idling. If I don't have my foot on the brake it will sometimes just up and go or lurch forward with no help from me."

Another variation: "My car won't slow down when I take my foot off the gas at 40 mph. When I release the pressure on the accelerator, the car keeps rolling merrily along."

Add rough idling to the above and you have some of the most common of all complaints I receive.

These problems have been prevalent in some of the newer computer-controlled cars. Although I doubt there is a simple blanket answer for each and every complaint, a recent article I came across in a technical training newsletter issued by Allen Testproducts in Kalamazoo, Michigan, might provide a simple solution to at least some of these frustrations.

In the newsletter, Tim Cooper, one of the Allen technical trainer engineers, wrote:

"My '88 Ford 3.0 liter Taurus gave me little to complain about. But I'd been living with this annoying little surging problem since I bought the car a year ago.

"I noticed the surging five to 10 minutes into my morning drive to work, usually while idling at a traffic light or stop sign. If my foot wasn't firmly on the brake pedal the car would actually lurch forward. The problem had gotten progressively worse and always seemed more noticeable in cold weather.

"Since the car was under warranty, I took it back to the Ford dealer for service a couple of times. During the second visit they installed a new IAC solenoid and assured me it would take care of the problem. It didn't.

"So I decided to take the matter into my own hands. And I mean to tell you, I cleaned and tinkered with everything I could think of—twice. It got to the point where all I could do was wait for the problem to run its course—a few weeks ago it did. I was shocked to find out how simple it was.

"One night last week I left my office to go home. I walked out to the parking lot, got in my car, and turned the key. It cranked twice and died—no lights, no radio, no nothing.

"My negative battery terminal and cable were badly corroded so I thoroughly cleaned them with a wire brush. Not only does the engine crank and start faster, but the idle quality is vastly improved and the surging problem is gone!"

But how can a little crud on the battery terminal cause a surging or rough idling problem? If you remember your high school physics it's a simple matter of Ohm's Law.

In this case the extra resistance in the negative ground battery cable caused a one-third drop in the amount of available current! The cold temperatures outside added to the problem because cold always exacerbates automobile problems.

In the case of the Ford, the onboard computer is grounded at the battery and what probably happened was that the crud on the negative battery terminal caused the surging because of the high resistance that occurred in the onboard computer's path to ground. The corrosion and gunk on the battery terminal blocked much of the computer's normal path to ground, and the current looked for an alternate path to follow.

All computer-controlled vehicles are quite susceptible to stray electrical current. The current in this case, which should have been grounded at the battery's negative terminal, found its way blocked by the dirty terminal and sought the path of least resistance. It chose the computer circuit that caused the car to surge and idle rough.

Because the computer control system has such low tolerance to electrical change, it was the first system to show signs of trouble, i.e., surging and rough idle. If ignored for a longer time the corroded battery terminal would also have caused problems in the car's charging system.

This little explanation, albeit a bit technical for this column, shows the value of simple preventive maintenance. Nothing is more basic—or easier—than keeping battery terminals clean and tight. One might not think that a dirty battery terminal could cause a computer-controlled car to surge, suddenly accelerate, or idle rough, but in this case it did.

Keeping battery terminals clean and tight is an elegantly simple way of avoiding many possible computer control system-related problems. Don't ignore the old-time basics just because you have a new-time car.

Air Bags Can Help You Drive It Forever

Air bags. I've known a few in my day and for the most part they have proved harmless. They let out a lot of wind but little substance.

Air bags. Of a different ilk. I haven't had the dubious honor of meeting one face-to-face or chest-to-face, but if this meeting should prove necessary I hope it will also prove harmless.

Automobile air bags have been the subject of much debate for a number of years. But there is now little argument that air bags, in combination with a three-point seat belt, provide maximum driver protection in the event of a head-on crash. In the past, air bags have been available as expensive options on selected cars; only recently have we seen manufacturers include driver's-side air bags as standard.

For 1988 Chrysler Corp. made driver's-side air bags standard on six of its models. In general, most air bags operate similarly to those in Chrysler cars. So using the Chrysler air-bag deployment process as a guide, let's see how an air bag works and what it can and cannot do.

An air-bag system consists of an air-bag module, a modified steering column and steering wheel, special wiring assemblies and wiring components, collision sensors, a diagnostic module, and a readiness indicator.

The air bag is made from neoprene-coated nylon—the neoprene keeps the bag from deteriorating—and has a volume of about 2 cubic feet when fully inflated. It is folded and mounted on the steering wheel where it is protected by the steering-wheel trim cover. This cover is designed so that it will separate when the air bag deploys.

The air-bag module itself has a couple of other important components, the igniter and the inflator, two high-tech units that had their origins in aerospace technology. Rounding out the components are the collision sensors. These are electromechanical switches that determine when the air bag will deploy. They respond only when sufficient deceleration (a head-on collision) is present.

These sensors are usually located in the front portion of the car (Chrysler places two sensors on the radiator support panel; other models vary in sensor placement). A third sensor is located in the passenger compartment, in Chrysler's case in the diagnostic module (engine computer).

For the bag to deploy, either one or both of the front sensors, in addition to the passenger-compartment sensor, must be activated.

The passenger-compartment sensor is a kind of check valve for the entire operation. It ensures that a sharp hit near one of the front sensors won't unnecessarily deploy the air bag. The impact must be of sufficient magnitude to set off the passenger-compartment sensor. When two sensors react thusly, the diagnostic module supplies the needed voltage to activate the igniter which, in turn, triggers the inflator. A mixture of sodium azide, molybdenum disulfide, and sulfur generates nitrogen gas that instantaneously fills the air bag.

What's amazing is that this entire process takes place in milliseconds.

It's great to see air bags becoming standard on more cars. But, above all, it is important to remember that an air bag is meant only to protect in the event of a head-on crash. The three-point seat belt remains the primary restraint system in collisions where an air bag is not intended to deploy (rear-end, rollover or side-impact crashes).

Air bags should not give you a false sense of security. They are not a cure-all and do not "injury proof" a driver. You must still wear your seat belt just as I've been telling you all along.

Always Be Safe with an Anti-Lock Brake System

ABS: If those three letters stood for Always Be Safe, they wouldn't be too far off the mark. They stand for a new anti-lock brake system (ABS) that is appearing on many cars. With ABS, chances are a lot better that you and your family will Always Be Safe.

Recently, I had some firsthand experience with the ABS in a variety of driving conditions. Saab engineers had set up a course requiring various types of braking and steering maneuvers using a Saab 9000 equipped with ABS. The tests were conducted at the Saab test track in Trollhattan, Sweden. But before we try the ABS, let's take a look and see what ABS does and how it benefits safety.

A number of anti-lock brake systems are available on the market, but they all work in much the same manner. Most systems consist of three main parts: sensors placed at each wheel (the fingertips of the system), electronic controls (the brains of the system), and a hydraulic aggregate.

The sensors measure the speed of each wheel. When excessive force is applied to the brakes (as in an emergency stop), the sensors note the change in wheel speed, then apply and release pressure on the brake at each wheel to keep them from locking. This on-and-off pressure happens hundreds of times per second. It's like having a speed demon pump your brakes super-fast to keep them from locking.

So what's the big deal? With an ordinary braking system, the brakes will lock, which, in turn, locks the wheels. Once the wheels lock, you can't steer the car. If you can't steer the car you can't control it; if you can't control it, disaster could be your companion.

That's the beauty of ABS. It allows the driver to maintain control of the car while applying full pressure to the brakes. Steering isn't affected. The ABS system on the Saab 9000 worked just as it was supposed to, and even went my expectations one better.

Now back to the test track. Three types of stops were required of the drivers: a straight-ahead stop on dry concrete, a stop on dry concrete with a sharp turn immediately after the brakes were applied, and a stop while driving with the right wheels on a long rubber mat covered with oil (the left wheels were on dry concrete). All three stops were approached at speeds of between 100 to 120 kilometers per hour (about 65 to 75 mph).

The third test was the most interesting, because it mimicked everyday driving situations in which two wheels might be gripping while the other two are in contact with icy or wet surfaces.

I found out quickly that the trick with ABS is to apply full force to the brake pedal and keep it there until the car stops. This is true even when one wheel is on a dry surface and another is on a slick surface.

The results? The car stopped quickly and smoothly in all cases. There was no undue skidding, and I never lost control of the vehicle. I was always able to steer, even during the oily rubber and sharp-turn conditions. In each case, with full pressure applied to the brake pedal (you can't push too hard!), the car was brought to a safe stop.

The ABS will be activated in approximately 2 percent of your braking. The other 98 percent is covered by your normal brake system. But when the chips are down and you must stop and keep control, it's nice to know ABS is on your side.

ABS is one of the most significant advances in automotive technology and safety ever made. More and more manufacturers are including it as standard, but even if ABS is offered as an option, it's more than worth the money.

ABS. Don't leave home without it.

12

Tires:
Life on the road
can be rough

MANKIND AND MYTHS GO HAND IN HAND. Myths that have been handed down from generation to generation have helped us define and understand nebulous areas of existence and heightened our awareness of the mystical; they have been explanations for things or events we couldn't explain any other way.

Myths still abound; they are persistent, relentless, and without time limits: the Loch Ness Monster, Bigfoot, the Abominable Snowman, the Lost Dutchman Mine.

But other kinds of myths are also handed down. Although not as melodramatic as the above, they can and have proved costly—even harmful. I'm talking about tire myths. Of all areas of a car, perhaps the least known and therefore one of the most susceptible to myths are the tires.

"It's unfortunate that so much incorrect information about tires and tire care still persists," says Dave Laubie, Bridgestone Tire's director of engineering. "Unfortunately, many people still rely on family 'experts' for advice."

Bridgestone engineers have put together a list of tire myths with the corresponding facts. I think it is helpful.

Myth: Radial passenger-car tires should only be rotated straight from front to back (left front to left rear, for example) and vice versa. Cross rotating tires damages the tires.

Fact: Passenger radials may be rotated using either method, whether they are rib-type or all-season tires. Cross rotation does not cause damage to radial tires. Follow the advice of your tire dealer.

Myth: Steel-belting in radial tires prevents punctures and flats from nails, glass and other debris.

Fact: Any pneumatic tire can be punctured and lose air. While steel-belted tires are durable, they are not indestructible. Avoid road debris and visually check your tires regularly to catch air-loss problems.

Myth: A tire size larger than what originally came on my car will wear longer and be safer.

Fact: That couldn't be further from the truth. Tires and cars are designed to work together. Not only will a tire larger than the size recommended for your car result in incorrect speedometer readings, a larger tire might change the balance of your car, resulting in poor handling. In addition, a larger tire usually costs more and provides no additional benefits.

Myth: New valve stems are an unnecessary expense when buying new tires.

Fact: The valve stem is the primary air seal on a tire and wheel. Valve stems are made mostly of rubber, with a steel mechanism inside that lets air in and keeps it in the tire. With age, the rubber can get old and brittle and fail, causing a sudden loss of air pressure. The valve core—the steel mechanism inside the valve stem—could rust or just wear out. Extra money spent on new valve stems gives you that added measure of confidence in your new tires.

Myth: All-season radials are a good substitute for snow tires.

Fact: In general, all-season tires are not designed for use in deep snow. They will not grip as well as true snow tires. All-season tires work great in moderate-to-light snow and are excellent in the rain. If you live in a rural area that receives little plowing or road clearing during the winter or in deep-snow country, stick with true snow tires.

Myth: You can drive as fast and as long on a temporary or compact spare tire as you can on a regular tire.

Fact: Common sense tells us this isn't true but, unfortunately, some drivers are lacking this commodity. Temporary tires are designed to get you to the nearest service center for repair or replacement of your flat tire. They are not designed for high-speed or long-term use. Never drive faster than 50 mph on a temporary spare; replace it as soon as possible with a regular-size tire.

Myth: Special repair methods aren't needed for steel-belted radials.

Fact: The proper method for repairing steel-belted radials requires that the tire be removed from the wheel, the hole filled with a plug-type repair inserted from the outside of the tire, and a patch be placed over the hole from the inside of the tire. Be aware of the repair method used: If the tire isn't removed from the wheel and a patch placed on the inside, it is an improper repair.

Myth: My car came with speed-rated tires—tires that can go 130-plus mph. But I never drive over 65 mph so I don't really need to pay extra for them.

Fact: Speed-rated tires, besides being designed for high speeds, also provide better cornering, handling, and braking capability. You might save money by replacing them with non-speed-rated tires but you will lose in the handling ability of your car.

Myth: It is acceptable to mix different types or sizes of tires on a car.

Fact: No way! Radials should never be used on the same car with bias-ply tires, either on the same axle or front to back. Also, do not mix highway tires and all-season tires. You can, weather permitting, use a mix of snow tires with either all-season or highway tires.

Although a few high-performance cars use different size tires front and rear, most passenger cars come with the same size tire all around. Mixing tire sizes can affect the balance of the vehicle, change the suspension's capabilities, and alter ride characteristics. If you need to replace one, two, or three tires, use the same brand, model, type, and size as the remaining tire(s).

Bridgestone offers a consumer brochure, "Tire Tips To Keep You Rolling." It is packed with information about tire maintenance and tips on purchasing new tires. For a free copy, call toll-free 1-800-382-0600.

Be Sure Your Tires Aren't Tired

With summer's heat almost upon us, it might be a good idea to review a few basics and nonbasics about the care and feeding of tires. Tired of tires? You shouldn't be, because nothing less than your life is riding on them. And summer means vacation and more traveling, so you want to be sure your tires aren't tired.

The only contact your car has with the road is through four tiny tire "patches" about the size of your palm. The front two patches constitute the total surface area of the tires that feeds information back to the steering wheel. But all four patches must be in good condition to ensure that the car steers and handles correctly and gives the best performance.

If you look hard enough you should find a tire placard on the inside of the car's doorpost or on the inside of the glove compartment. This placard lists the maximum vehicle load and the proper tire size required for safe operation of the vehicle. If the placard is missing, this information should be in the owner's manual.

We have a tendency to overload our vehicles during vacation trips; not one driver in a thousand is aware that tires do not have infinite load-bearing capacity. Another tendency is to buy the wrong size. That can be foolish because tire size, type, and load range are carefully chosen to match the car's weight (when full and empty), handling capabilities, top speed, and a number of other parameters. Correct size and load range are very important.

All tires are designed to carry a specific load for any given inflation pressure. If you load the car, and thus the tires, with weight beyond its designated carrying capacity this could lead to premature failure of the tire.

I have always advocated inflating tires to the maximum allowable pressure printed on the sidewall of the tire. This gives longer tire life, allows the tire to run cooler (underinflation causes the tires to overheat), gives better gas mileage, and, because it doesn't have to work as hard to move the car, the engine will last longer.

But don't overinflate tires. Overinflation can be as dangerous as underinflation. Check the pressure in your tires when they are cool, and never exceed the maximum pressure shown on the tire. Don't worry if the pressure exceeds the maximum as the tire warms up. That's fine, because the expansion capability of the tire is figured into the maximum inflation pressure recommendation. In other words, a tire inflated to 35 psi maximum when cool can safely expand to higher pressures when warm. The maximum pressure is for cool inflation only.

Another thing to consider as summer approaches is the temperature rating of your tires—how well they can dissipate heat. For drivers living in Sun Belt areas this is an important consideration, and bearing in mind the heat wave we have been having the last few years, it's important for drivers living anywhere.

Tires are temperature-rated "A," "B" or "C." "A" is the best, "B" is midrange, and "C" is the government's minimum standard. Consider an "A" temperature-rated tire if you do a lot of high-speed summer driving. The temperature ratings are printed on the tire's sidewall and are one part of the Department of Transportation's Uniform Tire Quality Grading System (UTQGS) that also rates tread wear and traction.

When you are inspecting your tires don't forget to check the spare. It, too, should be inflated to maximum pressure. If you have a mini or space-saver spare you'll no doubt note that it takes much more air pressure than your normal-size tires. It's supposed to, so be sure you pump it up fully.

Almost every new car built today comes with radial tires, which offer advantages other than lasting longer, being safer, and giving better gas mileage because they create less rolling resistance (the radial tire patches move over the road more easily than conventional tires). According to the California South Coast Air Quality Management District, radial tires produce less air-damaging particulate matter per mile traveled than bias-ply tires do. If your car came with radials, stick with them. Changing to a bias-ply tire could compromise the safety of your vehicle. If you are now using bias-ply tires ask a qualified tire shop if switching to radials is permitted on your car. As you can see, radials are a smart choice for more reasons than one.

Don't Let Your Tires Lead a Soft Life

"Would it surprise you to discover that your tires are significantly underinflated? Chances are they are 8 pounds to 18 pounds less than what they should be. Of 100 cars we checked, only one was at the rated pressure printed on the side of the tire! Most were in the mid-20s, and quite a few were as low as 15 pounds. The record was a squat tire with only 8 pounds of air pressure."

So begins an Arizona Energy Office pamphlet on ways to save gasoline. Keeping tires at the tire manufacturer's recommended maximum air pressure is one of the easiest ways to save gasoline and increase tire life—and by far the cheapest.

Chances are your car's tires are suffering from the malady of underinflation. Underinflation as a government policy might be good; underinflation when it comes to tires isn't.

Drivers in mileage marathon competitions know that super-inflated tires are a must for maximum gasoline mileage. Rock-hard tires are standard for each vehicle entered in such competitions. Depending on the type of competition and the kind of vehicles entered, typical tire pressures will be in the 100-pounds-plus range.

But don't run out and put 100 pounds of air in your tires; that is only for special tires on marathon vehicles. What you can do, though, is make sure that your tires have the maximum allowable pressure in them at all times. Use the figures printed on the side of the tires (usually 32 pounds or 35 pounds per square inch, or psi). Those are the pressures recommended by the tire manufacturer.

Owner laziness is probably the prime reason many tires are leading a soft life. Most owners are just too lazy or preoccupied to spend a few minutes every two weeks to check the tire pressure. Think about it: When was the last time you checked yours? Gotcha!

The pamphlet mentioned above also notes that if your tires are usually inflated at 24 psi, and you increase the air pressure to a maximum of 32 psi, your gas mileage should increase by 3 miles per gallon, or roughly 16 percent, if you were averaging 18 miles per gallon. That can mean a saving of about $130 per year for someone who is now spending $800 annually on gasoline!

I recently had a letter from someone who was worried that if he inflated his tires to the maximum pressure when they were cold, they would then heat up beyond that range and be unsafe to drive on.

Not to worry. The tire manufacturer's recommended pressure takes into consideration that air pressure will increase as the tires heat up. A considerable safety margin is built into that recommendation.

If you don't have a tire-pressure gauge, by all means buy one or borrow one. Check the tire pressure frequently and keep it at the maximum figure printed on the tire's sidewall. Always check and adjust the pressure when the tires are cool.

No other maintenance practice costs so little and returns so much.

Properly Inflated Tires: Super-Smart Maintenance

I guess by now almost everyone who owns a car is well-acquainted with the fact that keeping tires at the proper air pressure (preferably the tire manufacturer's recommended maximum pressure) is a super-smart maintenance practice.

There are several reasons why this is so. Tires will last a lot longer, wear more evenly, and be a lot safer when properly inflated. Also, maximum tire pressure ensures that your car will get its best gas mileage. Low tire pressure can eat big holes in your fuel and rubber budget. Keeping tires properly inflated is the easiest of all maintenance practices—and by far the cheapest. And it pays handsome dividends.

Besides all the above, properly inflated tires can help—sometimes dramatically—extend the life of other components in the car.

How is that, you ask?

Maximum pressure in each tire eases the load on a car's entire drive train—the engine especially, the transmission and even the rear axle or transaxle.

The load on the engine is eased because properly inflated tires offer less rolling resistance to the efforts of the power plant.

The engine runs at a slower pace (fewer rpms), and this in turn requires less work from all components that drive the car. Even things such as the power-steering unit benefit because the car is easier to maneuver and requires less work from the unit.

If tires are not properly inflated, the car's mechanical parts work harder, wear faster, and expend more energy to get from point A to point B.

Still skeptical? Then drag out a bicycle, let some air out of the tires and take it for a ride. Upon returning, fill the tires to their maximum recommended pressure and take the bike for another spin. It is a lot easier, isn't it? Your body (the engine in this case) doesn't work nearly as hard to move the bicycle. You have energy and breath to spare.

It is no different with your car. Keep those tires at maximum pressure (the pressure printed on the sidewall), and your car will enjoy added energy and have pep to spare. Checking the air pressure once a week, or even once every two weeks, isn't too much to ask for all you will get in return.

There is really no excuse for underinflated tires. Proper tire inflation is a no-lose proposition: Both your car and your wallet are surefire winners. This is one type of inflation even President Bush supports.

Why You Should Care a Lot for Your Tires

Have you ever used a tire-tread depth gauge? No, not an air-pressure gauge, but a tire-tread depth gauge. Probably not. Most of us are familiar with air-pressure gauges—the wise motorist has one tucked away in the glove compartment and uses it regularly to make sure the tires are up to the tire manufacturer's maximum recommended pressure (printed on the side of the tire). This assures good gas mileage and long tire life.

This simple device should be a standard glove-compartment item in each car. A tread-depth gauge shows how much tread, measured in 32nds of an inch, is left on a tire. It also indicates how the tires are wearing, if one is wearing faster than the others, or if an irregular wear pattern is beginning to establish itself on one or more of the tires.

This gauge, if used periodically, can spot tire-wear irregularities in their embryonic stage, long before they are apparent to the naked eye. Regular measurement of tread depth is also an excellent way to determine if the air pressure in your tires is the best for your car and your type of driving.

A tread-depth gauge should be used every month or two. It takes only two or three minutes of your time—surely a small amount to protect an expensive investment. You should check each tire and keep a record of the readings. Measure each tire in three places: left, center, and right side of the tread.

Place the gauge into the tire's tread and observe and record the depth. Your record should contain the three readings and which tire (left front, right rear, etc.) they were taken from and the date and mileage at which the readings were taken.

Equipped with this periodic dose of information, you will be able to see precisely how each tire is wearing by observing and comparing the readings. Ideally, all 12 readings (four tires, three readings per tire) should be the same, demonstrating that all the tires are wearing evenly across the width of the tread. In reality, though, this is not usually the case.

If your record of tread depth shows that one tire is beginning to wear faster than the others, or that one is wearing abnormally on one side or in the middle (a reading such as: 8/32, 6/32, 8/32 or 8/32, 8/32, 6/32), it's a sign that corrective action in the form of more or less air pressure, a wheel alignment, tire-balancing, or other front-end work is required. A tread-depth gauge is especially valuable because it will spot many tire-wear abnormalities before they can damage the tire or wear it out before its appointed time.

Tire Jargon Valuable Source of Consumer Information

When it comes to tire sidewalls, the differences are more dramatic than just that between black and white. The numbers, letters, and wording on the sidewall of a tire can provide a consumer with all the information he or she needs to know about a particular tire, and then some. It's a valuable source of consumer data, if only you know what it all means. Let's take a look at a typical modern tire and decipher some of the sidewall lingo.

Perhaps the first thing you will notice is the name of the manufacturer and the brand name, such as Goodyear (manufacturer) Eagle (brand). This is usually the most prominent lettering on the tire. Next in line is the tire's dimensions or size. Today, nearly all tires are marked with the metric designation. Let's say it's a P195/75R14. The letter "P" designates the tire is a passenger-car tire. The number 195 indicates the tire's width in millimeters. The 75 is a numerical ratio of the tire's height to its width; in this case it is 75 percent. The "R" indicates the tire is of radial design; it can also be a "B" (belted bias) or a "D" (diagonal bias). All radials must also have the word "radial" imprinted on the tire. Fourteen is the tire's rim diameter measured in inches.

Somewhere on the tire will be an imprint indicating if the tire is tubeless or requires a tube. "M/S" indicates the tire meets the requirements for a mud and snow tire. The country where the tire was made is also stamped on the side. A quality grading placard gives treadwear (how long the tire will last when compared to another tire), traction (its braking ability in wet conditions), and temperature ratings (how well the tire dissipates heat). The DOT stamp stands for the Department of Transportation, the U.S. government agency responsible for the tire's safety ratings.

Usually after the DOT stamp is the manufacturer's code, known as the tire serial number. For instance, the designation CU is the code name for the tire manufacturer, which is not always the same as the manufacturer's name on the tire. For example, Sears does not manufacture Sears tires. There are books in which you can look up manufacturers' codes and see who actually made the tire. This can be helpful, because you might be able to buy the same tire with a different brand name at a better price.

The manufacturer's code is followed by the code for the tire size, such as L2. Tire design is given in the UM8 code, and the double or triple digit number that follows indicates the week and year the tire was made —168 means the 16th production week of 1988.

Some of the most important consumer information are the carrying capacity index and maximum-speed rating for the tire. The letter "S" before the "R" designation—SR—indicates the tire is rated for speeds up to 113 mph. TR—119 mph; HR—130 mph; VR—150 mph; and ZR—150-plus mph. Any of these speed-rated tires is more than adequate for highway driving.

The maximum-load rating at the maximum tire-inflation pressure is another piece of helpful information for the car owner. Maximum load 635 kg at 240kPa means the tire's load limit is 1,400 pounds (635 kg) and the maximum cold-inflation pressure is 35 pounds per square inch (240kPa). This means that four tires inflated to maximum pressure can carry a maximum load of 5,600 pounds divided evenly among them.

Tread description is noted as such: "Tread, 6 plies (2 rayon, 2 steel, 2 nylon)." Sidewall construction is also marked: "Sidewall: 2 plies rayon." This means the tread is made up of two layers of steel belt sandwiched between layers of rayon and two layers of nylon. The sidewall is made of two layers of rayon. Of course, these descriptions can vary depending on the type and quality of the tire.

Check Your Tires: Don't Be Left Flat

I remember being very impressed a few years ago when I came across a U.S. government report that listed the three most common causes of highway breakdown. There was nothing highfalutin' about the statistics, but their cold, clear message was *prima facie* evidence that most drivers ignore many simple and basic tenets of automotive maintenance and care.

The survey showed that the number 1 cause of highway breakdown is running out of gas. Talk about something that is completely avoidable! Talk about basics of automotive maintenance! The number 2 cause was tire trouble of one sort or another, while number 3 on the list was cooling-system problems. It's the second one, tires, that I want to discuss.

Not that we haven't all had tire problems; however, with today's superior tires, blowouts, tread separation, or other maladies that plagued older, less sturdy tires are far less common. But things still happen on the highway and cars are still disabled by tire problems. Just witness their high ranking on the disabled list.

The highway patrols that gathered data for that study reported another finding that didn't surprise me. The people who had tire problems couldn't get going again because they either didn't have a spare tire or if they did it was flat. A spare is something we don't give much thought to. Buried back there in the trunk, it leads a cloistered life that would be the envy of a contemplative monk. Nobody bothers it; in return, it doesn't bother anyone else. Until the car has a flat, that is.

Then see if no one is bothered. There is no more sinking feeling than to be out on the highway with a tire problem, open the trunk, and find the spare is flat. And the only reason it is flat is because you didn't take time to check it out periodically. All a spare asks is a once-a-month check.

Don't just look at the tire: You can't tell if it is inflated by just looking. Don't just feel it, either. That can be misleading. Get your tire pressure gauge out and verify that the spare is fully inflated. If you don't have a gauge, there's no better time than now to purchase one. That's all a spare asks. And I don't think it's too much.

Checking on the spare is such a simple and basic task that we tend to ignore it or we have that all-too-human tendency to think that it won't happen to me. But when it does we find ourselves woefully unprepared. Perform an in-the-trunk check each month. While you're at it, see that you have an operational jack and lug wrench too. A fully inflated spare is no good if you don't have the equipment to put it on with.

If you own a newer car with the funny tire spare (a mini space-saver spare) remember that once it is put on the wheel you should limit your speed, usually to under 50 mph. These spares are not meant for normal use and should be taken off as soon as possible. They are meant to be used only until the regulation tire is repaired. Please remember to follow the owner's manual procedure for changing a flat tire. Procedures can vary considerably from car to car.

And don't find yourself stuck for another reason. Newer cars have little lug wrenches that are usually placed in the glove box. If you don't know what it's for, it is used to take off the wheel covers. (It's an anti-theft device.) If you can't get the wheel cover off, you won't be able to change the flat. Be sure you have the hubcap removal tool and know how to use it. Your owner's manual contains all the information about using the mini spare and removing the hubcap wheel covers with the special wrench.

I know, I know. Many of you are saying that this is simple, elementary stuff and why waste space on it. If it were so elementary, tire problems wouldn't be the second most common cause of grounded cars. So don't get caught with your second tire flat. No time like right now to go out there and make sure it doesn't leave you flat when you need it most.

What Ever Happened to Whitewall Tires?

What ever happened to whitewall tires? You remember whitewall tires don't you? Maybe one of the reasons we don't see them much anymore is because people are poorer drivers than they were when whitewalls were in their heyday.

With black-wall tires you don't notice scuff marks on the black side wall, stark evidence of someone behind the steering wheel who can't park or maneuver in tight spaces. But a whitewall tire is unforgiving. Make an error in judgment, be off by only a few inches when parking the car, and the whitewall lets you know—in black on white.

Remember how the slightest blemish on their pristine, snow-white sides would send the conscientious car owner scurrying for the nearest pail of water and a Brillo pad? It was unthinkable to be caught with blemishes on your whitewalls.

Was there ever more of a sense of accomplishment than to scrub those whitewalls and see them covered with soapy, metallic, splintered mush, then take a hose and sponge and rinse off the glop? Presto! As if by magic, pure white appeared again. No matter how many times they were scuffed there always seemed to be enough white underneath ready to come front and center. Try that with today's black-walls. Somehow spraying a rubber protectant on the black-wall and seeing the black glisten just doesn't do it.

I don't mind lots of European stuff on cars, nor do I mind Euro-styling and Euro-this and that. But did we have to go whole hog and adopt their bland black-walls? So we're not racing types if we use whitewalls. So we don't exude Continental flavor. Big deal. Hey, whitewalls were the one hallmark that shouted loud and clear that the car is American, not European, not Japanese. To me, they were worth the price of the car alone.

And for those of us who couldn't afford whitewalls, there were port-a-walls. Remember port-a-walls? They were portable whitewalls. For about $10 or so for a set of four you could turn a set of black-walls into glistening white. Like big flat white rubber Hula-Hoops, they hooked between the tire and tire rim and were hard to tell from the real thing—until you got moving at high speeds and sometimes the wind would get underneath one and started it flapping.

But then again—digressing to the driving-skill bit for a moment—I have to admit we had curb feelers back then. Curb feelers and whitewalls went hand in hand, or tire in curb. You remember curb feelers, don't you? Those little springs that stuck out from the right front and right rear wheel wells and scraped the curb when you got within about 6 inches of it. They let out a sound more than befitting their size, like a garbage truck picking up trash cans in the early morning. You couldn't ignore their warning, those best friends of the whitewall.

Sure, curb feelers were cheaters, but the wise motorist always had a pair dangling from the passenger's side wheel wells. Besides, it was cool to have them. Today's drivers have passenger side-view mirrors. That's even more of an advantage because you can actually see where you are going, not just hear.

Remember whitewall tires? Oh, I've seen some pale imitations in the past few years: thin red and blue "whitewalls." Red and blue whitewalls? OK, then make that bluewalls and redwalls. Somehow it just doesn't sound the same. And there are even whitewall imitations. But you can't really call them whitewalls, those pencil thin stripes of white that pass for a whitewall. That's like some of these grocery shelf products that claim to be such and such but in reality have only a whiff of what their names conjure up.

What ever happened to whitewall tires? Oh, they're still around—in memories anyway.

13

Behind the wheel

A RACE-CAR DRIVER'S ULTIMATE AIM is to cross the finish line first. Sometimes just crossing is quite an accomplishment. But he or she still must drive in a way that conserves fuel, the engine, and other mechanical parts. The best race drivers drive conservatively on their way to the finish line.

The consistent winners, the ones who collect the big paychecks, are also the ones who seem to drive in an unspectacular fashion. They are intent on conserving their car and fuel and not making unnecessary maneuvers on the way to the checkered flag. On the way to the grocery store you should follow their lead—no, not get there as fast as you can—and drive conservatively.

Three-time world-champion race-car driver Jackie Stewart says, "My overruling passion has always been to drive as spectacularly as I can in an unspectacular fashion." Think about that a while. True professionals behind the wheel drive so that no one notices them.

"Light is right," says Stewart, referring to a driver's touch on the accelerator and steering wheel. Those are three excellent words to keep in mind when you are driving. They are important keys to extending the life of your car and getting maximum miles per gallon from it. It's right if it feels light.

I recently attended the Silverstone 1,000 race in England and marveled as two Jaguars and a Mercedes dueled neck-and-neck for the entire 1,000 kilometer (621 miles) race—that's 121 miles longer than the Indy 500.

The two Jaguars were in the top positions for the entire race until the last few laps when, because of an error in calculating the amount of gasoline left, one of them ran out of gas. But the other Jaguar had its gas figured down to the last liter and went on to win that prestigious race. The driver had enough skill and foresight to nurse his car to the finish line by driving with the light-is-right touch. He had less than a liter of fuel left at the finish.

You don't have to be a race-car driver to drive with the light touch. Light on the accelerator. Light on the brakes. Light on the steering wheel. If the wheel begins to feel heavy and cumbersome you know you are doing something wrong.

According to Stewart, "You should strive to drive like the world's finest chauffeur." Finesse and gentleness should be an integral part of your everyday routine. Backseat passengers should be able to drink a cup of coffee and read the paper without being unduly aware of your stops and starts. Combine gentleness behind the wheel with driver awareness of what is happening around you and you will cross every line first, be it at the grocery store or Silverstone.

Father Time Takes His Toll

A recent stint at the Bob Bondurant School of High Performance Driving taught me a lesson I was not yet prepared to accept.

One portion of the training held at the Sears Point International Raceway near Sonoma, California, consisted of driving through the "accident simulator." Students line up in their cars and take turns driving down a straightaway toward three red lights positioned about 10 feet above the road. Each light hangs directly over one of three cone-lined lanes that serve as exits from the course. The student has three choices: directly ahead, the left lane, or the right lane.

As the cars build up speed to the maximum of 45 mph they cross an imaginary line approximately 80 feet from the lights. At that point one of the instructors changes one of the red lights to green. The student's job is to guide the car into the green exit lane—it could be any of the three—without using the brakes and without knocking over the lane-marking cones.

Sounds pretty easy, but you'd be surprised how fast 45 mph seems when the lights (or a potential accident) are only 80-odd feet away, and how fast those lanes approach even at a speed most of us consider pokey. The first day was a breeze; I never missed a light, never trampled a cone.

Day two on the simulator was a different story. I had partied a bit the night before and wasn't feeling as chipper as I would have liked when I arrived at the track. When it came time to practice the accident simulator, I did OK at lower speeds, nursing the car into the correct lane as the light changed, but at 45 mph I seemed to freeze at the wheel, choosing the wrong lane each time and plowing through a gaggle of cones. I couldn't believe I was doing this. Just yesterday I sailed through the simulator like a pro; today, there was only a shadow of my expert self behind the wheel. I went 0 for 3. Talk about being embarrassed. Others were scooting through with no problem, but I couldn't find a clean exit.

I parked the car and sheepishly went over to talk to the instructor. Were they rigging the lights to fool me or not flashing the green until I had passed the 80-foot mark? No such luck. Everything was on the up-and-up. So what was I doing wrong?

I confessed to having hit the sack rather late after an evening of partying. The instructor's knowing smile told me he had the answer. This wasn't the first time this had happened.

The few drinks combined with staying up late and getting up early had taken their toll on my half-century old body and mind. My eye and hand coordination wasn't as keen as it was yesterday, and my reaction time was lessened by a split second or so. I wasn't doing anything wrong, but my reflexes were off by a hair. It was enough to make a dramatic difference in how I handled the accident simulator.

Bondurant instructors tell their students to imagine a truck laden with nuclear bombs crossing in front of them as they approach the simulator. If that were really so, Sears Point would have been only a memory that fuzzy morning.

But it taught me a lesson: Because I am getting older, my reaction time isn't what it used to be. That's not easy to accept. Couple that with the late night, and you have the reason why I couldn't equal my performance of the previous day. It drove home the point of how truly dysfunctional a legally drunk driver must be behind the wheel. But that's another story.

We aren't what we used to be, no matter how well we take care of ourselves. It's a lesson all drivers can benefit by. Temper your driving as you get older. It's tough enough avoiding a potential accident at 45 mph; think what it must be like at 65 mph. Snug and safe in our silent whooshing environments we are lulled into complacency and lose proper perspective of high speed and what it can do.

If you are tired, have something weighing heavily on your mind, didn't sleep well, or are hung over, please exercise extreme caution when driving. Better yet, let someone else drive. Or take the bus.

I'm not saying that as you get older you should quit driving. On the contrary—these can be some of the best years. You are more aware of yourself and your capabilities and will have sense enough to forget the macho stuff and re-evaluate your driving habits and adjust them to compensate for the ravages of Father Time.

Slippery Roads? New Tips on How to Handle a Skid

I recently finished a three-day driving course at the Bob Bondurant School of High Performance Driving at Sears Point International Raceway near Sonoma, California. And brother, did I learn a lot. Think you're a good driver? A couple of days at Bondurant will convince you otherwise.

Through the many experiences I had during those highly charged three days, a couple of things stood out as being of special value in everyday driving. And with Old Man Winter peeking around the next corner, these suggestions could prove invaluable in the event you find yourself losing control of your car on icy, snowy, or wet roads.

We've all heard the old adage that if your car goes into a skid, turn the steering wheel in the direction of the skid to help bring the car under control. Well, that's true, but one thing has always bothered me: How does a driver determine the direction the car is skidding? That question is not as silly as it sounds.

If the car goes into a skid and the back end kicks out toward the curb, then the front end would be aimed at the center of the road. OK, which way are you skidding and which way should you turn the wheel to bring the car back under control? Not as easy as you thought, is it? Well, forget about turning in the direction of the skid. Bondurant instructors take this confusion and turn it into advice everyone can understand: No matter what direction your car is skidding, turn the steering wheel (and thus the car) in the direction you want to go. It's that simple.

If the skid is taking you into oncoming traffic, turn to the right, out of the way of the oncoming traffic. If the car begins to skid off the road onto the shoulder, turn the wheel to the left to get the car back on the pavement. And it doesn't matter if you are driving a rear- or front-wheel-drive vehicle. The rule applies to them all.

There are other things to consider when attempting to bring a skidding car under control. A skid is usually caused by too much braking or too much throttle. Let's say you are in a skid and turn the wheel in the desired direction and nothing happens—the car just continues in the same direction. This is a case of too much brake being applied, which has caused the front wheels to lock. You can't steer a car when the front wheels aren't rolling. You should ease off the brake pedal until the wheels unlock. When you do this two things happen to help you regain control: The front wheels start rolling again and gain traction, and your steering input will take effect. The car now steers where you want it to.

Too much throttle going into a turn or under adverse conditions can also cause the car to skid. If in a front-wheel-drive car you find the front wheels spinning uncontrollably, ease off the gas. This shifts the car's weight to the front and allows the wheels to gain traction. Again, point the car in the direction you want to go.

In a rear-wheel-drive car too much brake pressure shifts the car's weight to the front and causes the rear wheels to lock. If this happens, the rear end will skid. Get off the brakes fast and steer in the desired direction. The rear end will begin to swing the other way, sometimes violently, and you must correct the reverse skid by steering where you want to go. A skid or spin caused by fast spinning rear wheels can be corrected the same way.

Bondurant instructors emphasize that a person tends to steer in the direction he is looking. If caught in a skid, always look ahead to where you want the car to go, and you will almost automatically steer in that direction. Being aware of what you should do to control a skid gives you a head start in extracting you and your car from a potentially dangerous situation.

Don't Be Lazy: Downshift!

Have you ever lugged your car's engine? I don't mean taking it out of your car, lifting it on your shoulder, and carrying it around. I'm talking about a more insidious kind of lugging—and you don't have to be a weight lifter to be guilty of it. Most drivers of cars that have manual transmissions do lug their engines occasionally; some make a bad habit of it.

What exactly is lugging?

A vehicle's engine lugs when it strains to operate in a gear that is too high for the driving situation. A classic example is coaxing a car up a hill in high gear when it should be shifted to a lower, more economical (in this case) one.

The main culprit in the lugging game is driver laziness; we don't want to bother to push in the clutch and shift to a lower gear. The main victim of this laziness is your engine.

Lugging is extremely detrimental to any engine and can cause premature wear of internal engine parts. When an engine is lugging, the accelerator is usually pushed all the way to the floor to try to urge more power from the unit. This causes gasoline to pour into the engine, where most of it remains unburned and wasted. The little that is used fails miserably in trying to keep the car running smoothly.

This is one of the times that tries the engine's soul. Valves clatter and ping, bearings knock, and the car, in some cases, begins to vibrate. Lugging puts unnecessary demands on the engine, gasoline and oil, demands that could be cut to the quick by downshifting. By doing this, the accelerator position is immediately raised, cutting the wasteful flow of gasoline, and the engine operates more efficiently and economically. The gears take over the job the engine was trying to do.

Lower gears are there for a purpose. Use them; don't let them atrophy from driver neglect. Never ask your engine to do a job that is meant for the gears. Always downshift at the first sign that the engine is lugging. You are always better off wear-wise and fuel-wise to shift to a lower gear than to stay in a high one that would cause the engine to labor and lug.

Be especially diligent now that it is cold. Lugging a cold engine will do even more harm because you are putting pressure on parts when the engine oil hasn't warmed sufficiently to give up-to-par protection.

Tips and Tricks for Easier Driving

When I lived in western Pennsylvania, I always welcomed anything that would make winter driving a bit easier. Not one to forget my roots, here are some tips and tricks that will do just that and make it a little more economical and safer too.

If you drive a manual-transmission car be sure to depress the clutch—even though the shift lever is already in neutral—before trying to start the engine. This is helpful at all times, but especially when it is cold, because depressing the clutch frees the transmission and the starter has less work to do when trying to start the engine.

This is a good practice to get into anytime, and it has safety implications also. If the clutch is in, the car will not accidentally lurch if inadvertently left in gear. On many newer cars the clutch must be depressed before the car will start.

Whether you drive a front- or rear-wheel drive vehicle, it has a differential (that hump underneath the car) between the driving wheels. (The driving wheels are the ones the engine's power goes to.) The job of the differential is to distribute power to the wheels: The ones with the least amount of traction get the most power.

If you have ever been stuck in snow you know what this can mean. one wheel will spin while the other that has grip remains stationary. Here is an old trick—courtesy of Saab—that allows you to fool the differential and get it to deliver equal power to both wheels when you are stuck and one wheel is spinning. (To use this method your parking brake must act on the driving wheels of the car. Check your owner's manual to see how your parking brake works.)

Apply the parking brake a few notches until it just begins to grip. If the brakes are correctly adjusted the braking effort will then be equal at both driving wheels. This will cause both wheels to turn at the same speed and your car will instantly revert back to a two-wheel drive instead of one. The extra traction might be just what the doctor ordered to get you out of the snow or ice.

Don't apply the parking brake too hard and don't keep it engaged too long because it can wear the brake pads.

If your car is equipped with an anti-lock braking system (ABS), always apply full pressure to the brake pedal during an emergency stop or a skid. This might be hard to get used to because it is just the opposite of what you should do with conventional brakes.

With standard brakes try practicing threshold and cadence braking so you'll be prepared for driving on slippery surfaces. Pick an isolated spot on a slippery road and apply the brakes only to the point where they begin to lock up (the threshold) then ease up. Rapidly repeat the procedure over and over. This keeps the wheels from locking and keeps you in control of the car. It used to be called "pumping the brakes."

Remember, if the wheels lock up, you can't steer the car. So keep those wheels turning by applying the brakes just to the point of wheel lock up and then release the pressure. This is an excellent braking technique on wet and icy surfaces.

Many drivers believe in letting some air out of the tires come winter, reasoning that the softer tires allow for better traction on slippery roads. Actually, just the opposite is often true. Fully inflated tires—especially snow tires and all-season radials—allow the tires and car to handle as they were designed to. Underinflated tires could compromise handling and the car's traction and stopping capabilities.

Remember that tires naturally lose about 1 pound of pressure for each 10 degrees drop in temperature. Adjust tire pressure frequently during winter driving and don't keep them on the soft side—no matter what your neighbor tells you.

Tips for New Drivers

You're 16 and have just passed your driver's exam. In your pocket is a bona fide driver's license, a document issued by your state that allows you to operate a vehicle on the nation's streets and highways. Your range of travel is now limited only by the amount of road in front of you—and perhaps by your parents.

What a great feeling it is when you first get behind the wheel alone. It's just you in complete control—no coach sitting alongside you to critique your driving. It is a rite of passage for almost every teenager, one that drivers fondly remember and relish.

Enjoy and cherish your new license. All new drivers should because there is no comparable feeling of mobility and independence anytime, anywhere. It's a once-in-a-lifetime thing. Go ahead, pinch yourself. It's for real.

But new responsibilities are part and parcel of new-found freedom. Tough driving decisions face today's new driver, and more skills and judgment behind the wheel are needed than ever before. Traffic is more congested; freeways are nightmares for even experienced drivers.

Be aware, new drivers, that although you think you know how to drive a vehicle, you really don't know how to drive. That can only come with hours spent behind the wheel honing your skills. Only by driving in everyday situations and recognizing and correcting your mistakes can skill and an intuitive reckoning come your way.

Learn to drive defensively. Don't assume the other driver is going to do what is right and proper or that he or she is adept behind the wheel. You'll soon find out it doesn't work that way. Drive with a heightened awareness of what is happening around you. Keep your young senses keenly tuned to all the activity in front, to the side, and to the rear of your car. Driving means continual monitoring of everything around you as you guide the vehicle to your destination.

Remember that driving is a privilege and not a right. And that the privilege can be taken away if you take undue liberties with it. Obey the laws of the road regardless of what others may do. Laws are there to protect both you and me.

And make two vows right now as you read this. First, to never drink and drive. Nothing will ever heal the heartache you and your victim's family will feel if you injure or kill someone while intoxicated. Plant this in your head and nurture it until it becomes part of your psyche. Second, to always wear your seatbelt and encourage others to do likewise.

And finally, remember that each one of your passengers—and each person in every car you share the road with —- has entrusted you with nothing less than his or her life. You'll never have a greater trust than that.

It's a great time in your life as you assume new adult responsibilities. Take them seriously. That doesn't mean you can't have fun with a car, because you can and will.

Public Vehicles Deserve Better Treatment

I was driving down the highway the other day, cruise control set on 55, when a car whizzed past me doing 70 or 75. I glanced up and saw that it had official state plates.

I was in town, making a left turn at an intersection, when a car cut in front of me. I noticed this one bore the official county seal.

I was driving by a city work crew last summer and noticed two municipal vehicles idling with the windows rolled up. No doubt the air conditioner was running to keep the car cool so the inspector or boss could get back into a comfortably precooled car.

I was at a stoplight sitting next to a city-owned truck. When the light turned green it took off as if shot from a cannon.

City, county, state, and federal vehicles don't belong to these faceless entities but to you and me, the taxpayers. And many drivers of these vehicles—not all of them, mind you—don't care about how they treat or drive them because they don't own them.

I care. Those are my cars and trucks, they're your cars and trucks. That's our money those irresponsible drivers are wasting. Not the city's, not the county's, not the state's, not Uncle Sam's, but ours—yours and mine.

Countless gallons of fuel are wasted because the drivers of these public vehicles don't care about or don't practice or aren't aware of proper driving techniques. Who pays for this fuel? You got it.

Every driver of every government-owned vehicle should be required to drive with both safety and conservation in mind. No breaking the speed limit, no pedal-to-the-metal antics, no unnecessary car-wasting or fuel-wasting maneuvers, no unsafe driving.

Many drive that way because we let them get away with it. No one seems to care. I do. It pains me to see my tax dollars wasted. It pains me to see finite resources consumed unnecessarily.

More stringent training of drivers in the public trust is needed. The U.S. Department of Energy DECAT (Driver Energy Conscious Awareness Training) program broke the ice a few years ago by teaching various local and federal employees how to drive more efficiently. (I was instrumental in helping begin DECAT.) But the program needs reinforcement and constant vigilance. Anyone who routinely drives a public vehicle should be required to undergo periodic driving tests for safety and energy conservation. Safety, economy, and car-conservation driving programs are necessary.

Every driver entrusted with a public vehicle should be required to set a good example in the above areas. If violations are reported, the offenders should lose their right to drive for a specified period. Too harsh? No way.

There is so much waste in other areas that some things may appear to be insignificant or not worth the bother. Maybe this is one of them. But it seems to me that safety on our roads, saving our precious fuel, conserving our public vehicles, and putting otherwise wasted money to work elsewhere might just be worth the bother.

Avoid Neck Injuries: Adjust Your Headrest Properly

If you are taller than 5 feet 10 inches, you are considered tall by today's standards. Tall is supposed to be a desirable attribute in our society. Take "tall, dark, and handsome," for instance (I qualify for one out of three of those, the tall bit). Witness our many looked-up-to sports figures: You got it, tall. Being tall is supposed to give a person a number of advantages. Why this is so I don't know, but that's the way it seems to be.

Well, I am 6 feet 2 inches and I know being tall isn't all it's cracked up to be—especially when Mr. or Ms. Tall is driving a car. I can't drive a Japanese car in comfort; there is rarely enough headroom. And many foreign and domestic cars don't give a tall person enough legroom up front. And the backseats of most new cars? Forget it. Cramp city. There is only a handful of cars I am comfortable in.

Being tall has another disadvantage when it comes to cars, one that can really be a pain in the neck. Saab, the Swedish car manufacturer, recently released the results of a study of 1,000 accidents in Saab cars on Swedish highways. Seems that if you're tall—they don't specify what is meant by tall, but you get the idea—and your headrest isn't adjusted high enough, you are susceptible to a neck injury in the event of a rear-end collision.

The word "headrest" implies a place to rest one's head, and a lot of drivers take this literally, adjusting the headrest so that they can drop their heads back on it and rest. "Headrest" is really a misnomer; it should be called a head stop, because that is its main purpose. It is meant to stop the head from swinging backward with force, thus preventing whiplash-type neck injuries.

If you are tall, chances are the headrest will be at the back of your neck, exactly where it shouldn't be. Headrests—for all drivers—should be adjusted so that when you move your head backward, the center of the headrest squarely meets the back of your bead. Your neck should not be in contact with the headrest.

This is no problem for shorter people because this is usually where a headrest will be. But in some cars, even with the headrest adjusted to its maximum height, a tall person will still find his neck meeting the headrest, not the back of his head.

For maximum protection always adjust the headrest as described above. Even though that ideal position might not be possible for you in some cases, the closer the headrest comes to the back of your head, the better off you are.

Make Sure You Can Drive It Forever:
Don't Drink and Drive

"Drinking (and driving) has: Drained more blood, slain more children, blinded more eyes, twisted more limbs, dethroned more reason, wrecked more manhood, dishonored more womanhood, blasted more lives, driven more to suicide, and dug more graves than any other scourge that has ever swept the world."—Evangeline Booth in *Good Housekeeping*.

Jerry Cartin is one of the lucky ones. He survived an encounter with a drunken driver. But Cartin, a Tucson, Arizona, lawyer and chairman of the Pima County chapter of MADD (Mothers Against Drunk Driving), has paid dearly. The two years he spent recovering from an accident that nearly took his life are but cobwebs spun in a dark cellar. Cartin remembers little of that portion of his life, memories taken from him by a drunken driver.

But Cartin is one of the lucky ones.

A 12-year-old boy, a woman of 23, and an 81-year-old man didn't have luck on their side. They are among the 57 people in Pima County who won't start 1987 with their families. That is 10 more casualties than 1985's total.

Altogether, 25,000 people won't be around to enjoy 1987. That's how many die nationwide in an average year due to drunken drivers. Fifty-seven thousand men were lost in Vietnam, but in the same period 260,000 people were killed by drunken drivers. Let that sink in for a while.

In fact, more than 11 million American families have had a member killed or seriously injured by a drunken driver in the past 10 years.

The loss to society exceeds $24 billion each year. The drunken driver hits your pocketbook, too. More than 25 cents of each auto-insurance dollar goes to pay for damage he or she does.

All these people were killed because someone didn't give a damn. This isn't a plea to stop drinking. Nor does MADD or any other group concerned with drug- or alcohol-impaired driving want you to stop. That's your decision to make. What they do want you to do is to stop drinking and driving. It's that combination that is so deadly.

One of man's greatest responsibilities begins when he or she takes the wheel of a couple of thousand pounds of hurtling steel. To assume that responsibility in an intoxicated state shows gross contempt and disdain for your fellow man. Perhaps we have become numb to the devastation a car can wreak in the hands of a drunken driver.

No, none of those special people can be brought back now; we can't do a thing about what has already happened. But we can do something about keeping it from happening again. Each and every one of us can decide never to drink and drive.

And what better time to make that commitment than now? What better resolution than to not get in your car and attempt to drive after you have had your fill.

To paraphrase Robert Benchley: "Drinking (and driving) makes such fools of people, and people are such fools to begin with . . ."

Especially if they drink and drive. Just ask Jerry Cartin.

Drive Carefully and Drive Long

If you knew the areas along highways or city roads where accidents are most likely to happen, you would be in a much better position to take evasive action in the event it became necessary. Right?

Given that the above is true, it is possible for every driver to help cut down on accident rates that are a shame to this country.

One statistic hasn't changed much during the past few years: Almost 50,000 people are killed each year in automobile accidents. Think about that—137 people every day. And think about this: According to the National Safety Council a full 85 percent of all those accidents were avoidable.

One way we can reduce those tragic figures is to be aware that most accidents happen at intersections. Intersections are the killers supreme, be they the in-town or highway variety. In fact, upward of 40 percent of all city accidents (it's higher in some cities) take place at intersections.

You can make sure you don't become one of the statistics by being especially aware when nearing an intersection.

○ Never try to run a yellow or red light. Are the few seconds you save worth the risk to life and limb and car?

○ At any non-traffic-light intersection remember that the car to your immediate right always has the right of way. You are supposed to yield to that driver. Never assume that the other driver knows this rule. Many times they don't, or if they do, don't care about it. Drive defensively: Always assume the other guy is not going to follow the rules.

○ Even though the light is green and you have the right of way, slow down and check the intersection prior to driving through it. Never speed through an intersection. Approach it with the idea that an accident might be about to happen: foot off the gas and at the ready near the brake pedal.

○ Always look out for the car in front of you when entering an intersection. Don't assume the driver will go through. If the light should turn yellow, be prepared to stop, because the driver in front of you might suddenly apply his brakes.

○ Watch for cars making left turns in the oncoming traffic lanes. Many times these drivers will try to beat you across your lane of traffic. Again, never assume the left-turners will wait to make their turns until you have passed.

○ Practice being a courteous driver. Make at least one attempt each day to extend some courtesy to another driver. Soon it will become a habit. And if everyone did it, most accidents would be a thing of the past.

We know that most accidents happen at intersections. And we know that if we are prepared we can avoid becoming a participant in one. Remember those stats: 85 percent of accidents are avoidable. Be extra careful at all intersections and take the precautions outlined above. It's just plain dumb not to.

Trains Can't Stop; You Can

I was dumbfounded when the Norfolk Southern rail people sent me a copy of their regularly issued compilation of articles highlighting train/ vehicle crashes. I never thought much about the accidents that occur at railroad crossings, but after reading some of the material, I realize the subject is not one we should take for granted. It's incredible how many people are maimed, injured, and killed at railroad grade crossings throughout the country. Even more incredible is that each and every incident could have been avoided. Included with the latest compilation of accident reports was a brochure issued by the Amoco Motor Club and Operation Lifesaver, Inc., an industry organization that promotes safety at train crossings.

One of the more sobering statistics and pieces of advice in the brochure simply said, "Trains can't stop—you can." Now we all know that trains really can stop, but what they mean is that the stopping distances for an average freight train do not even closely resemble those for a loaded car going the same speed. A car's stopping distance can be measured in multiples of 100 feet. A train's? Nowhere near that.

Consider this: A freight train traveling at a modest 30 mph must use up over 1/2 mile of track—.6 miles to be exact—before it can be brought to a halt. At 60 mph, the distance required to stop the big iron stretches to 1.4 miles. So now you see what they mean when they say that trains can't stop, but you can.

It's easy to misjudge the train's speed and distance from the crossing. Because of the large size of the train, it appears to be moving much slower than you think. Kind of like a bull elephant on the charge. If you have any doubts, stop and wait for it to pass, whether it be an elephant or a train.

Here are some other tips to keep in mind when you approach a train crossing. As common-sense as these might seem, drivers disobey them daily and many pay with their lives and those of their passengers.

○ Never race a train to a crossing. It's not like track and field because you will never have a second chance if you lose.

o Watch for vehicles that must stop at railroad grade crossings. Be prepared to stop when you are following buses or trucks that are required to stop.

o Be especially watchful at night for railroad-crossing warning signs. At night it is particularly difficult to judge speed and distance. If you have any doubts, it is always better to be overcautious than sorry.

o Expect a train on any track at any time. Most trains do not travel on a regular schedule. Be cautious at a grade crossing at any time of the day or night.

o Don't get caught on a grade crossing. Never drive onto a grade crossing until you are sure you can clear the tracks. Once you have started across the tracks, keep going, especially if you see a train approaching.

o Never drive around gates. Gates are the red-and-white-striped poles that lower to close off traffic lanes at a crossing. If the gates are down, stop and stay in place. Do not cross the tracks until the gates are raised and the lights have stopped flashing.

o Watch out for the second train. To me this is one of the most important precautions. When you are at a multiple-track crossing and the last car of the train passes the crossing, do not proceed until you are sure that no other train is coming on another track, especially from the opposite direction.

o If your vehicle stalls on a crossing, get everyone out and off the tracks immediately. If a train is coming, stay clear of the tracks. If no train is in sight, post lookouts and try to start the vehicle or push it off of the tracks.

There must be some deep-seated psychological reason that impels some drivers to flaunt danger and try to beat a train across the tracks—something I'm sure psychologists and train people have an explanation for. But to me this ultimate game of "chicken" seems the ultimate high in stupidity. Nobody wins this game: There can only be losers, even if you make it across, even if you beat the system.

If you have a younger person with you and he at some time tries to mimic your action, perhaps it will be he who will pay with his life for your foolhardiness. Think about that the next time you try to outwit a train.

Amoco Motor Club and Operation Lifesaver, Inc. say that many tragic railroad accidents could have been prevented if the above safety tips had been followed. Study them and pass the column along to family members and friends. No one should ever have to consider the consequences of meeting a train, except maybe to pick up a visiting relative.

Drivers' Excuses Are No Laughing Matter

A couple of months ago I attended an awards banquet sponsored by a local county's traffic-survival school. Drivers who have had their licenses suspended for having three moving violations in one year, or one moving violation if they are under 18, are sent there to have their driving skills honed. Needless to say, traffic-survival school gets the hard-core cases. Most states have some type of similar "school."

Sifting through a packet of information from the school, I came across a sheet with some excuses drivers had used after being in an accident. These were explanations given to an insurance company.

They are enlightening, hilarious, and scary because they show the kind of people on the roads—people you and I have to contend with in our daily driving, and the kind of people regularly sent to the school to be made better and more aware drivers. Listen to some of these doozies:

- Coming home, I drove into the wrong house and collided with a tree I don't have.
- The other car collided with mine without giving warning of its intentions.
- A pedestrian hit me and went under my car.
- The guy was all over the road. I had to swerve a number of times before I hit him.
- The accident occurred when I was attempting to bring my car out of a skid by steering it into the other vehicle.
- To avoid hitting the bumper of the car in front, I struck the pedestrian.
- When I saw I could not avoid a collision, I stepped on the gas and crashed into the other car.
- An invisible car came out of nowhere, struck my car, and vanished.

Funny, huh? But there is a serious undercurrent that flows through them: A lot of incompetent drivers are on the roads, a fact of which most drivers are aware. They are the main reason for traffic schools. Get rid of the bad drivers, and the schools will disappear. Somehow, though, I have the feeling that traffic-safety schools will be around for a long, long time.

Are You a Road Warrior? Take the "Driver Stress" Test

If you drive to work, do me a favor and take this simple quiz:

1. Do you frequently drive through yellow or red lights?
2. Do you get impatient with other drivers for going slowly?

3. Do you curse, pound the steering wheel, or make obscene gestures while driving?
4. Do you drive to work or home in the shortest possible time?
5. Do you often "fight" the traffic driving to work or home?
6. Do you frequently read, dictate, shave, apply makeup, etc., while driving or stopped at a light?
7. Do others tell you that you get overly upset or annoyed while driving?
8. Do you worry about being late?
9. Do you drink or take drugs while driving?

If you answered "yes" to one or more questions, you have symptoms of driver stress, according to psychiatrist Martin Brenner. But don't feel like the Lone Ranger. A recent Connecticut Department of Transportation (ConnDOT) survey found that over 40 percent of the more than 1 million Connecticut commuters experience stress on the highway.

Dr. Brenner worked with ConnDOT to promote his "Stress Care Driving Program," which is aimed at helping commuters become happier, healthier and more relaxed drivers. According to Brenner, not learning to cope with traffic congestion can lead to elevated blood pressure, negative mood swings, reduced tolerance for frustration, and even more aggressive and impatient driving habits. In other words, we become "Road Warriors" instead of alert, considerate, and competent drivers.

"Aggressive driving behavior often reflects a problem with stress at work or home, too," says Brenner. And children who note a parent's aggressive driving might pick up from it and start acting aggressively themselves.

We can learn to cope with gridlock, heavy traffic, and everyday commuting problems by following some of Dr. Brenner's suggestions:

○ Ride together to work. Join a car pool or van pool, or take a bus or train (even if it's only one or two days a week). It will take your mind off the commute and you'll have the freedom to do work or use the time more productively. And you'll save money—up to $2,000 a year (which can help relieve financial stress). You'll also help reduce the traffic congestion that adds to the stressful environment.

○ When you must drive alone, think of the car as your refuge, a place to get away from the pressures and demands of life.

○ When you drive, don't do anything but drive. Don't try to read, dictate, work, or put on makeup. You won't do a good job, and it's dangerous.

○ Listen to relaxing music; don't constantly switch stations.

○ Don't use the car to think about work or problems—enjoy being bored.

- Buckle up your seat belt; you'll feel more secure.
- Give yourself extra time. Eliminate the need to rush. But if you're late, you're late. People will understand.
- Stifle the urge to be a "Road Warrior," trying to take charge of drivers you feel are doing the wrong thing. Stay calm and keep away from the erratic drivers. Drive defensively.
- Avoid tailgating, quickly changing lanes, going through yellow or red lights, cursing, screaming, or making gestures at other drivers.
- Don't fight the traffic. Give in; go with the flow. The struggle isn't worth it. And, I might add, it's a great way to not get anywhere fast.
- Believe that you are the master of your behavior. You can control the way you drive and the way you live and avoid being controlled by the actions of others.
- Never drive while drinking or taking drugs.

I might add a few of my own tips to the above:

- Take a course in defensive or performance driving. You might think you are a good driver; a professionally taught course will show otherwise. You'll be amazed at how much more you have to learn about handling a car and behaving properly behind the wheel.
- Don't blast music; it takes your mind off your driving. It also distracts other drivers. If you have a boom box, do me and a lot of other drivers a favor—give it a toss.

Try these tips for a week to see if you can become an Easy Rider instead of a Road Warrior. You'll see how much less stressful commuting can be. And when you see that these suggestions really work, you'll want to be sure they become a regular part of your daily driving routine.

Courtesy Is Contagious—Try to Catch It!

The old man turned the corner slowly, carefully, waiting until the way was clear before making his move. His wife, sitting next to him in the car, was helping. I could see her craning her neck to check traffic. Between the two, a driving team had emerged. I followed behind them as we both drove east to the intersection. At that point they moved correctly into the right-turn lane, turn signal showing their intent well before the act.

They had moved slowly on the road—or so I thought at the time—but a glance at my speedometer showed me that they were going about the legal limit. All the other cars whizzing by us at above-the-speed limits made my pace and theirs seem ponderous.

As I, too, moved into the right-turn lane, a car suddenly cut in front of me and tucked itself on the older couple's rear bumper. They were waiting for traffic to clear or for a green light before turning right. But it wasn't good enough for the guy who had cut between us.

Middle-aged, suit and tie, in an upbeat, with-it car, he fidgeted and fussed, his neck muscles bulging as he puffed furiously on a cigarette and strained at his shirt collar. Heart-attack city, I thought. Then he leaned on his horn, impatient at the older couple's patience, urging them to get out into traffic.

The couple looked around to see what was the matter. I could sense their concern. The suit and tie kept leaning on the horn. He was going to get through, over or around the car, come hell or high water.

He kept blowing. It only confused the older couple. I could see they were becoming flustered and didn't know what to do. Finally, perhaps thinking that there was an emergency in the car behind them, the old man meekly acceded to the blaring demands of the red-faced driver and pulled up and over the curb to his right. Beet-red roared off, content, I'm sure, in getting his way and showing that man and woman how to really drive on these roads.

The man and his wife never knew what the commotion was about. I signaled them to get back on the road and followed them a short distance until they pulled into the medical center. Who, I wondered, had the more pressing engagement?

The incident started me thinking. Wouldn't it be nice if each of us would go a little out of our way for older drivers? The elderly man had done nothing wrong, but he paid an unfair price for being cautious.

He might have lost a bit more confidence in his driving skills because of the impatience of the beet-red driver. Sure, he was careful. It is probably one of the reasons he and his wife have been graced with their extra years.

What is wrong with extending some extra courtesy to older drivers? (Or any other drivers, for that matter?) Are we embarrassed to wear our concern on our sleeves? Are our affairs that pressing that they hinge on a few seconds' delay? Were the few seconds the driver saved worth the price he made the older man pay? What indeed is the big hurry? Courtesy is contagious; give it a try.

Be a Better Driver: Respect the Pedestrian

Question: What do drivers and pedestrians have in common? Answer: With few exceptions almost every driver has been a pedestrian and every pedestrian is, has been, or will be a driver.

It's funny that when we are the pedestrians we tend to view all motorists as potential adversaries. But when we switch hats and become drivers, the story is different, isn't it?

Then we see pedestrians as thorns in our sides, a nuisance we must grudgingly put up with, a hindrance to our getting from point A to point B in the shortest possible time. We forget, of course, that just a few minutes ago we were that very person we now disdain.

Funny creatures, drivers. We forget completely how it felt to be unprotected and vulnerable now that we have securely wrapped ourselves in a blanket of moving steel. In a one-on-one confrontation with a pedestrian, we're invincible. Some of us even drive as if we're invincible regardless of what comes our way.

Cars, trucks, motorcycles, bicycles, buses—we are ready to take 'em on. Some of us drive as if we are impervious to the laws of physics that say when two moving objects, or one stationary and one moving object meet, something has to give. Unfortunately, many times it's a life.

No creature that inhabits our roadways is more vulnerable than the pedestrian. When behind the wheel, we owe it to ourselves and others to be considerate and courteous with these ambulating roadies. Remember, they don't stand a chance if challenged by a moving vehicle.

No matter how arrogant the pedestrians, no matter how much time they take crossing our paths, no matter if they purposely seem to slow down when they hit the crosswalks—and most important—no matter how in the wrong they might be, we drivers must respect their vulnerability. Who knows? The person you go out of your way for might someday be the driver who goes out of his or her way for you when you are pounding the pavement.

You bet it takes a lot of patience.

For sure you will become irritated at times.

No doubt it can be very bothersome.

But as drivers we are entrusted with the serious responsibility of looking out for those who are on foot. When you think about it, the pedestrian must have complete trust in our assuming that responsibility.

A little courtesy, patience, and politeness can go a long way. It makes you a better all-around driver, a safer driver.

Safe Off-Road Driving

One of the automotive phenomena of recent years has been the burgeoning popularity of sport/utility vehicles. According to Range Rover of North America Inc., distributors of the off-road Range Rover, it has become the fastest-growing segment of the American automotive market. Four-wheel-drive vehicles aren't limited to warfare and construction anymore, and you are as likely to see a woman loading one in a supermarket parking lot as a lumberjack using one in the Oregon backwoods. Practical, go-anywhere, roomy, and durable, it's no wonder these sporty four-wheelers have caught the fancy of the automobile-buying public.

But few drivers really know how to handle an off-road vehicle in an off-road environment. Once they get off the pavement anything goes. And a lot of times it is the vehicle that "goes."

Whether you drive through snow and ice, desert sand, or tropical swamps, the way you drive will help put you on or off the road to fun and safety. What follows are some tips on how to properly drive a sports/utility vehicle off-road. Although they are meant for those with four-wheel-drive vehicles, many of them apply when you take your two-wheel-drive vehicle off the main highway, as many of us often do.

So here are 16 driving suggestions from an expert in off-road manners, Range Rover's demonstrations chief Bob Burns:

1. Get to know your vehicle and its performance potential. Squeeze the accelerator to avoid wheelspin.
2. Survey difficult terrain on foot to reduce the risk of encountering an unexpected hazard.
3. Select "low" range on the transfer box and a suitable gear before tackling a difficult section. Avoid the temptation to play safe by selecting a gear lower than the terrain warrants.
4. Keep use of brakes to an absolute minimum so wheels won't lock on wet, muddy or loose surfaces. Descend steep slopes in the "low" range and first gear, then rely on the engine braking.
5. Reduced tire pressure improves traction in very soft conditions, especially sand—but consider the subsequent loss of ground clearance. Reinflate when on the pavement!
6. Follow the fall line to climb or descend steep slopes. Traveling diagonally may result in a broadside slide.
7. Do not oversteer along rutted tracks. Front wheels sliding through mud while pointed in the wrong direction can suddenly regain traction with potentially serious consequences.
8. Always tackle a ridge at a right angle to the crest so front wheels and rear wheels cross at the same time.
9. Cross ditches at an angle so that three wheels assist the fourth's passage.
10. Check terrain carefully for sudden depressions and other hazards if a slope must be traversed. Load cargo as low as possible. Place passengers on the uphill side of the vehicle.
11. Make slow, steady progress through deep water to create a bow wave "cavity" in the engine bay to minimize the risk of drowning the engine. Check brakes after immersion.
12. Do not wrap your thumbs around the steering wheel. They can be broken if the wheel kicks back on rough ground.
13. Avoid prolonged wheelspin if the vehicle comes to a halt.
14. Cleaning clogged tire treads improves traction. Use brushwood, sacking, and the like in front of the wheels if they are stuck.
15. If the vehicle has dug itself in, jack it up and replace the ground under the wheels to obtain clearance.
16. Respect private property and the environment. Only drive off the pavement with permission or on roads designated for off-road vehicle use.

Here are some additional off-road guidelines I gleaned from a Range Rover video.

Always wear a seat belt. Read the owner's manual, because the four-wheel drive in your vehicle might be different from another you have driven. Forget high speeds and clowning around when four-wheeling. Drive with finesse. Remember that good off-road technique rarely involves using the foot brake.

If wheels start to spin in slippery conditions, back off the accelerator until they regain their grip. Consider shifting to a higher gear because wheelspin is often caused by using too low a gear.

Most easy to moderate off-road conditions can be successfully tackled in third gear, low range. If you need to use the foot brake often you are probably in too high a gear and should shift down. Always use first gear, low range, for steep downhill sections.

And finally, drive within the limitations of your own knowledge, skill, and experience. Don't drive in situations that are uncomfortable for you. That's just good common sense no matter what type vehicle you drive or the conditions you drive it in.

Detours Are Costly for Motorists

The type of roads you travel plays an important part in determining how long your car will last and how good its gas mileage will be.

As I pondered this fact while driving over a seemingly interminable detour on my way to town, it occurred to me that I—along with thousands of other drivers who use that road—am paying an expensive price in wear and tear on my car and myself because a new housing development is being built.

Why should our cars suffer by being routed over unpaved, rutty, rocky, dusty, and sometimes muddy detours? If you don't believe cars are affected, you are kidding yourself—or you must be a new-car salesman.

It is not so bad, I guess, if the inconvenience lasts only a few days or maybe even a week or so, but this detour has been on my side of town for months.

A long dose of detours makes your car hurt and ache all over. The tires take a beating as sharp rocks and potholes gang up on them. They don't like being treated that way and respond by becoming weaker and out of balance. The suspension, shocks, ball joints and steering take some pretty good shots. The whole undercarriage is constantly pummeled by rocks, dirt, and mud.

Chances are, by the time the road is back to normal your car won't be. Start checking the ads for those alignment and shock-absorber specials.

And how about the car's finish? If the detour is dusty, the paint gets covered with an abrasive coating. If it is wet and muddy, you get a nice mudpack—not the beauty kind—over much of the finish. At best, you have to wash the car more frequently. Money out of your pocket, a bit of gloss off your car.

Hold it! Don't forget the engine. Abrasives—dirt, dust, sand, and grit—are the number 1 cause of engine wear. After a few months of construction detours, this stuff will find its way into your engine, even if they do wet the road every so often. Remember that on a dusty road the engine can inhale as much as 2,000 times more dust as on a paved road. Think about that.

Be aware, too, that you are getting minimal gas mileage when forced to drive over rough roads. A gravel road can cut fuel economy by 35 percent. A dirt road with rocks and ruts and hills, where slow stop-and-go is the rule, will cut at least 55 percent off your top mileage for that period of travel. Multiply 55 percent by the number of times you use the road each day, then multiply that figure by the number of cars that use the road, and you have a whopping number of extra gallons of gas used.

Maybe I am crabby, but it is unfair that drivers—and their cars—must pay so a few can have their way. We can't hold back progress, but we can channel it so as not to inconvenience so many for so long.

And how do we do that? If the detour is expected to last more than, say, a month, the developers should pave the road with a cheap, temporary surface. This doesn't seem unreasonable and should be relatively easy and inexpensive to accomplish. The surface could be removed when the main road is ready for traffic.

The other alternative would be to set up a tollbooth. Whoever is responsible for our misery would station an employee with a fistful of dollars at the beginning of the detour. As each car enters or leaves the obstacle course, he would slip the motorist a buck or two for his inconvenience, thanking him for his understanding and forbearance.

Somehow, though, I think the builders would prefer the former.

14

Squeezing the most from every drop

WHAT'S HAPPENING AT THE GAS PUMPS should be familiar to those of us who have been driving for about 10 years. (Has it been that long?)

Of course, I'm talking about the most recent gas "crisis." This one, like the past two, has its roots in the Middle East.

Suddenly, conserving fuel and getting more miles per gallon are in vogue again. Talk—and sales—of smaller, more fuel-efficient cars is again on the rise. Our thirst for larger, more powerful, gas-thirsty vehicles is temporarily put on the back burner. Blown by rumors of war we are like reeds in the wind, again doing a 180-degree turn and bending toward fuel efficiency and conservation.

But politics isn't this column's bag; our goal is more miles per gallon and more miles per car. Over the years I have consistently offered my readers fuel- and car-saving information, crisis or not. Conservation is always smart and shouldn't be taken out of the closet and dusted off only in emergencies.

Why most Americans, once a crisis has past, go right back to the old inefficient and wasteful ways of driving and maintaining their cars has always been a mystery to me. Economy driving and longevity mainte-nance practices aren't reserved for fuel shortages or high gasoline prices or for when cars become so expensive that we have no other choice.

It's smart to save money, smart to save on repairs, smart to conserve our nation's resources, smart not to add to our burgeoning air-pollution.

I don't know what will happen to gasoline supplies and prices in the near future. But here are a number of fuel-saving ideas that will lessen the impact of the suddenly high gasoline prices:

- The most economical driving range, on average, is still some-where between 35 mph and 45 mph.

- You can get almost 100 miles per gallon by *decelerating*—foot off gas, car in gear—into any mandatory stop from as far away as prac-tical. Don't rush up to the stop and then slam on the brakes. Instead, take advantage of a super high-mileage situation.

o On newer cars a malfunctioning EGR (exhaust gas recirculation) valve or O_2 (oxygen) sensor can be a vicious gas robber. A sudden dramatic loss of fuel economy can often be traced to one or the other. Make certain yours are serviced and operating properly.

o On older and newer cars the PCV (positive crankcase ventilation) valve must be clean and working properly. A stuck or clogged PCV costs mpgs.

o Catalytic converters can become clogged. This increases engine back pressure and can cut fuel mileage dramatically. If yours is getting near five years old, have it checked.

o Gas-saving gadgets galore will start appearing around the country. We have exposed some in this column. A good rule of thumb is that they don't work, especially the ones that promise "too-good-to-be-true" results. You can be sure they will live up to that claim.

o A cold engine will get only a fraction of the fuel economy it gets when warm. The faster the engine warms the better the fuel economy. Engine heaters help. A correct temperature thermostat and a working heat riser valve hasten warm-up.

o Malfunctioning or stuck automatic chokes are notorious fuel wasters. A tuneup should correct any problems.

o You still save gas in 1990 by obeying the 55-mph speed limit.

o Short trips with a cold engine use more gas, create more pollution, and cause more engine wear than any other single driving mode.

o If yours is a two-car family, use the car with the warm engine for that necessary short trip.

o Not driving is the greatest fuel saver of all. Public transportation, car and van pools, bicycles, and walking are, and will continue to be, the very smart alternatives.

o Idling gets you nowhere at a substantial cost. When possible, do away with unnecessary idling.

o Keep tires at recommended pressure. It's one of the easiest ways to increase gas mileage. And don't ignore tune-ups. Although your new car might not need them as often, that doesn't mean they should be ignored.

o Use a quality gasoline of proper octane; remove any unnecessary objects from the car (weight costs mpgs); consolidate shopping; and don't warm the car by idling.

Conservation is smart and easy. If every driver in the United States would follow the above suggestions, losing the oil supply from Iraq would little affect us. What's your reason for not joining the club?

Think Economy!

Think economy! Those two words can save you hundreds of dollars each and every year if you follow their simple directive.

Think economy! Two words of advice which, if followed, will guarantee better gas mileage, a long-lived car, and a more safety-aware driver.

Think economy! Two words that should be the crux of your automotive driving and maintenance techniques.

When you drive, think economy. When you maintain, think economy. The upshot is that you'll take great joy in thinking about all the money you are saving by thinking economy.

Most of us are subject to the myriad foibles that constantly plague the human race. Laziness and forgetfulness are prime examples, especially when it comes to our cars. We want to do right by them, but we forget; when we do remember, we are too busy or too lazy to do anything about it.

Car owners should be aware that fuel conservation and automobile life-extension practices are mental concepts. As with most worthwhile things, you must mentally commit yourself to the goals before you are able to achieve them. one of the best aids for the motorist is a little reminder—two little words written on a piece of paper and taped on the dash near the speedometer: THINK ECONOMY!

This visual reminder, taped in a conspicuous spot, will prod you to be more aware of your driving and to implement conservation and preservation techniques you have mastered. Each time you get into the car, you are reminded by the words on the dash to do a variety of things: obey the 55 mph speed limit, keep proper air pressure in the tires, reduce engine idling. While driving, a glance at the dashboard automatically brings the THINK ECONOMY! sticker into view, reminding you to be aware.

When you drive for economy and longevity, you are also driving and thinking safety. They go hand in hand because each asks the driver to commit himself or herself to total awareness while behind the wheel. This alone should be reason enough to think economy at all times.

Make sure your THINK ECONOMY! sign doesn't block your view of any gauges or lights. You will be pleasantly surprised at how effective those two words can be in helping you become a better, more efficient and safer driver.

Out of Gas? Try the Mileage-Marathon Technique

Have you ever wondered how those experimental high-mileage vehicles made and used by college students in marathon competitions achieve the phenomenal miles-per-gallon figures they do? They can get from 100 mpg to 3,000 mpg. I wonder what their EPA rating would be?

These student-built vehicles use a very small lawn-mower-type engine, a light, aerodynamically designed chassis, and bicycle tires inflated to the point of bursting. To allow for more efficient aerodynamic design, the driver might even lie on his belly while driving the vehicle.

Each vehicle has one thing in common: Their drivers use a special driving technique that makes these high-mileage figures possible. It's a trick that was used many years ago by drivers in the old Mobile Marathon. It's called the coast-accelerate-coast method, and you can use it in your own car if it becomes necessary. I'll explain.

Let's say it's late at night and you're driving on a deserted stretch of road. You are very low on gas because the last station you saw was closed. The map indicates another town a few miles ahead, and you decide to keep going and fill up there. But when you reach the town, you hit the panic button. There's nothing there but a few deserted buildings and a railroad crossing.

You look at the map again. The next town is 50 miles away! You estimate that there might be about a gallon of gas left in the tank, and you know your car gets about 25 mpg on the highway. Not very encouraging. You will never make those 50 miles on 1 gallon of gas.

Wrong! Not if you know what I call the "emergency economy method." That gallon will get you to the next town, and you might even have a little left over. How do you do it? You follow the technique of the mileage-marathon boys and begin to coast-accelerate-coast.

Accelerate slowly to about 25 mph, then quickly shift the car into neutral and turn off the ignition. Let the car slow down to about 5 mph, restart the engine, place it in gear, and repeat the process of accelerating slowly to 25 mph. Repeat the process over and over again until you reach your destination. Simple? You bet—and extremely effective.

Although this emergency economy method is impractical—and illegal—for everyday use, it's comforting to know that if you are caught in an emergency low-fuel situation you can coax many extra miles from a gallon of gasoline. I believe it's better to be safe and secure in your car going between 5 mph and 25 mph than to be out of gas, stranded, and at the mercy of anyone who happens by. If you must use this trick only once in your lifetime, you'll be glad you knew it.

Special note of caution: Do not use this method when driving down steep grades. Turning the ignition off will render power brakes much less effective, and in many cases make them almost impossible to engage.

And if your steering wheel locks when the ignition is turned off, as in many newer cars, you might be unable to use the method for obvious reasons. Check your steering wheel to see if it operates when the ignition is off. Be sure to do it with the car standing still. If it locks, try the ignition in the accessory position. Many times this will turn the engine off but will still allow you to steer. If this works for you, then use the accessory position when you must use the emergency economy method.

With luck, it will be one mileage-improving ploy you'll never have to use.

Drive Conservatively: Save Fuel, Save Energy

One of the things that makes war hellish is the inability of the hundreds of millions of people at home to influence the outcome. As we sit and listen to or watch reports of the Persian Gulf conflict, many of us feel frustrated and helpless, but I think almost all of us want to do something to help.

It's not the same as it was during World War II. During that prolonged global strife many Americans contributed at home by working in defense factories, buying war bonds, easing our consumption of war-necessary products, and even saving leftover cooking fat.

But the war in the Persian Gulf is different. Seems all we can do is watch and listen. But I think there is something each of us can do that will say we care and are doing something, albeit token, to help the cause.

What I'm proposing isn't just tying a yellow ribbon on your car aerial. We can reinforce our commitment to drive conservatively, to save fuel, to save energy. If we aren't already committed there is no better time than now to begin. It's something we should have been doing all along and, indeed, many of us have. Everyone who owns a motor vehicle uses petroleum products and about 50 percent of those products come from foreign sources.

I wonder if the gasoline we wasted during the past 10 years is somehow partly to blame for our current predicament? I don't know the answer to that, but I feel we all share some of the responsibility, and I do know we can reduce our dependence on foreign oil by beginning to conserve fuel right now, the very next time we get into our vehicles.

Longtime readers of this column know that mine has been a voice crying in the wilderness whenever I offer fuel-saving tips. Through the years my readers have seen many columns on how to save fuel—crisis or no crisis.

No matter what our stance on the war, whether we think it right or not, surely each of us supports our troops now that the battle has begun. By saving fuel we might not change the outcome of the war, but we will be helping. And I think that's important.

I know many readers have read some of this before and, I hope, already practice it, but here are some tips that will put you on the way to helping reduce our dependence on Mideast oil and show our men and women in the armed forces that we care:

○ Decelerate into all mandatory stops. When you decelerate (foot off gas, car in gear) the car gets its maximum possible fuel economy for that period, sometimes as high as 100 mpg!

○ Don't warm your car by extensive idling. That just wastes fuel. After about 15 seconds of idling—a bit more if temperatures are below zero—put the car in gear and get moving. Go slowly at first, then gradually increase to desired speed.

- Drive in the "economy" 35-mph to 45-mph range when possible. This is the speed range at which most vehicles attain their best fuel economy.

- Keep highway speeds sensible. For every 5 mph over 55 mph, an average vehicle pays a 1.5-mpg penalty.

- Use an energy-conserving II motor oil. These fuel-efficient oils provide a 2.7 percent or greater increase in fuel economy compared to non-energy-conserving oils.

- Add a solid lubricant to the oil at the next oil change. Many of you have done this since I wrote about the efficiency of solid lubricants in increasing fuel economy and extending engine life.

- Keep tires inflated to the maximum pressure printed on the sidewall of the tire, usually between 32 pounds and 35 pounds per square inch (psi).

- If you are not using radial tires, consider buying a set the next time you need tires. Radials can give up to 10 percent better mileage than non-radials.

- Install an engine heater. Not only will it help save fuel, it will cut down on toxic tail-pipe pollutants.

- Consider a vacuum gauge. These $10-$30 marvels will "teach" you how to drive economically at all times and spot engine problems before they become major.

- Give up your vehicle at least one day a week and use public transportation. Better yet, join a car or van pool to and from your job.

My new book, *Car Tips For Clean Air*, has many other gas-saving ideas.

Next month another book, *How To Get More Miles Per Gallon In The '90s,* an updated version of my best-selling book of the late '70s, will be published by TAB/McGraw-Hill. It contains more than 300 workable and easy fuel-saving ideas.

Vacuum Gauges Help Boost Mileage, Reduce Wear and Tear

Wouldn't it be nice if every driver could have a personal driving instructor along at all times?

I'm not talking about a driving instructor per se, but an economy and wear-prevention driving instructor. If you made a mistake, the instructor could immediately correct it, and in a short time every driver would become proficient at getting maximum mileage while incurring minimum wear-and-repair bills.

Alas, it would be too costly to employ a full-time expert to ride with us, and it wouldn't be practical either (backseat drivers don't count!). But there is a way we can get almost all the benefits of an instructor in the car at little cost. How's that? By installing a vacuum gauge.

I personally feel that no car should leave the factory without a vacuum gauge as standard equipment. Unfortunately, the auto makers don't share this view, and only a few select sports and high-performance cars are thus equipped.

What is a vacuum gauge? It is a simple instrument that measures engine vacuum, which indicates the efficiency of the engine. A glance at the gauge tells you whether you are driving efficiently or wasting gas and, consequently, whether the engine is experiencing unnecessary wear. It can also detect when an engine is in need of a tune-up and can spot mechanical problems in their embryonic state when most can be easily repaired.

A panacea it's not, but a valuable aid to economy and wear-efficient driving it is. By trying to keep the gauge at or near its highest vacuum reading, you maximize fuel efficiency and engine life. This is the basic thrust of the gauge: High vacuum readings indicate top efficiency, while low vacuum readings show the engine is wasting fuel and, in the long run, harming itself. There are exceptions to this rule, but they are minor.

A dash-mounted vacuum gauge is not expensive (a basic gauge can be purchased for about $10) and will pay for itself many times over not only in fuel saved, but also in repair bills avoided and in extended engine life.

Vacuum gauges are available at almost all automotive-supply stores, and are relatively simple to install. And if you sell your vehicle, you can easily remove it.

Installation instructions are included with all gauges, and many also include a chart that shows what engine condition is indicated by various fluctuations of the gauge—carburetor set too rich, valve sticking, clogged exhaust pipe, and many more.

If you decide to purchase a gauge, make sure it is one that can be mounted on or under the dash. The numbers should be easy to read and it should light up for nighttime driving.

Vacuum-gauge driving is an easy art to master, and after a while you will find yourself driving proficiently without much help from the "instructor." It is one of the best "add-ons" I can recommend.

Gas-Saving Devices: Flimflam!

A recent letter from a reader in Santa Barbara, California, included a couple of ads for "gas-saving" devices. "If these two products do indeed perform as advertised," the reader asked, "wouldn't they be hailed by the media? Please address yourself to the validity of the claims made. I am sending this letter on behalf of myself and several friends. We would certainly appreciate if you could respond in your syndicated column."

One of the items the reader was inquiring about was a type of gas-saving device that has been popping up under different names all over the country. Advertisements for these gas-saving and pollution-reducing devices are everywhere, including my mailbox.

Although they have different names, the ones in question claim to work by using magnets or "dissimilar metals" to rearrange the molecules and ions in the gasoline so it burns more efficiently and with less pollution. Brother, if you believe that one, you deserve to be stung.

I have advised my readers throughout the years to be on guard against such flimflam, no matter what the products claim. Now the attorneys general of several states agree with my caveats. Perhaps the answer to the above reader's query can best be found in a recent Associated Press release about these alleged gas-saving magnetic devices. The article, headlined, "Iowa's Attorney General Sues Over Device to Save Gas That's 'Too Good to Be True,' " was as follows:

> Attorney General Tom Miller has sued the marketers of a product that claims to be a gas-saving breakthrough.
>
> "Our lawsuit can be summarized in five words," Miller said Friday. "Too good to be true."
>
> Marketers of the PetroMizer claim their product produces substantial fuel savings by using a magnetic field to reorient the molecules in the gasoline.
>
> "The U.S. Environmental Protection Agency has concluded that there is no technical basis to expect that the PetroMizer would improve either emissions or fuel economy," Miller said.
>
> The suit asks the court to prohibit any further marketing of PetroMizer in Iowa, assess a civil penalty up to $40,000 and order refunds to any Iowans who bought the devices.
>
> PetroMizers were advertised at $59.95 for 4- and 6-cylinder cars and $79.95 for 8-cylinder cars.
>
> The PetroMizer ads claim the device has been tested, used and endorsed by such organizations as the U.S. Army.
>
> "This isn't the first allegedly phony gas-saving device we've tackled," Miller said. "Unfortunately, with the surge in gas prices it probably won't be the last scam, either."
>
> The attorneys general of Missouri and Minnesota were filing simultaneous lawsuits against PetroMizer.

Devices of this kind have been proliferating recently. What's worse, people have been buying them. I recently turned over to the Arizona attorney general's office for investigation information on a similar device called the Vitalizer that retails for more than $100.

And just yesterday as I was reading my November issue of *Popular Mechanics*, lo and behold, I came across a full-page ad for another one of these magnetic devices, this one called the "Gas Saver 2000." But the price of this baby will knock your hat in the creek: Try $189 plus $4.50 shipping! Even if it did work, how long do you think it would take to break even on the fuel you save?

I'm surprised that an excellent and informative magazine such as *Popular Mechanics* would run an ad for these devices. To my way of thinking, it's a kind of offhand endorsement for the product; i.e., "If I saw it in *Popular Mechanics*, it must be OK."

I'm always amazed that even after people have been burned time and again by gas-saving gadget scams, they line up for more.

Many years ago Mr. Barnum told us why they act this way, and human nature hasn't changed. We still crave those "too good to be true" items and the con men are all too willing to oblige.

Save your money, gang. As I've said before, you'll go a lot farther on a tank of expensive gasoline than you will with one full of wishful thinking.

Caveat Emptor: High-Mileage Carburetors

One hundred-plus miles per gallon! That's what Richard Goranflo says he gets on his big 1977 Cadillac with a V-8 engine. Goranflo and his Cadillac are for real; the 100 mpg might be another matter.

Florida-based Goranflo, who has conducted seminars on building a high-mileage carburetor like the one he has invented, says many people across the country are getting that kind of super mileage with his invention. His conversation is peppered with mileage figures that go all the way up to 200 mpg. Are these high-mileage carburetors used on a routine basis?

High-mileage carburetors have been around since 1930, so the idea has had time to cook. In the early '30s, Elmer Nay built his "Nay Box" and said it got almost 100 mpg. In 1936, Charles Pogue patented and demonstrated his now-famous Pogue carburetor, which allegedly got 200 mpg in one trial. Recently, Tom Ogle of El Paso claimed 110 mpg while Ray Covey, also of El Paso, reportedly has a system that can do almost as well. In fact, it is even claimed that some World War II tanks were equipped with Pogue carburetors and delivered an astounding 70 mpg. Is there any credibility to any of these claims, or are they nonsense?

Goranflo's Cadillac is equipped with a system that supposedly uses the principle of gasoline vaporization: Liquid gasoline is turned into vapor by passing through a super-heated element. The engine then uses the vapor rather than the liquid. Theoretically, this allows for almost complete burning of all gasoline, eliminating the tremendous waste common in all internal-combustion engines.

Gasoline vaporization is a valid idea. High-mileage carburetors exist; I have examined a number of them.

The main problem encountered when investigating their merits is that no one has offered any viable proof that high-mileage carburetors actually do what they're supposed to—boost mileage. Instead, all a person has to go on is the word of the inventor.

There are a number of simple, quick, effective ways to check (fill your tank and check your mileage, or have your automobile emissions examined), but curiously, most proponents—Goranflo included—balk at having their systems scrutinized. In my book, that leaves a lot to be desired.

To me, the question is whether these high-mileage devices actually live up to their claims. Until we see positive proof of their effectiveness, they will continue to exist in that shady realm of wishful thinking and, until then, caveat emptor.

Test Your Miles-Per-Gallon Knowledge

With gasoline readily available and cheap, many drivers have taken the hard-earned lessons of the fuel crisis and put them on the back burner. That is a no-no.

Conservation should be a habit, practiced daily because it benefits both your car and your pocketbook. Here is a 10-question quiz to see how much you have remembered, how much you have forgotten and how much you never knew.

1. Americans do much of their driving on trips of:
   a. 100 miles or more
   b. 50 miles or more
   c. 15 miles or more
   d. 5 miles or less
2. At speeds above 45 mph, open windows help increase gas mileage by allowing the onrushing air to flow smoothly through the car, thus reducing wind resistance. True or false?
3. Mileage-marathon drivers pay close attention to which of the following?
   a. Minimizing rolling resistance
   b. Increasing engine efficiency
   c. Improving driving techniques
   d. None of these
   e. All of these
4. In general, the narrower the tire tread, the better mileage it will provide. True or false? (And you thought these were going to be hard questions!)
5. One of the least costly, easiest, and most effective ways to increase gas mileage is to:
   a. Get an engine overhaul
   b. Have the engine tuned
   c. Keep tires at recommended air pressure
   d. Borrow your neighbor's car
6. One of the best gas-saving techniques for city driving is to:
   a. Try to be first at the next stoplight
   b. Start very slowly from all traffic lights and stop signs
   c. Decelerate when approaching all stops and slowdowns
   d. All of the above

7. It is more fuel efficient to turn off the engine, then restart it if the period of anticipated idling is going to exceed:
   a. A few seconds
   b. 15 seconds
   c. 30 seconds
   d. 1 minute
   e. 2 minutes
8. The time of most pronounced engine wear and maximum gasoline consumption is the period immediately after you start your car's cold engine. True or false?
9. Moderate acceleration to desired speed is one key to achieving good gas mileage from your vehicle. True or false?
10. For every 5-mph increase in speed over 45 mph, most cars will pay a mileage penalty of how many miles per gallon (mpg)?
    a. $1/2$ mpg
    b. 1 mpg
    c. $1^1/2$ mpg
    d. 3 mpg

Answers

1. (d) These trips really eat the gas.
2. False. At 55 mph open windows can dent your gas mileage by 10 percent.
3. (e) These three are the tenets of the mileage-marathon boys.
4. True. High-mileage experimental cars all have bicycle-width tires.
5. (c) Air is free so use it; (d) is a close second.
6. (c) Almost 20 percent of all city driving is done in the deceleration mode; i.e., the car is coasting to a stop or slowdown.
7. (a) New evidence has shown that it is better to turn off the engine immediately.
8. True. Everyone who reads this column knows that one.
9. True. Jackrabbit and turtle starts both waste fuel. Moderate acceleration is best.
10. (c) Speed doesn't pay; it costs.

15

Before buying a new or used car

AMERICANS SPEND ABOUT $85 BILLION each year to buy more than 17 million used cars, according to government statistics. That's a lot of jack and a lot of cars. If it's been a while since you've bought a used car, you might be surprised at the protection buyers now have, courtesy of the Federal Trade Commission's Used Car Rule. This rule requires all used-car dealers (new-car dealers who sell used cars are also included) to post a Buyers' Guide in the window of each used vehicle they offer for sale.

Used vehicles coming under this rule include automobiles, light-duty vans and light-duty trucks. It's interesting how Uncle Sam defines a used vehicle: "One that has been driven more than the distance necessary to deliver a new car to the dealership or to test drive it." Incidentally, all "demonstrator" cars are also covered by the rule.

The Buyers' Guide will tell the prospective used-car buyer:

○ Whether the vehicle comes with a warranty and, if so, what specific warranty protection the dealer will provide.

○ Whether the vehicle comes with no warranty; that is, it is being sold "as is" or with implied warranties only.

○ That you should ask to have the car inspected by your own mechanic before you buy.

○ That you should get all promises in writing.

○ What are some of the major problems that might occur in any car.

If you purchased a used car from a dealer you should insist on receiving the original or a copy of the Buyers' Guide that appeared in the window. It should reflect any changes in warranty coverage you might have negotiated with the salesman. Remember that the Buyers' Guide becomes an important part of your sales contract and overrides any contrary provisions that might be in the contract. Let's touch on some of the more important points covered in the Buyers' Guide.

Roughly one-half of all used cars sold by dealers come without a warranty, or as is. If the as-is box on the guide is checked, it means the dealer has no responsibility for the car once the sale is complete and you drive off the lot.

Implied warranties   In most states almost every purchase you make is covered by an implied warranty unless the seller specifically states in writing that implied warranties do not apply. A common type of implied warranty, the *warranty of merchantability*, means the seller promises that the product will do what it is supposed to. In other words, a car will run; a washing machine will wash. Another type, the *warranty of fitness* for a particular purpose, means that if you buy a light truck to pull a trailer, it should be able to do exactly that.

Even though the vehicle doesn't come with a written warranty, it is still covered by an implied warranty unless you purchased it as is. Some states, however, do not permit as-is sales. In these states vehicles must be sold with implied warranties.

If you have problems that are not covered by the written warranty, check on the protection provided by the implied warranty. It varies from state to state. Consult your state consumer protection office to see what is covered.

If the used vehicle is being sold by the dealer with only an implied warranty then "Implied Warranties only" will be printed on the Buyers' Guide in place of the as-is disclosure box. This box then should be marked by the dealer.

If a warranty is offered on the vehicle then the "Warranty" portion of the Buyers' Guide must be filled out. You should check this closely to see what is covered and what is not. In addition, if the dealer makes any verbal promises to repair the vehicle that are not listed on the Buyers' Guide, you should have these added in writing to both the Buyers' Guide and the sales contract. The sales contract must also include other specific information about your warranty.

More about the Used-Car Buyers' Guide

Last week I introduced you to the used-car Buyers' Guide, a large sticker that must be placed on the window of any used vehicle sold by a dealer. It contains a wealth of information about the car, is consumer-friendly, and is something any prospective used-car buyer should be familiar with. This week I'll finish talking about the Buyers' Guide, beginning with those all-important warranties.

If the warranty box on the Guide is checked, see if the warranty offered is full or limited. A full warranty provides the following:

○ Warranty service will be provided to anyone who owns the vehicle while it is under warranty.

o Warranty service is free and includes such costs as returning the vehicle or removing and reinstalling any system covered.

o If a dealer is unable to repair a warranted system after a reasonable number of tries, you are entitled to a replacement or a full refund.

o Warranty service is provided without requiring you to return a warranty registration card.

o No limit is placed on the duration of implied warranties.

Now, if any one of the above statements isn't true, then the warranty is a limited one. A limited warranty means that the buyer will have to assume some of the costs and responsibilities for systems covered by the warranty. It is important to remember that a full or limited warranty need not cover the whole vehicle, but the actual repair costs a dealer will assume for individual systems should be marked on the Buyers' Guide.

The systems covered by either warranty must be listed in the appropriate area of the Guide, as must be the duration of the warranty for each specified system.

If the used vehicle is still covered under the manufacturer's original warranty the dealer may add, "Manufacturer's Warranty Still Applies" in the warranty section of the Guide. Ask the dealer to let you examine any unexpired warranty on the vehicle.

One section of the Buyers' Guide has an important warning: "Spoken promises are difficult to enforce. Ask the dealer to put all promises in writing. Keep this form."

That speaks for itself; the copy of the Buyers' Guide you should receive will act as proof of the written promises.

Another section of the Guide covers service contracts or, as they are sometimes misnamed, *extended warranties*. These are different animals: Warranties are included in the price of the car, while service contracts cost extra.

Should you consider a service contract? It depends on a number of things. Does the present warranty include repairs you might get under the service contract? Is the vehicle likely to need repairs, and what might they cost? How long is the service contract? Does the dealer honor his contracts? If a service contract is offered with the vehicle, the box provided will be marked. Some states, however, regulate service contracts, and the dealer is not required to include this on the Guide.

The Buyers' Guide also suggests that you ask the dealer for permission to have an independent mechanic inspect the vehicle either on or off the lot before you purchase it. Not a bad idea. It also lists the 14 major systems on a car and some of the problems that could occur with them. This list can be helpful when comparing vehicles or evaluating their mechanical condition.

Finally, the back of the Buyers' Guide lists the name and address of the dealership and the person you should contact if troubles arise after the sale.

OK, I know what you are thinking: What if I buy a car from a private individual? Private sellers are not obligated to use a Buyers' Guide. Most cars are sold as-is, and the seller assumes no further obligation once you get the car out of his driveway.

But that doesn't mean you can't use some of the information here to your benefit. For instance, is the car covered by a service contract or unexpired manufacturer's warranty? You might even be able to talk a private seller into offering you some type of warranty.

What You Need to Know about Service Contracts

A major service-contract company advertises its contracts as: "The inflation-beater . . . for pennies a day you can have peace of mind." The appeal to the pocketbook and the promise of no hassles are undeniably effective. An estimated 50 percent of new-car buyers purchase *service contracts*, also known as *extended warranties*. There is a lot of confusion about service contracts, so let's see if we can clear up the muddle and determine if they are a wise buy.

Many car buyers are under the impression that service contracts are available for new cars only. Not true. They can be purchased for both new and used vehicles.

A service contract provides for a specific time during which the service contractor agrees to repair or maintain your car for an agreed-upon price. You purchase it separately and don't have to buy it from the car dealer.

How do you know if a service contract is a good deal? To make a smart decision, you need to read and understand the contract—before you purchase it. Here are some points to keep in mind:

Who is responsible for the contract? If a company that offers service contracts goes out of business, it might not be able to repay claims. If this happens, you will be out in the cold.

Many dealers offer their own contracts on new and used cars. Most of these dealers have independent companies administering their service-contract program. While some dealers set aside funds or buy insurance to cover future claims, others don't. Even if the dealer has a service-contract company administer the program, you should find out if that company will honor your contract if the dealer goes out of business.

Some car makers also offer service contracts, generally only for new cars. These service contracts are frequently sold through dealers or the manufacturer.

What is covered? A service contract might cover some or all major systems of the car. Some dealers and manufacturers offer a choice of plans, from the least-expensive covering a few systems to the most expensive covering many systems. Also, a service contract might cover all the parts in those systems, or it might cover only the expensive problems. Sometimes a potentially expensive repair is excluded. You should assume that the contract doesn't cover anything resulting from misuse or failure to maintain the car.

Aside from repair costs, some contracts provide reimbursement for towing and rental-car expenses. Be sure to see how much these contracts cover.

What will my service contract give me that my warranty won't? Your warranty coverage and your service contract might overlap, especially with some new cars with multiyear bumper-to-bumper warranties. If they do, you should compare the coverages and decide whether the additional expense of the service contract is worth it.

How will my repair bills be paid? Your service-contract company might pay the dealer or mechanic directly, or you might have to pay for the work and ask for reimbursement.

How long will I keep the car? As a rule, service contracts are not transferable from car to car, but can sometimes be transferred from owner to owner. If you don't plan to own the car for a long time, a long-term service contract probably won't be practical unless you can obtain value for it from the buyer of your car.

Where can I get service? What happens if I am traveling or if I move? Most service contracts require that your car be serviced by the selling dealership. In some contracts you may use any mechanic you choose. Manufacturers have dealerships nationwide, and service may be available from any of their dealers. And most dealer contracts are part of a network that offers nationwide service, so you may be able to get service if you travel or move. Other companies give you service in only a specific geographical area.

How much does the service contract cost? While manufacturers' service contracts generally offer the same coverage for all their new cars, the price varies according to car model. Independent and dealer service contracts base the price on car make, model, condition (new or used), what is covered, and length of contract. Any dealer might offer more than one type of contract. You might be able to choose your coverage and cost.

What other costs will I have? After you pay for the contract, you might have other expenses. Service contracts, like insurance policies, have deductible amounts. Many contracts charge you for each unrelated repair. Some contracts charge you one fee per repair visit, no matter how many repairs are made. Contracts frequently limit the amount paid for towing or rental-car expenses, and you remain responsible for the costs of maintenance and repairs not covered. You might also have to pay cancellation or transfer fees if you sell your car or wish to end the contract.

Tips for Used-Car Buyers

Two of every three car buyers will purchase used vehicles this year, according to the Automotive Information Council in Herndon, Virginia. The decision-making process can be an anxiety-filled nightmare if you don't know what to look for when shopping for a used car.

The council recently published a "Used Car Checklist." It contains worthwhile basic information for anyone looking for used iron. I think it is valuable to repeat some of this information; I will add my own recommendations in a later column.

Shop with someone who knows cars. Don't be intimidated by a seller eager to rush your examination of the car.

Look for signs of body work or frame damage that might indicate an accident. Check for dents, ripples in the metal, and mismatched paint. These often signal that the car was in an accident or was rusted through and repaired. Look for rust on door bottoms, fenders, wheel wells, and under floor mats.

Check for breaks or rust in the frame or signs that it has been welded. These could indicate a weak vehicle understructure. While underneath, check the condition of the exhaust system.

Check the car's suspension system on level ground, noting if it sags in front or back. If one corner is lower than another, one of the springs could be worn or broken. Push down hard on a corner of the car; if it continues bouncing the shocks are probably worn.

Check the car's tires for tread wear. Unevenly worn tires could mean problems with the steering, the suspension, or the brakes. Also, check to see if the spare tire, the jack, and the lug wrench are in the trunk.

Check all glass. Cracks or scratches often enlarge and require expensive replacements.

Thoroughly check the underside of the car while it is parked on a clean surface. Do it with the motor on and off. Any fluid dripping from the underside is a sign of trouble (air-conditioning condensation excepted).

Next, open the hood and thoroughly check the major engine components. Check the oil and transmission dipsticks. The oil should be free of water or coolant droplets, and the transmission fluid should be pink or reddish; if it isn't, the car may have problems.

Look for frayed wiring, leaky hoses, and worn fan belts. Examine the condition of the battery and its cables. Look for rust on and in the radiator and any metallic-looking sludge in its coolant.

Carefully inspect the car's interior. Worn upholstery, carpeting, seat belts, pedals, and ignition keys indicate heavy vehicle use. Be sure all dash controls and accessories (including heat, air conditioning, wipers, and lights) work properly. Check inside lights and all warning lights on the dash. All gauges should be functional. Also, check the brake pedal; it should be solid and show no excessive downward movement under pressure. If it does, there could be a leak in the brake system.

Examine the odometer. If the digits do not read in a straight line or if scratches or pieces of broken plastic appear in the speedometer case, it might have been tampered with.

Start the engine and take the car on a test drive. The engine should start easily and run smoothly. Start it up several times.

Test the car in both stop-and-go traffic and on the highway. Note any vibration in the steering wheel, which might signal front-end trouble. Be alert to wandering and drifting. The car should stop smoothly without veering to either side. Test the brakes on a quiet street for noise or a grabbing or mushy feeling.

Finally, before shelling out your hard-earned cash, take it to a reputable mechanic and get his opinion. It is cheap insurance. And, to top it off, call the National Highway Traffic Safety Administration auto-safety hot line at 800-424-9393 to find out about any safety defects or recalls on the model car you are considering.

Used Cars: To Buy or Not to Buy

Are there times when it would be better for a prospective new-car buyer to consider purchasing a used car? Now, I don't want to upset new-car dealers, but there are reasons why a used car should receive equal consideration when it comes time to lay your cash on the line.

Once a car leaves the new-car showroom it begins to depreciate in value. Some cars depreciate at a faster rate than others, but the average loss of value through depreciation for domestic cars during the first year of ownership is approximately 30 percent of the purchase price. The previous owner has already absorbed much of the depreciation on the used vehicle.

Because depreciation is the single largest new-car expense, you will lose more money if you buy new and sell used than if you buy used and sell used. After the first two years a car depreciates at a slower rate. Best bets are low-mileage cars two to three years old.

Payments are likely to be less on a used car and so are other fixed costs such as insurance, license and registration fees and state taxes. Overall ownership and operating costs are generally less on a used car than a new one, providing the used car is in good condition.

Used cars have a track record. Their repair and recall history are known, as is their reputation for durability and fuel economy. This allows you to pick and choose from cars with good serviceability, endurance, and economy backgrounds.

A potential used-car purchaser should call the NHTSA (National Highway Traffic Safety Administration) hot-line number (800) 424-9393 to inquire about safety-related recalls on the vehicle they are considering. Manufacturers can also be contacted about non-safety recalls.

Guarantees, warranties, and service contracts: Just as with a new car, a quality used car, if purchased from a new- or used-car dealer, will probably come with some type of warranty, although it usually won't be as long or as encompassing as a new-car warranty. However, many dealers offer service contracts on used cars in addition to whatever warranty is offered. A used car purchased from a private party may also have an assumable warranty.

A used-car buyer will also inherit the remainder of the manufacturer's new-car warranty. In most cases, the outer body rust-through warranty can also be assumed by a new owner for a slight fee. With today's extended new-car warranties, this is good news for a used-car buyer.

Used cars cost less than new ones. This can be a very important—if not the most important—consideration for many buyers. What you can afford to pay should be determined before you begin to look for any car, used or new. A car purchase should be able to fit comfortably into the framework of your finances. Used cars often fit the bill easier than new ones.

You can get more car for the dollar when buying used. Example: For what you'd pay for a no-frills econobox, you can get a used and guaranteed performance or luxury car with numerous amenities.

You have a whole range of makes and models from which to choose—usually all on one or two lots. One dealer might have many models of used cars but carry only one model new car. It consolidates your shopping and gives you greater selection.

Most new-car dealers save the cream of the trade-in crop for their used-car lots. These cars are checked thoroughly and usually backed by long-term guarantees. Again, a good way to consolidate shopping.

You can add aftermarket items options of your choice if the car doesn't have all the desired equipment. The advantage here is that you can add the items at your leisure or when you have the spare cash. Another plus: New-car options usually come in packages.

To get one item you want you might have to take a few you don't want. With a used car you can choose the exact aftermarket options you want.

A one-, two-, or even three-year-old used car can be nearly identical to a new one in both looks and mechanical components. It's rare for car manufacturers to completely redo a car every year or two. More than likely they are given face-lifts or "freshening" treatments: add or change a trim piece, offer more paint colors or interior fabrics selection. So for a lot less money you might get a model that is almost identical to a new one.

All that Glitters is Not Gold

You are in the market for a good used car and have already looked at several vehicles, both privately owned and at the used-car lot. So far, none has filled the bill. Undaunted, with a fistful of long green, you press on.

Finally, you spot the car on a dealer's lot. The obliging salesman opens the hood and you are greeted by a glittering array of seemingly new or near-new engine components. The engine compartment is spotless: no oil leaks, no grease, no coolant stains, no battery gunk. It looks too good to be true.

The car's paint glistens, the interior is spotless, and it almost smells like a new car. The trunk is the cleanest you have ever seen; even the thick rubber on the spare shines with Marine Corps spit and polish. This baby,

Detailed w what has been done to make
the car look better (painted engine hides
leaks, etc)

you reason, has had exceptional care. It's by far the best one you have seen.

Indeed, the car does look good, not because it has had tender loving care from a previous owner, but because it has recently come from a detail shop. Many new and used-car dealers detail some of their questionable iron before putting it on the lot.

A detail shop can work wonders. Steam-clean and paint the engine and accessories. Vacuum and shampoo the interior. Rejuvenate the dash and rear deck. Wash, rub out, and wax an exterior finish. Touch up nicks and scrapes. Brighten white walls and blacken black walls. Go through the trunk with a fine-tooth comb. Presto! What was a back-of-the-lot question mark is now a proud front liner, with a price reflecting its newborn status.

Detailing, like makeup, can either accent desirable features or draw attention away from less desirable ones.

When buying a detailed car, what you see might not be what you are getting. Detailing can cover up symptoms that otherwise would have been detected even by inexperienced eyes. This is especially true when it comes to a detailed engine.

An engine that looks too clean and smells of fresh paint should be approached with caution. Engine detailing can cover up and gloss over many conditions (oil leaks, coolant leaks, etc.) that otherwise would have been obvious. This could spell trouble later. And even though these covered-up spots might not be indications of something wrong, on a nondetailed engine you would at least have the option of checking and questioning them. Then, once you were convinced that the car was a good one, you could have it detailed yourself, if you wished.

You Shouldn't Have to Write a Thank-You Note

It wasn't something you see every day, the small ad that caught my eye in the business section of the local paper: "In appreciation of courteous service from William T. Schaup at Fred Willis Motors shown to Susan Pestalozzi. Thank you."

It cost Susan $207 to run the ad for three days. I contacted her and asked what prompted her to do it. "There is so much negative stuff out there that I felt very strongly the positive needs to be reinforced. It was my way of saying thanks to William and letting him know how much I appreciated what he did." What Bill Schaup did was what every car salesperson should be doing but, unfortunately, isn't.

When Susan Pestalozzi walked into Fred Willis Motors in Tucson, Arizona, she saw the exact white hatchback she had been searching for. During her concentrated four-month "serious car shopping" experience she had seen other equally attractive vehicles, but overzealous salespersons or nagging sales managers had driven her out of the showrooms.

Willis Motors turned out to be different. There she met William T. Schaup, one of the salesmen at the dealership. From the very start, Susan noted, he was extremely courteous, answered all her questions, told her everything about the car and let her test-drive the car on her conditions. "He directed his energy toward me," says Susan. "He wasn't belittling, he talked directly to me, making eye contact at all times, and he was genuinely interested in me and the car and had nothing negative in his makeup."

A day or so after buying the car Susan had problems with it. But she liked it so much she was willing to pay to have it fixed. Schaup and Willis stepped in and fixed the car—an $800 repair bill—at no cost to Susan. "That did it," says Susan. "I just had to express my thanks in some other way than just by saying thanks. The ad in the paper was my small way of showing how grateful I was for an experience so refreshing, so unique."

One of the complaints I hear most often from women car buyers is that salespeople ignore them or talk down to them, even though they are the ones with the money. Unfortunately, a macho what-do-women-know-about-cars? attitude still prevails at many dealerships. And, whether they know it or not, that attitude costs them a bundle.

Smart operators recognize that women are involved in more car-buying decisions than are men. Ford Motor Co. estimates that women play a major decision-making role in about 75 percent of all new-car purchases and make about 50 percent of all new-car purchases as sole proprietors.

Shaup, a car salesman for the past 18 years, says this is the first time anything like this has happened to him and nothing in his career impressed or affected him as much as what Susan did. It's obvious he loves what he does, and he tries to accommodate his customers and give them what they want and need. "High-pressure salespeople are dinosaurs, things of the past. We must share information with the customers, tell them all they want to know, and we will have a happy marriage of people."

Shaup makes an important observation. "When a dealer meets his obligations (to the customer) it is so much easier for a salesperson to treat their clients right."

Fred Willis, owner of the dealership, concurs. "I try to instill in every employee the fact that each customer should be treated in the same way he or she would want to be treated—the Golden Rule, if you will. If a salesperson or technician or receptionist feels uncomfortable at any point when dealing with a customer, he is doing something wrong."

But perhaps the best way to sum up Willis's philosophy is with his parting words: "I keep telling all my employees that the customer is really the one who signs the payroll checks; I only countersign them."

Remember, if you are shopping for a car, be it new or used, you don't have to endure being treated like a second-class citizen. You are the one with the money and you, as Fred Willis noted, sign the payroll checks at the place you choose to buy. Keep shopping around until you come across a salesperson who will treat you as Bill Schaup does.

And you won't even have to run a thank-you ad in the local paper—unless, of course, you want to.

New-Car Options I Like

Buying a new car often turns into a sobering experience when it comes time to select options. It doesn't take long for a $12,000 base price to rocket over the $15,000 or $16,000 mark. But a car without options is like, well, a day without sunshine.

After years of testing and driving new cars of every make and model, here are some of my favorite new-car options. Most are practical; some are strictly self-indulgent, and many might not seem like the traditional options you have grown to know.

Anti-lock braking system (ABS) When offered, ABS is usually optional. I think it is the single most important mechanical advancement in cars in the last few decades, maybe even the last half century. ABS stops the wheels from locking under hard braking, allowing you to keep control of the car at all times. For the most part, skids, under any road conditions, are avoided. And for the vast majority of drivers, ABS will bring the car to a quicker stop than conventional brakes. Any new car I'd buy would have ABS on it. It's number 1 on my list of new-car options.

Upgraded all-season steel-belted radial tires No single item will affect car handling, ride, and suspension more than a good set of tires. Tires such as the Goodyear Eagle GT+4, a current favorite among car manufacturers, add a new dimension of safety, stability, and driving pleasure to any new or old car.

Remote trunk/hatchback/fuel lid release Sometimes these are standard, sometimes not, but they are a great convenience.

Air conditioning Because I live in Arizona, this isn't an option but a necessity. Anywhere else it can add much enjoyment to summer driving, especially on those humid days. And, who knows, the way we're going the rest of the country is going to be one big Arizona pretty soon. Air conditioning also boosts the resale value of any car, so you do get back some of the initial investment.

Upgraded stereo radio/cassette If you haven't test-driven a car with one of the new super sound systems, such as General Motor's Delco-Bose stereo system, just attend the next performance of your local symphony. They sound about the same. Concert-hall-quality systems that are tuned to the individual car's interior acoustics give you unbelievable listening pleasure. I guarantee you'll extend your drive so you don't have to turn off the stereo.

Four-speed automatic overdrive transmission If you are choosing an optional automatic transmission, why not go with one with an automatic overdrive? The cost won't be that much different, but you'll save on engine wear and gasoline for the life of the car. And the entire power train will be quieter at highway speeds.

Upgraded front seats for the driver and passenger You can choose from power lumbar adjustment (nice for that bad back and for long trips), heated seats (wonderful on those cold mornings), and seat memory (push a button and the seat returns to your favorite position).

Leather-wrapped steering wheel and shift knob   Leather feels good and gives you a nice grip on the wheel.

Engine heaters   Did you know that many new car makers offer built-in engine heaters as an option? Don't leave your dealer without one. For the money, one of the best investments you will ever make for your car.

Light and door-open packages   Such things as interior or exterior light delay (the lights stay on until you get to your doorstep), remote interior lights (turns interior lights on from far away), and remote door opener (works like your garage-door opener). Besides the convenience they offer, these are great security and safety options.

Power windows and door locks   Although these have been around forever, I wouldn't be without them for both security and convenience. They are a plus, especially if you have small children.

Trip computer   Gives you fingertip information on miles per gallon (mpg), average mpg, miles traveled, average speed, time, date, temperature (outside and inside), and a host of other information that makes driving more enjoyable and informative.

Although many of these options are available only as part of an option package—for the most part, you can't pick and choose like in the old days—they are ones my car wouldn't be without.

Look for these Safety Features when Car Shopping

I test-drive new cars every day of the year. Each week finds one or two current pieces of iron at my front door. It isn't a bad job.

One of the areas of great improvement over the past few years has been in automotive safety features. Here are some of the safety features I would like on my new car and ones you might consider for your next car:

Three-point seat belts in front and rear seats

Three-point simply means the belts attach at three points, usually on the floor on each side of the driver/passenger and again on the B-pillar or, in the case of backseat passengers, near the C-pillar. Virtually every car made has three-point seat belts up front, but you might have to search a bit to find them for the rear passengers.

Passive seat belts

All car manufacturers are required to include passive seat belts in a certain percentage of their vehicles. These are seat belts that automatically engage with no help from the driver/passenger—thus the name.

As a rule, only the shoulder harness engages and the driver must manually buckle the lap belt. Although the driver/passenger, as in an active system, must still engage one buckle, the movement of the passive belt is a good reminder to do so.

Driver or driver's and front passenger's air bags

The classic passive restraint. If you read about the recent head-on collision between two Chrysler LeBarons in which both drivers walked away, you should be convinced of the efficacy of air bags. But as helpful and desirable as they are, air bags aren't panaceas. For maximum front- and side-impact crash protection seat belts should also be used.

Knee bolsters

These are padded areas on the vertical portion of the dash that absorb the energy of passenger/driver impact and can save your patellas.

ABS brakes

Antilock Braking Systems can bring a car to a safe, sure, and straight stop under adverse conditions such as icy or wet roads. This system automatically pumps the brakes faster than the driver could and keeps the wheels from locking and the car from going into a skid. The driver must apply full brake pressure; the ABS will do the rest.

Four-wheel disc brakes

These brakes are better in stopping ability than disc brakes on the front axle and drum brakes in the rear. Four-wheel disc brakes are usually optional except on more expensive vehicles. Also, ABS systems are usually installed on vehicles with four-wheel disc brakes.

The best tire offered by the manufacturer

No one feature can affect the handling and safety characteristics of your car as much as tires. The few extra dollars invested in the best tire (it will probably be an option) not only ensures maximum road safety, but also better handling, performance and ride.

Dual-side power mirrors

Don't drive a car without a passenger's side-view mirror. Make sure your car has two mirrors, even though the second might be optional. Fingertip control of both mirrors allows you to scan the side in question before making a move.

Delay headlamps

Delay headlamps keep the headlights lit for 30 seconds or so after you've turned off the ignition. This helps light the way into your home or a strange parking area.

Good headlights

Not all cars have comparable lighting systems. I have test-driven vehicles with headlamps that seem twice as efficient as others. The only way to tell is to drive the vehicle at night. A night test-drive should be on every new-car buyer's list.

Theft/alarm systems

Except on higher-profile cars, these systems are optional. Most of the current ones really raise a ruckus.

Five-mph bumpers

Such bumpers absorb minor impacts and keep you away from the body shop.

Ingress/egress lighting

Usually this means a light on the inside of the doors that illuminates the way in and out of the car. Some vehicles also have red warning lights on the open door.

Four-wheel drive: selectable or full-time

If you live in an area where bad weather is the norm, these systems could prove valuable.

Good washer/wipers

A good windshield washer and a set of good wipers, including one for the rear window, are important in any car.

A powerful engine

Your engine should have enough power for passing or emergency situations. Even though you won't always use the power, it's nice to know it's there, just in case.

Tinted windows

Tinted windows should be on your list if you are bothered by glare.

Although you might not be able to find all the above features on any one car, each one you include in your car will help make it a safer place to be.

Low Cd: Better Mileage, Quieter Car

Have you noticed how tough it is to tell new cars apart? Line up a Ford, Chevy, Chrysler and AMC automobile and, without name tags, you are pressed to tell one from another. Legislated blandness? A much-desired design? Not really.

Blame it on aerodynamics. Blame it on laws that require certain cars to deliver certain miles per gallon by certain dates. It's sure not like the old days. There was no way you could mistake a '57 Chevy for a '57 Ford.

Personality abounded. Today's cars sacrifice looks for efficiency, pizzazz for gas mileage.

The problem is there's only one shape that is best suited to meet aerodynamic demands: the wedge-shaped cars we now see coming into prominence. Low front, high back, with a chopped-off tail.

The efficiency with which a car slices through the air is directly related to its shape and can be numerically measured. The car's rating is called the *coefficient of drag*, or Cd for short. The lower a car's Cd, the less affected it is by wind drag and the easier it moves through the air. Thus a car with a Cd of 0.35 is less affected by the air mass in front of it than a car with a Cd of 0.40.

Envision a very thin 4-by-6-foot piece of sheet metal sailing horizontally through the air. It would meet with little or no resistance. Engineers give this hypothetical situation a Cd of 0. Now turn the sheet of metal so that it is standing on edge and try sending it through the air with its flat 4-by-6-foot face turned in the direction of movement. Much harder to do. The sheet metal, in this case, is given a Cd of 1.0. The Cd of all automobiles will fit somewhere between these two extremes.

Why all this talk about coefficient of drag? Simply because it is an important—and usually overlooked—factor to consider when buying a new car. It is especially important that you study your prospective car's Cd if you anticipate using the car for a lot of highway driving. This is where less wind resistance will mean getting better gas mileage and a smoother, quieter ride.

If you are tired of whistling windows and doors, road noise, and being buffeted by every gust of wind that comes along, look for a car in your price range that offers a low coefficient of drag. With a low Cd, the car sheds wind quickly and smoothly as the air is routed up, over and around the vehicle in a more efficient manner. The car holds the road better, is less affected by wind, drives easier, and is quieter and safer.

So don't forget to look at the car's Cd number the next time you go shopping for a new one. Cds, once the exclusive province of sports- and race-car enthusiasts, are now published for almost every model car. Study them, check them out.

And remember, Cd doesn't stand for those things you have tucked away at the bank. Cd in this case means a smoother, quieter, safer car, and—unlike those other kinds of CDs—the lower the number, the better.

Auto Reviews: One Man's Opinion

You pick up a newspaper or magazine and start reading a review of a new car. You are especially interested in this review because the car is one you have recently purchased. After you finish the article you put down the paper, wipe the sweat from your forehead and say, "Hey, this guy is crazy. I own the same car and very little he says about it is true." Ever happen to you? Ever wonder why the test-driver seemed so far off base? Read on, please.

The expert's review should be taken for what it is: One man's opinion about a certain car driven under specific conditions. But that review should be given credence, because evaluating a new car is tricky business whether you are a professional driver or a consumer looking for the best car for the money. It's rare for even professionals to see the same car the same way, so it shouldn't be surprising that a reader's opinion differs with the writer's critique.

But let's look at some of the advantages the professional has and why you should pay attention to what he or she has to say. First, the expert test-driver is reviewing new cars all the time, in my case every day of the year. Different cars: big and little, sports and sedans, expensive and cheap. The entire spectrum is presented in a never-ending parade of new iron.

The tester has at his disposal a memory filled with facts about other cars. He can compare and compare and compare. So although he is testing one car in particular, he is always contrasting it to others he has tested in the past. That gives the regular reviewer an advantage.

Of course, you can approximate what the pro does by test-driving many different cars prior to purchasing one. It's one way an untrained buyer can imitate the veteran. There is no great secret to it, just time and effort to drive and pay close attention to as many cars as practical. It will soon become obvious to even the novice that some cars are better than others.

A car should live or die on its own merits. The keen driver is able to interpret the information the car is giving him, compare it with facts culled from other cars, and make a judgment.

Reading reviews helps. If one car gets consistently glowing reports, it is for a good reason. If one gets lukewarm or noncommittal reviews, there is a reason for that, too. Many new-car reviewers disdain an outright pan of any car—they don't want to offend the manufacturer or the dealer who advertises in the publication carrying the review. Instead, they offer mild condemnations of unimportant features. These middle-of-the-road evaluations—not much good or bad said about the car—are quite common but offer little substance for the reader to sink his teeth into. However, some of these are legitimate, because there are many new cars about which you must search hard to find something to say, good or bad. They exist, they do their job, and that's about it. You shouldn't expect outright raves or pans in every review. The cars themselves see to it that that doesn't happen.

Keep all the above points in mind and remember that the expert is human and can make mistakes. Most reviewers don't have the luxury of looking at the car for an extended period to assess whether or not it can hold up over the long run. That may be why the guy at the beginning of this piece disagreed with the review he had just read about a car he owned. He had had the time to shake the rattles and rolls out of the car and to see things the average reviewer never will. A reviewer, with a new car at his disposal for seven to 10 days, can't judge the long-term merits of the vehicle.

So read that review with an open mind. It's subjective, sure, but the writer should be trying—if he is honest—to be objective and fair.

Tips for a Thorough Test Drive

1988 saw new-car buyers shelling out on average $14,000 for their purchases. And five will get you 10 that many of them ignored the most important part of buying a car: a thorough test drive. It's amazing how people will lay big bucks on the line without so much as driving the car around the block. Indeed, salespeople I know regale me with stories about buyers who plunked down their money without even getting into the car. I hope you're not one of them.

The test drive is your main opportunity to get to know the car beforehand. Take advantage of it. Single out a few cars your pocketbook qualifies for, then get serious. Here are some suggestions—I drive and report on a different new vehicle each week in another syndicated column—that will guarantee that your next new car is the one you want and not the one a salesman wants to sell you.

Take the family along on the drive if it's going to be a family vehicle. Listen to their input, their pros and cons. Is it roomy enough, are the seats comfortable? If others in the family drive, let them take turns behind the wheel and note their observations.

When I get in the driver's seat I look for a number of things. Headroom and legroom are important if you are tall. Ease of access—some cars are a pain to get in and out of. Visibility—are you able to see all around without craning your neck? Some aerodynamic-looking cars have limited front and rear visibility.

Is there sufficient storage space up front? Look for map pockets, glove compartment, console storage, and cubbyholes. The more the better, in my opinion. Check the trunk or hatchback to see if it is roomy and easily accessible. Thirteen or more cubic feet of storage space is nice to have if there are more than two in the family.

Try all the controls—not just some of them. Don't take for granted that everything will work just because the car is new. Most new-car manufacturers laud their car's *ergonomics*, the position of the instruments and controls in relation to the driver, and most are pretty good. Everything should be within reasonable reach: wipers, air conditioning, radio, lights, power windows, mirrors, locks, gear-shift lever, and other frequently used controls. All gauges should be easy to read—also check them at night, if possible. Sometimes an important gauge is tucked behind the 10 o'clock or 2 o'clock portion of the steering wheel.

It's important that you be comfortable behind the wheel. Does it feel good, is it the right height, is it adjustable? Are the seats too firm or too soft? Can they be positioned to your liking? Remember, you are going to live a long time with your decision. Don't ignore signs of discomfort, no matter how good-looking the car is. You'll drive to regret it.

Don't be afraid to put the car through its paces. Does the engine have enough power? Does it hesitate or stumble? Take it on some hills, then test its passing ability on a freeway. Are the brakes adequate? Pick a straight stretch of road, accelerate and brake hard. The car should stop evenly without pulling to one side or dipping its nose.

Evaluate the suspension by cornering hard on a traffic-free street. The car should not lean excessively nor should it feel as if it is getting away from you. Are you comfortable with the handling and do you have confidence in the car?

Try maneuvering in and out of tight parking spots or slipping through heavy city traffic. And be certain the car will fit in your garage or carport.

Listen, listen, listen. Sounds tell you a lot about a car. For my money, a quiet car is a better car. Don't settle for a car that has excessive interior wind noise at highway speeds or a lot of rattles, ticks and groans. Take it over a rough road and see how it reacts. Listen to the engine. Can you live with the amount of noise it makes? Don't let the salesperson talk you into a city-only, around-the-block smooth drive. That's not going to tell you anything. Rough up the car.

Check the fit and finish; it's a clue to the car's overall quality. Body parts should fit evenly and snugly. Don't assume it will have a good paint job. Quality varies.

I asked a salesman friend of mine what is the biggest mistake new-car buyers make. His answer didn't surprise me: They test-drive the vehicle with the stereo on, more interested in a $500 option than the $14,000 car. Of course, he doesn't mind because the sound system can mask other noises and give the buyer a false sense of euphoria about the car. Turn off the sound when test-driving.

And remember, if you don't feel right about the car, don't buy it. There are too many others you will feel right about.

Before You Buy, Take a Test Drive at Night

If I was a betting man, I'd lay a considerable sum on the line backing my contention that not more than one in 1,000 readers have had the following notion. Let's see how much money I'd win.

When you purchased a new or used car, did you ever take the time to test-drive the vehicle at night? I didn't think so. But I'm quite serious about it; this is on my list after I have determined that the car is attractive in price and looks, is in good mechanical condition, has the features I desire, and drives and handles the way I like. After these preliminaries have been established and I have test-driven the car during the day, I always give the car a run in night-driving conditions. There are a number of reasons for this.

I want to be certain that my vision when driving isn't obstructed by nighttime conditions. Daylight can often mask what will become an obvious imperfection in vision during night driving. For instance, I once tested a new car at night that would pick up reflections of oncoming car lights and somehow relay them onto the glass covering the instrument panel. From there it was reflected into my eyes. It was bothersome and something I would not care to drive with on a regular basis. I would not have purchased the car because of this glare. And I wouldn't have spotted the problem if I hadn't driven the car at night.

If you don't drive the car at night, can you be sure the lights are adequate for your vision? Some cars have much more efficient lights than others. Some are quite marginal. You won't know until you test the lights.

Bright taillights are important for safety if you do a lot of driving, as are powerful backup lights.

Interior lighting is also quite important. I hate groping in a dimly lit interior trying to find something. Only way to check the interior is to drive at night.

One of the more important considerations is how the dash and instrumentation light up. Are all the gauges and controls fully visible, or do you have to strain to see the information the car is giving you? Are the lights on the dash aesthetically pleasing, or do they irritate you?

I personally enjoy a dash with amber lights. They are easy on my eyes and have a handsome look. On the other hand, vacuum fluorescent digital dashes are a bit too harsh and cold for my night-driving tastes. Your preference might be just the opposite, but you will never know until you test-drive the car at night.

Most of us spend time behind the wheel after the sun goes down. The exterior and interior lighting should be as comfortable and pleasing as possible. You need every advantage you can get to make driving easier and safer during the time when accidents are more likely to occur.

Remember, the differences in the nighttime behavior of cars can be as striking as between, uh . . . night and day.

Buying a Car? Turn Off That Stereo!

I had lunch recently with a friend of mine, a man of considerable automotive savvy who has sold new and used cars for the past 30-odd years. The conversation, as it always does when we get together, turns naturally and easily to cars. As we chewed the fat over a cup of coffee in a local greasy spoon, it dawned on me what better person to ask about the ins and outs of buying a new or used car.

And so I asked him to comment on consumer habits he had observed over the past three decades while on the selling end of the transaction. I was particularly interested in his thoughts on the most common mistakes consumers make when buying a car. He pulled hard on the black stuff and took a deep breath.

"The single biggest mistake almost everyone makes when buying a car is that the first thing they do is turn on the radio. Younger buyers especially can't wait to blast the stereo, check out the number of speakers the car has, play with the cassette or fiddle with the numerous electronic buttons and gadgetry found on most newer cars. Compact-disc players have added to their choice of playthings. From the moment they get behind the wheel it's usually the sound system that interests them most. The car just happens to be attached to it."

That's the biggest mistake?

"By far and away, and it's one that car salesmen encourage. And if someone doesn't turn on the radio, we politely do it for them."

OK, I know what you're getting at.

"I know you know because we've talked about it before. If you can get the person hooked on the sound system, selling the rest of the car is relatively easy. And remember, when you turn on the radio—and when most younger people turn it on, they blast it—it masks other sounds you should be listening for."

For example?

"Well, things such as wind noise around the windows, engine noise, air-conditioner or heater-blower intensity, and any scraping, grinding, or other noises coming from anywhere in the car."

Aren't you being a little underhanded when you turn on the radio for them?

"Not really, because for most people it's the single important part of the car, bar none. When we get a buyer who turns it off we know we have a smart buyer, a tough cookie who knows what he wants and how to look for it. Of course, we love it when we get a buyer who turns on the stereo and keeps it on for the duration of the test drive. They seldom ask questions, rarely pay attention to the car and how it drives, and bop their way to my office afterward where it doesn't take much to get the signature on the line."

I finished my coffee and picked up the tab, something I'm not in the habit of doing too often. But in this case it was well worth it because here was some solid info I could pass on to my readers.

As I got into my car I thought about an automotive writer who occasionally is the butt of other writers' jokes because he, too, is overinfluenced by the power of sound. When referring to his reviews, other writers jokingly note that so-and-so test-drove another stereo.

So if professionals can do it, be wary; it will be even easier for you to be influenced by the sound of music. Turn off the stereo when you get into a car you are considering buying. You can listen to it later when you have thoroughly evaluated the car. And the salesperson will know you mean business.

16

Rip-off
tip-offs

ONE OF THE MOST-PUBLICIZED, most-read articles ever published by *Reader's Digest* was a May, 1987, article of mine called "Highway Robbery: The Scandal of Auto Repair In America." Its findings were quite revealing. I traveled across the United States and visited 225 repair shops of all kinds to determine the kind of treatment an average motorist could expect. My problem was a simple one: a loose spark-plug wire.

I received a fair and competent repair in only 28 percent of my stops. When a mechanic did work on the car, I got a satisfactory repair only 44 percent of the time. At the remainder of the stops, I was victimized by incompetence, cheated, sold unnecessary parts or work, overcharged, and lied to.

Since that article appeared, many repair shops have changed the way they treat their customers and many repair-shop customers are more aware of how to find a good mechanic and what to do if they encounter shoddy service or a rip-off. As a result, both consumers and the repair industry have benefited.

The article attracted so much publicity that the *Canadian Reader's Digest* asked me to do a similar investigation of automotive repair facilities throughout Canada. Last summer my family and I went on a coast-to-coast trans-Canada excursion checking out Canadian repair shops. From Halifax to Vancouver, through eight provinces, with stops in virtually every major Canadian city, we traveled over 10,000 kilometers.

I made random stops at 152 repair shops of all kinds: small and large independents, dealerships, service stations, and chain automotive outlets. My report, called "Highway Robbery: Canada's Auto Repair Scandal," appeared in the February 1990 issue of the *Canadian Reader's Digest*.

The names of these two articles aren't the only things that are similar. The results of the Canadian investigation virtually paralleled those of the American. Listen to this: In the American *Reader's Digest* story I found that only 28 percent of my stops resulted in a correct diagnosis and repair of my problem (a loose spark-plug wire). In the Canadian study, where I loosened a connection at the idle air control (IAC), a unit that sits in clear view on top of the engine, the figure was 27 percent! At the other 73 percent of the stops I couldn't obtain service or was victimized by dishonest or incompetent operators.

In the United States when a mechanic did work on the car I got a satisfactory repair only 44 percent of the time. North of the border the number was 43 percent, only a 1-percent difference. In the United States the other 56 percent of the times mechanics either overcharged, performed unnecessary work, tried to sell me unneeded parts, charged for work they didn't do, or fixed the car and lied about the kind or amount of work they had done. In Canada it was 57 percent.

I find it amazing that the statistics of both investigations were nearly identical. Although I'm neither a statistician nor a mathematician, it seems that these numbers are saying that international borders can't contain human nature. Crossing into Canada for nearly two months of road work showed that I received virtually the same treatment in Canadian shops as I did in the American ones.

Is it inevitable that the consumer stands only a 43 percent or 44 percent chance of having an automotive problem fixed at a fair price on the first visit when making a random stop? The results of these two independent studies seem to suggest just that.

There were other parallels:

- ○ As in the United States, small-town and rural Canadian garages treated me better than big-city shops.

- ○ A shop that employed "certified" mechanics wasn't necessarily an honest shop.

- ○ Shop appearance meant little; I was ripped off in neat, clean places and got treated fairly in grubby shops.

- ○ Honest, competent technicians always found a way to help, even if they were busy.

Consumers must take the initiative to up the paltry good-repair-on-first-try odds. Knowledge of your car is the most important weapon you have in your anti-rip-off arsenal. Regular preventive maintenance, such as I constantly emphasize in this column, is another important weapon. The better shape your car is in, the less likely it is that you will need major repairs and the less often your car will be in a shop.

When you do need repairs:

- ○ Be specific when describing the car's symptoms. Try to speak directly to the mechanic who will work on your car. If major work is recommended, get a second or even a third opinion before committing yourself to the repair. Don't leave the shop without a written estimate, and don't allow extra work to be done without your permission.

○ If you think you have been ripped off, **complain**. Go to the shop first and explain your problem. Many times it can be amicably solved and might be no more than a simple misunderstanding.

○ If the rip-off is obvious, notify the Better Business Bureau and the consumer-fraud units of the local or state government. Write or call any national organization connected with the shop, such as the American Automobile Association or the Canadian Automobile Association.

So many readers have asked me how to find a good mechanic that I put the complete answer in a book. Drawing from the invaluable insights and knowledge I gained from both cross-country investigative trips, I wrote *Rip-Off Tip-Offs: Winning The Auto Repair Game*. Published by TAB/McGraw-Hill, it's the definitive book on the subject.

The Garage Attendant Cometh—With an Ice Pick

Ice picks are very versatile. When I was a kid, I marveled at the way the iceman performed magic on a huge block of ice—whittling, chipping, and carving out the exact size needed by his customer. All he ever used to accomplish his task was an ice pick.

Ask any air-conditioning ductwork installer what one of his most useful tools is, and no doubt he will reply, "an ice pick." They are just perfect for punching holes for starting sheet-metal screws.

Put an ice pick in the hands of a good bartender and he or she can scalp a lemon without drawing a drop of juice, a prerequisite to the ideal lemon twist.

Put one in the hands of an unscrupulous service-station attendant, and an ice pick becomes the perfect tire-punching tool.

Normal expenses on a driving vacation trip eat heavily into the bankroll, what with the current prices of gasoline, rooms, and meals. What you don't need are unnecessary expenses, the kind that some highway service-station attendants are more than willing to dole out.

A classic situation: You pull your out-of-state car into a service station and tell the man to fill it up and check the oil. While he is busy at your car, there is a mad rush for the rest rooms and refreshment machines as the whole family scatters helter-skelter. Upon your return to the car, the attendant greets you with a $25 tab for the gasoline and the bad news that one of your tires is leaking air.

You never noticed anything wrong on the road but, upon inspection of the tire, you find that there is indeed a leak. The tire is taken off the car and the attendant, after looking at its innards, says the puncture can be fixed but the tire's safety is questionable. Concerned about the safety of your family, you agree to buy a new tire, slightly thankful that the puncture was spotted and didn't develop into a blowout at high speed. A hundred dollars lighter, you pull away, feeling you did the right thing.

Unfortunately, you were just ripped off. An unattended car is a joy to behold, money in the bank for dishonest service-station workers. It takes only a second to puncture a tire with an ice pick or slash it with a pocket knife. A concealed screwdriver or wrench can be used to quickly loosen hoses, causing fluids to leak and giving the engine the appearance of a major disaster area. There are a number of other quick, easy, and nefariously effective scare schemes a deft roadside magician can perform.

But there is a simple solution that will halt automobile molesters in their tracks. Don't leave the car. Stay with it until it has been gassed and serviced. Get out of the car. Hound the attendant, track his every move. If he is honest, he shouldn't mind a bit. Always leave an adult guard with the car. Take turns at refreshing. If you are driving by yourself, have the car serviced first, then pull it over to the side near the rest rooms, lock it, then refresh yourself.

Simple? You bet. But very effective. It could save you and yours many dollars and much anxiety—dollars that can be used for what they were saved for, vacationing—and anxiety that can be saved for when you get back to work.

So the next time you are on the road and you hear someone say, "The iceman cometh," just make sure he doesn't have grease on his overalls.

Avoiding Unnecessary Transmission Repairs

Summertime. Believe it or not, it's just around the corner. For the majority of us summertime means vacation time. And that means getting the old buggy up to par so we can travel unhindered by repairs.

It's wise to have the car completely checked, serviced, and tuned before leaving home on an extended trip. And one of the major mechanical components that should be looked at and serviced (if it hasn't been the last year or so) is the automatic transmission. Automatic transmissions are quite hardy, and only minimal service and care are needed to ensure that this unit will perform trouble-free for many thousands of miles.

But too many times having an automatic transmission serviced can end with your pocket being picked. Many of us are attracted by the low-cost transmission-service specials only to find later that they become high-cost nightmares. Your smooth-operating automatic transmission needed hundreds of dollars in repairs, perhaps all unnecessary. But that needn't happen if you know what to expect and what to look for.

Advertised service specials almost always include all or some of the following: check level and condition of fluid, test-drive car, check under-the-hood-transmission linkage and obvious external leaks, remove transmission oil pan, drain transmission fluid in the pan, adjust bands where required, clean screen or replace transmission filter.

Remember that the cost of fresh fluid, pan gaskets, and filters are often added to the special price. Ask what the total cost will be if these parts aren't included in the price.

A dishonest mechanic might bring you the transmission pan and point to the many fine metal particles and other friction material in the pan. This wear debris is not necessarily a sign of transmission trouble. In fact, in most cases it's perfectly normal to have a moderate amount of debris in the pan.

Or the repair person might point to the discolored transmission fluid and ask you to smell it, saying that the burned smell and brown or dark-colored fluid is a sign that the internal condition of the transmission should be investigated. However, many times all that is needed to correct this is to change the transmission fluid. ˙

One key point to remember (and this applies for any type of repair): If the transmission was working satisfactorily when you took in the car for service or inspection, chances are nothing is wrong with it.

It is at this point the consumer should tread with caution. If the shop suggests that the transmission be torn down so they can see what repairs will be needed, insist that they put in writing why it is needed. It's also very wise to take the car to another shop for a second opinion.

Don't let someone tear down the transmission just to inspect it—especially if it was working fine when you took it in—because it's going to cost you big bucks to have it put back together. In the event a "tear-down" and major repair are necessary, be certain you get on the estimate the maximum amount it will cost before you give your OK.

Remember, the money you save by avoiding unnecessary transmission repairs will go a long, long way in paying for that summer vacation.

Roadside Vultures Are Ready to Pick Your Pocket

A friend and I had just pulled into a large gasoline station in Tucson, Arizona. I was filling the tank while my friend, the car's owner, busied himself washing the windows.

The car, with out-of-state plates, was only two years old and had a mere 23,000 miles on the speedometer. It had had excellent care and, although dirty from traveling, was in top mechanical shape.

As I pumped gas into the tank I saw one of the station attendants check the plates, then walk around to the right rear of the car. I thought he was checking the air pressure in the tires. But he wasn't. I looked again and saw him underneath the rear portion of the car. I asked him what he was doing.

"You got problems," he replied.

"Problems, what kind of problems?" I inquired.

"Your coil springs are bent real bad. They are leaning way over to one side."

He pulled out a tire gauge, extended the measuring portion, and bent it to demonstrate how the springs were bent. "It could be dangerous traveling on those," he cautioned.

My buddy and I exchanged glances. Let's play his game was the unspoken message. "Let's run the car in and check it on the rack," I suggested.

The car was hoisted and the attendant, now starting to squirm a bit, tried his best to point out how the coils were bent. They weren't, but we played along. "We don't want to travel on bad springs," I said. "How much to replace them?" He eagerly totaled the amount. "One hundred twenty-five dollars will get you going and I can have it finished in 20 minutes," he said.

"Do you have the right size coils in stock?" I asked. Before the last word was out of my mouth, he produced a shiny new pair of coils from a box on a shelf. "These are the exact ones you need," he said.

To make a long story short, we extricated ourselves from the situation. We didn't buy the coils, of course, because the ones on the car were perfect. The attendant made a strong play to rip us off for $100 or so, but, lucky for us, we both knew enough about cars to realize what he was doing.

But what about people who don't know any better? What would have happened then? These car vultures are adept at placing doubt in the minds of the uninitiated. They are pros at questioning the safety of your car.

If you don't have any mechanical knowledge, you are at their mercy, especially if you are on the road. Sure, we didn't fall for the ploy, but how many others will?

I got a glimmer of just how much a good, honest mechanic is in demand when, while writing a local newspaper column a number of years ago, I offered a list of reader-recommended mechanics. These were garages that readers had found to be honest, fair and competent. Nearly 5,000 people wrote for that list!

We know there are good mechanics but, unfortunately, there are a lot of vultures too. They still prowl, still lurk, still set traps for the unsuspecting. They are all too happy to take your money.

Auto-Parts Competition Good for the Consumer

"The installation of imitation parts . . . could place your vehicle in noncompliance with federal safety standards," a Toyota brochure is quoted as saying in a pamphlet put out by the Ohio Insurance Institute (OII) of Columbus, Ohio.

"Sorry. That's just not true," says the OII. "The fact is, there are no federal safety standards for replacement crash parts (bumpers, fenders, hoods, etc.) except for headlight assemblies."

What they are talking about is replacement body parts, the kind a body shop uses to repair your car after it has been in a crash. So what's going on here? Is the consumer being caught in a squeeze play between the new-car industry and the parts concerns? According to OII, that might be the case. Referring to the Toyota quote, the Institute goes on to say, "It's one example of the kind of myths being perpetuated by the auto industry for the sake of protecting their replacement-parts business.

"The real issue in auto replacement parts isn't safety. It's competition and choice—your choice. And the automakers don't seem to like that."

OII continues: "The automakers would like you to believe that unless you purchase their brand-name replacement parts, you're taking away from your car's safety and quality in every case. Instead of innuendo, why don't we deal with facts?

"Crash parts are not critical to vehicle and driving safety. According to the Insurance Institute for Highway Safety, 'The source of cosmetic parts used to repair cars has little to do with the possibility of injury in those cars after they've been repaired.'

"In recommending competitive parts, are the insurance companies in any way jeopardizing the safety of repaired cars? It would hardly make sense to approve any repairs that threatened your car's safety.

"After all, an insurance company is going to insure your car after it has been repaired. An unsafe vehicle could make your insurance company liable for even greater damages later on, and no company could survive doing business like that.

"Competition in the replacement-parts business is not a new idea. Competitive replacement parts from sources other than the auto makers have been used successfully for over 50 years, with vital parts such as brakes, suspensions, batteries, spark plugs, and oil filters all replaced without compromising quality or safety.

"Actually, competition has, in some cases, resulted in higher quality in replacement parts and warranties. For example, auto makers did not provide anti-corrosion warranties except in response to the growing challenge of replacement-parts manufacturers.

"Consumers are saving money, thanks to parts competition. Repair costs have been reduced by 25 percent to 40 percent, depending on the type of repair involved. And that has helped keep auto-insurance premiums as low as possible."

Aries fender:

1983, manufacturer $221, competitor none
1984, manufacturer $180, competitor $140
1985, manufacturer $87, competitor $86
1986, manufacturer $87, competitor $79

Omni fender:

1983, manufacturer $165, competitor none
1984, manufacturer $140, competitor $120
1985, manufacturer $76, competitor $74
1986, manufacturer $79, competitor $67

Corolla fender:

1983, manufacturer $117, competitor none
1984, manufacturer $117, competitor $78
1985, manufacturer $79, competitor $79
1986, manufacturer $61, competitor $61

"Notice the effect of competition on one crash part. In 1983, when there was no comparable competitive part; the price of a Dodge Aries fender was $221. By 1985 the manufacturer's price for the same part was $87, less than half the 1983 price. Notice that the competitive part price also went down after 1984 as a result of the manufacturer lowering his price.

"This price stabilization has been typical whenever competitive replacement parts become available. Healthy competition in crash parts is one of the best ways to control auto repair costs—and insurance premiums.

"When it comes to making a decision regarding auto 'crash' parts, the fact is, competition is good for all of us. And when it comes to analyzing what you read or hear about replacement-part safety, the facts speak for themselves."

Mitchell Wilson, director of public information for the Ohio Insurance Institute, says the important thing is that "consumers should know they do have a choice" when it comes to replacement auto parts.

We all know there is a huge and thriving aftermarket selling non-manufacturer automotive parts, accessories, lubricants, additives, waxes, and the like. Stiff competition has weeded out many questionable products and on the whole has been good for the consumer. It seems to me the same scenario would repeat if auto body-parts competition runs its natural course.

An editorial in *Automotive News*, a respected industry journal, sheds more light on the matter. "Privately, the manufacturers have been telling the people who make repairs that original equipment parts are essential for making accident repairs—and that any substitutes are inferior. This is pure hokum. Granted, there are a lot of cheap, inferior substitutes for factory parts out there . . . We make no brief for such junk.

"But there are also high-quality parts—lots of parts—that meet or exceed original-equipment standards from GM, Ford, Chrysler-Jeep-Eagle and their suppliers. And those parts often sell at rates 30 percent, 40 percent, 50 percent below those charged by OEMs (original equipment manufacturers).

"Let the marketplace decide whose parts to buy at what cost. That's best for independent body shops, best for dealers, best for consumers—and best for the country at large."

I would like to hear a manufacturer's response to these positions so readers can get both sides of the story. Is there a manufacturer out there who wants to answer?

Code of Ethics Helping to
Improve Auto-Repair Industry

Several months ago I was invited to be the speaker at the Congress of Automotive Repair and Services convention in Fort Worth, Texas. I looked long and hard at the invitation, because this was a national meeting of technicians who belong to the Automotive Service Association (ASA), the nation's largest organization of automotive repair people.

It came on the heels of a tremendous amount of controversy generated by an article I did for *Reader's Digest* called "Highway Robbery: The Scandal of Auto Repair in America." My findings on a two-month research trip across the United States weren't very laudatory to the repair industry in general, so I was a little taken aback by the invitation. But accept it I did.

And it turned out to be a gratifying experience both for me and for the hundreds of technicians and shop owners who attended. It didn't take long to see that these were the cream of the crop. They listened to what I had to say, and almost all agreed with the basic findings of that article: There is shoddy work being done on cars, and a car owner isn't immune to being taken by a dishonest operator.

But repair technicians like these guys and gals from ASA aren't the ones who are plaguing the repair industry. I went to some of the seminars attended by the technicians. It became evident that there was an ongoing commitment to excellence. The ASA itself keeps members informed of changes coming their way so they can prepare for them through never-ending schooling and study. I was impressed by the dedication to upgrading the repair industry in general.

There was a common thread linking these technicians with the many good shops I visited on the *Reader's Digest* trip, particularly those in California that belonged to the California Automotive Service Councils (ASC), an affiliate of the ASA. I received fair treatment at every one. But perhaps what stuck most in my mind was the code of ethics subscribed to by each and every member. It's worth going over. An ASA or ASC member promises:

To perform high-quality repair service at a fair and just price.

To use only proved merchandise of high quality distributed by reputable firms.

To employ the best-skilled technicians obtainable.

To furnish an itemized invoice for parts and services that clearly identifies any used or remanufactured parts. Replaced parts may be inspected upon request.

To have a sense of personal obligation to each customer.

To promote good will between the motorist and members of ASA.

To recommend corrective and maintenance services, explaining to the customer which of these are required to correct existing problems and which are for preventive maintenance.

To offer the customer a price estimate for work to be performed.

To furnish or post copies of any warranties covering parts or services.

To obtain prior authorization for all work done, in writing or by other means satisfactory to the customer.

To notify the customer if appointments or completion promises cannot be kept.

To maintain customer-service records for one year or more.

To exercise reasonable care for the customer's property while in our possession.

To maintain a system for fair settlement of customer's complaints.

To cooperate with established consumer-complaint mediation activities.

To uphold the high standards of our profession and always seek to correct any and all abuses within the automotive industry.

To uphold the integrity of all members of the Automotive Service Association.

Sounds pretty good, doesn't it? Sounds like the kind of shop you'd like to do business with. Of course, a code of ethics is only as good as a person's commitment to uphold it. But from what I have seen and the number of members I have talked to I believe that ASA is trying to abide by those self-imposed rules.

Now, maybe you can't find one of these member shops in your area, but you can do the next best thing. Take this code of ethics into the shop you choose and ask them if they abide by similar standards. If they don't, you can—and should—take your business elsewhere. Don't settle for questionable repair service. It's one way that you too can help improve an industry that needs all the help it can get.

The Mechanic's Lament

"Dear Bob: I recently attended a course in Ford computer-ignition systems. The instructor read us the enclosed poem. As an automotive technician, I think the poem is accurate about how the public views us. Please publish it in your column for all of us who work in the automotive field who don't feel that they get just compensation for their services."—G.L.

Dear G.L: Although I imagine many would disagree with that last sentence, I thought the poem made some good points. Here it is, not in its entirety, due to space limitations, but enough so you get the point. It was written by Jim Conners of Fred Frederick Chrysler-Plymouth in Laurel, Md.

> I'm a journeyman technician
> In an automotive shop.
> I'm supposed to know the answers
> From the bottom to the top.
>
> I should diagnose the problem
> With just a single look.
> And if I fail to fix it
> You think that I'm a crook.
>
> When I charge you for my labor
> You yell and scream and moan,
> And even call and threaten me
> Upon the telephone.

But technology in the auto
Is advancing every year,
And for the systems I must know
I simply have no peer.

Electronics now have made the scene
And more are coming yet:
Some models now will far exceed
Your television set.

In hydraulics I have more to learn
Than a specialist in pumps.
There's brakes and shock absorbers
To help absorb the bumps;

Torque converters and transmissions
With servos, valves, and gears,
With models by the hundreds
Introduced in recent years.

Fuel systems of a hundred kinds
I must adjust and meter,
Each far more complicated
Than your furnace or water heater.

I'm in welding, I'm in plumbing
For water, vacuum, oil, and fuel,
Compared to me, a plumber
Is a kid in grammar school.

There's alignment and there's balancing
And God alone knows what.
If I fix it, that's expected
If I don't, I'm on the spot.

There's models, makes, and systems
Some 700 strong,
And new ones coming up each year
To help the scheme along.

Now compare me to a doctor
Whose prices make mine meager,
Yet folks revere his expertise
Ever more impressed and eager.

The human body hasn't changed
In 20,000 years,
And every model works the same
From the ankles to the ears.

There's new equipment and techniques
And medicines for sure
But this is true in my field too,
As much, or even more.

There's lots of books he has to read
His procedures to define,
But for every page in his field
There's 25 in mine.

There's no comebacks and no warranty;
You pay for what you get.
And then come back and pay again
If he hasn't fixed it yet.

His mistakes are often buried,
While mine come back for free.
And he plays golf on Wednesday
While my customers hassle me.

Everybody has one body,
No one has more.
But when it comes to autos
You may have three or four.

But you'll go right on complaining
Of the way I run my show
With no appreciation
For the things I have to know.

And when your car cannot be serviced
I'll not hang my head in shame.
So you'd best wake up, America
And find out who's to blame.

17

The high-mileage club

CAN A CAR LAST A MILLION MILES? A million miles, that is, without any major mechanical repairs? I hear you; you say you have a tough time getting your vehicle to make it to the 100,000-mile mark, let alone a million.

Well, the million-mile car is not some fantasy conjured up by an automotive engineer under the influence. It's a reality. A number of present-day vehicles have done just that—gone a million miles. And one, at least, has gone the distance without any major repairs.

Actually, there's not much to getting a car to last a million miles. All you have to do is rack up the miles and replace the engine and transmission every 100,000 miles or so. The rear axle might make it to the 200,000-mile mark before it needs changing. The real trick is getting the car to go the distance without any major mechanical repairs. Impossible?

A man from Oregon recently had his 1967 Mercedes honorably retired by the company after it logged 1 million miles. They gave him a new one in exchange. The million-miler is currently used in displays and dealer showrooms to entice prospective Mercedes buyers.

How did he do it? Most of the miles logged were highway miles, the easiest kind on any car. He commuted 130 miles each way to work every day for years and, at that rate, it doesn't take long to tack on the miles. But he did more than just accumulate mileage; he paid close attention to many points this column stresses.

He was meticulous about changing the car's oil and filter on a regular schedule, and he never varied from it. In his case, it was every 3,000 miles. He followed the recommendations in the owner's manual for severe-service maintenance, at times even exceeding those rigorous recommendations. He kept his engine immaculate, reasoning that a clean engine runs cooler and more efficiently.

He took care of small problems as they arose, fixing them before they had time to blossom into major problems. Although that might sound simple, it's one of the most important things any car owner can do; it keeps your car from "getting away from you." You stay in control all the time.

Tune-ups were a must, using either a time or mileage schedule or, in some cases, when gas mileage fell below a certain figure. He wasn't afraid to spend some money on upkeep, reasoning that it's better to pay a little now than a lot later.

How long can your car last? It depends. It depends upon the kind of car you have. Some cars, because they are better built with better materials, will last longer. The Mercedes just cited is a case in point. The weather you drive in, the number of miles you drive, and the way you drive all play important roles in the longevity equation.

The kind and amount of care you give your car will be reflected in the number of miles it gives you in return. You can, if you choose, drive it a long, long time. Only you, however, can make the decision to do so; the car can't.

High-Milers Make Their Debuts

A number of weeks ago I asked readers who own trouble-free high-mileage cars (100,000 or more miles) to write and tell me about them. I was interested in such things as their cars' total mileage, maintenance schedule, type of oil, driving techniques, repairs made, and anything else they thought was pertinent to achieving high mileage.

Because these cars are running proof that vehicles can and do make it to high mileages in relatively trouble-free fashion, I thought a brief synopsis of one car per week in "Drive It Forever" would be valuable to readers. They would soon be able to detect a pattern in maintenance practices or products used, and would get a profile of the types of cars and engines that have made it to the big figures.

This could also be a valuable source to draw from when a reader is in the market for a used car. It would be nice to buy a car that you know has a proved record of longevity.

The response from readers with high-milers has been gratifying. I have been swamped with letters! This week's column will feature two of these vehicles, and each succeeding column—space permitting—will contain a brief synopsis of one vehicle. So without further ado, here are this week's high-milers.

J.A.'s 1972 Oldsmobile Delta 88 with a 350 Rocket engine:

○ Total mileage: 222,000 plus.

○ Bought used in 1977 with 92,000 miles.

○ Previous owner had done his own maintenance; there had been no engine or mechanical work except for standard maintenance. Only replacement parts were a water pump at 92,000 miles; an alternator at 103,000 miles; a radiator at 129,000 miles, and new head gaskets at 196,000 miles. There have been no major mechanical repairs.

○ Oil was changed between 3,000 and 6,000 miles using 10W-40 weight; a new oil filter was installed about every change.

o Air and gasoline filters were replaced at least once a year. Tune-ups were every 10,000 miles (every eight to 11 months).

o Engine has always run smoothly and averages about 16 miles per gallon (mpg); can get 20 mpg on the highway when tuned.

o The car has had one recurring mechanical problem: The U-joint has had to be replaced or rebuilt three times in the last 120,000 miles.

J.A.: "In general, the tune-ups were done by an excellent mechanic who would look over the car each time. This caught belt and hose problems before they could cause other problems. The basic tune-ups I do, but in the long run the extra cost of having an expert do it . . . has paid off handsomely in longevity, since he would make adjustments and fine-tune in ways that I couldn't."

T.J.'s 1976 Dodge Dart Sport with a 225 cubic-inch slant-six engine:

o Total mileage: 100,000.

o No major problems. The master brake cylinder was replaced along with the air-conditioning hoses and a new water pump at 97,000 miles. A leak in the transmission-switch fitting was fixed.

T.J. follows the owner's manual recommended maintenance schedule and has found that it has "proved adequate to keep the engine running smoothly."

o New oil and filter every 3,000 miles, using Pennzoil.

o Flushes the cooling system once a year and does the usual periodic check of filters and fluids.

o Keeps the car in the garage or under a car cover to preserve the original finish.

o 28 mpg on the highway with the 4-speed manual overdrive transmission.

T.J.: "It should keep right on going if I can keep it in parts. I've already had to go to salvage yards twice for a parking brake pedal and a brake cylinder piston. Wish me luck."

Good luck, T.J. Let's hear from you after the second 100,000. With the reputation for longevity that the slant-six engine has, I don't think you will have any trouble getting there.

High-Mileage Club Letters

With the average new-car price now above the $14,000 mark, car owners are looking for ways to make their present vehicles last without investing big repair dollars. It's not an impossible task. In fact, owners are achieving some phenomenal mileages from 4-, 6- and 8-cylinder cars, both domestic and imported. Here's how some members of The High Mileage Club have gone at least 100,000 miles without any major repairs.

From B.G., Rapid City, South Dakota: My 1977 Olds 98 Regency with a 350 engine has 182,600 miles. Its oil-using habits haven't changed since I purchased it new. It uses about a quart every 3,000 miles. I've used nothing but Pennzoil 10W-30 or 10W-40, depending on the time of year. Oil/filter/lube: every 2,500 to 3,000 miles.

Annually I do the following: flush the cooling system, change automatic transmission fluid, have wheels aligned and the engine tuned. Every two years the wheel bearings are packed. I wash the car every two weeks in a brushless car wash that cleans the underside also and wax the car about once a year with Turtle Wax.

I drive sensibly and never put a strain on the engine. When a problem arises I have it taken care of immediately. The only thing I can credit the car's long life to is TLC.

From R.K., Seattle, Washington: 1972 Volkswagen Beetle with 287,467 miles. It has had four paint jobs but still has the original engine. The car uses very little oil, and I always use a 10W-30 weight. We have used it heavily, in lots of bad-weather driving such as skiing weekends and vacations to Sun Valley, Idaho. I have used it to and from work all this time (about 14-20 miles one way).

One important factor is that we have had excellent mechanics who specialize in Beetles. I do drive defensively (carefully), and the car is kept under a cover. We have adhered to an overcautious maintenance schedule. Another important thing: I have been the only operator, no kids or others driving it.

From C.L., Burlington, Colorado: I know you won't believe this Bob, but I swear it's true. I own a 1974 Ford Grand Torino. When I bought it in 1976 it already had 174,000 miles on it! Most of these were highway miles. I now have 285,000 miles on the car and, don't laugh, the engine heads or pan or transmission have never been off for any reason. The last set of tires (Sears Roadhandlers) I had for 74,000 miles before I got worried about them.

I don't believe the rear brakes have ever been changed—not in the last 100,000 miles, anyway. I do change oil and filter every 3,000 miles and tune up the car every 5,000. I am going to keep this car because it can be worked on without metric tools. I wish they would take all those cars with metric bolts and nuts and put them you know where.

Maybe you won't believe this either, but 90,000 miles ago I bought a quart of Slick 50 and put it in the crankcase. Maybe that helped my engine, I don't know. Can you explain why the car is still running?

From B.R., Cupertino, California: Cars of the late '60s—American as well as imported—going over 100,000 are not uncommon. I know, because I've owned Volvos and have noticed their soundness at any mileage. But I've also run into owners of other models with high mileage. So raise your mileage requirements Bob, to 150,000 or 200,000, and separate the mice from the men. Also define what you mean by "major repairs" more precisely. My 1969 Volvo 145S has 207,000, the 1970 145S has 196,700 miles.

I've used only Castrol 20W-50 oil and changed the oil and filter every 3,000 miles. I stuck to the manufacturer's suggested maintenance schedule that came with the car. My preventive-maintenance attitude: Don't wait for it to break or die before you repair or maintain it.

I have an AAA club diagnostic check every year and repair anything they spot. The engine is tuned every year or when gas mileage drops under 20 mpg. Compression tests show very little wear on the Volvos. I am the only driver and use both the Volvos demandingly.

E.M.H.'s 1978 Ford E-150 van with 351-cubic- inch V-8 engine, automatic transmission, power steering and brakes, cruise control, and air conditioning. Total mileage: 580,000.

E.M.H.: "I was a self-employed contract hauler of newspapers doing 200 miles a night, seven nights a week, 365 nights a year. Every 30 days, or 6,000 miles, I changed the oil and filter and lubed it, using Texaco 10W-40, Motorcraft oil filters and a can of Siloc Tune Up in the crankcase. I retired two years ago and the van had just logged 400,000 miles. It still has the original spark-plug wires, electronic ignition, muffler, and tail pipe. The starter and valve covers were never taken off. This was the last year Ford made an E-150 to burn regular gas; I am sure this had something to do with the service I got—not too much clean-air equipment on it.

"Another man took over my route and the van now has 580,000 miles on it with no major repairs to the engine. It still has the original items mentioned above. It still doesn't use any oil.

"You can change the oil in the van, run it 4,000 miles and the oil looks just like new. Nobody understands it. We thought Ford was testing some special bearings, crankshaft, or cam, because none of those have ever been touched.

"Although most of those miles were on the road in southeast Georgia, I had to go through towns and cities each night to drop off the newspapers, so the van had some city miles too. It really pays to use preventive maintenance, especially when you work at night when everything is closed."

Since I started the High Mileage Club four years ago, I've had over 2,000 car owners write me about their vehicles that have gone at least 100,000 miles without major repairs (major repairs include engine overhauls or replacements, valve jobs, transmission rebuilds or replacements. Major repairs do not include replacement of parts such as the starter, alternator, battery, tires, or the like).

18

Everybody loves
an old car

WE ALL LOVE OLD CARS. In fact, the affection we show for older vehicles cuts across lines that might otherwise separate us. In this election year, Democrats and Republicans alike are wont to marvel at the glorious fins of a '59 Cadillac. And it's not hard to find everyone agreeing that a '39 Hollywood Graham is a sight to behold. Doesn't matter who you are or where you come from or how much money you make, everyone can marvel at the beauty of older iron.

Old-car collecting is hot. Auctions and swap meets draw record-setting crowds in every part of the country. No matter where you live, you aren't far from a gathering of old-car buffs. It's a great hobby, a great way to pass some time, even if your interest lies in only looking. But watch out, a couple of auctions, a swap meet or two, and you'll soon be bit by the bug.

For amateurs and professionals there are a couple of essential publications that cover the old-car hobby. It would be wise to delve into them before attempting to buy your first old car.

- *Hemmings Motor News* (Box 100, Bennington, Vt. 05201), a monthly publication, has everything you could possibly want to know about old cars, from parts and restoration services to thousands of ads offering for sale old cars of every type and price, to lists of upcoming auctions around the country.
- *Old Cars News and Marketplace* (700 E. State St., Iola, Wis. 54990) is similar but not quite as extensive, and is offered weekly for those who can't wait a month.

Although your heart might attract you to an old car, it's still a good idea to use your head when purchasing one. These publications can keep your heart in line with your head and pocketbook.

And it could be more than your heart that benefits. Old-car prices have risen dramatically in the last three years. For example, a 1957 Chevy Belair convertible in perfect condition sold for $26,000 in 1985. Last year the same car sold for $50,000. Not a bad return on the investment. Of course, not all of us have 25 big ones lying around, but don't let that stop you; there is a lot of good stuff currently selling for less than $2,000. If your spouse complains, you might counter with what Mitchell D. Kruse, auctioneer and president of Kruse International auto auctioneers in Auburn, Ind., recently said. Despite the extremely strong showing by old cars over the past three years, Kruse believes that "The (collector car) market is going to continue to go straight up. It is just in its infancy."

Ah, why fight it? New cars are nice, but will there ever be one quite as nice as your first car? Wouldn't you like just one more shot at owning it? Of course you would. And it doesn't hurt that you might make a buck out of all those memories, does it?

Collector Car Auctions

With the recent surge of interest in collector cars, there has been a proliferation of collector car auctions. Buyers and sellers are becoming increasingly concerned about the level of service within the industry and the standards and practices they should expect from a collector car auction company.

Auctions are a great place to buy or sell collectible vehicles, but they are only as good as the company that runs them.

The Barrett-Jackson Auction, one of the largest in the United States, has developed a list of guidelines aimed at educating consumers to possible pitfalls they might encounter when buying or selling a collectible auto.

According to Thomas W. Barrett III, an internationally recognized collector car expert, problems have arisen because "every other used car lot on the block thinks it's a collector car auction showplace. We don't want to see anybody get taken. It hurts the whole industry. Car collecting is a wonderful activity, but an unscrupulous, fly-by-night auction company can easily ruin that enjoyment for life."

Barrett and his auction co-organizers offer the following tips for buyers and sellers when dealing with a collector car firm or auction they are unfamiliar with:

Seller

An auction company should be expected to screen its bidders to the highest degree possible—including requiring bidders to present a letter of guaranty from their bank prior to check-in time, on bank letterhead, notarized by a bank officer and stating the bidder's account number and approved financial limit. This protects the cosigner from the possibility of the sale falling through due to lack of funds. It's not a good feeling to think you have sold a car and then find out the buyer doesn't have the funds to cover his or her bid.

The seller should expect to know for certain whether his car actually sold. Some auctioneers have been known to say "sold" to make the auction look more successful than it actually is and then tell the seller later that the car failed to sell.

The seller should expect to have his car on the block long enough to give it the best opportunity to sell at the highest price. About 3 minutes per vehicle is a good average time.

The best way to receive payment on a sold vehicle is through the auction company itself and not from a person the seller has never met. This avoids possible post-auction financial complications.

A seller should expect the auction to be reasonably advertised and promoted. Consignment fees normally pay for this advertising.

All auction rules, regulations, and fees should be presented up front, so that there are no misunderstandings or surprises later.

The seller should expect the auction company to limit the number of cars of the exact make and model of the seller's. The vehicle should be presented in its best light. Remember, supply and demand functions within the auction as it does in the outside market.

Buyer

A buyer should expect the vehicle he purchases to have a good, negotiable title—no salvage titles. Each car should be inspected by the auction firm to verify that title and serial numbers match.

The vehicle should perform mechanically as described on the consignment form and on the car window card. If, in the auction company's opinion, the mechanical condition has been misrepresented, the buyer does not legally have to complete the transaction.

Buyers should expect to purchase the actual vehicle they think they are buying. Cancellation of the sale or negotiation should occur if any of these four problems are undisclosed prior to the fall of the gavel:

1. Incorrect engine made to appear correct.
2. Car rebodied to a different style and not stated.
3. Low mileage stated and found to be incorrect.
4. Claims or documentation of previous ownership by a famous personality found to be false.

All advertised cars should be at the auction. Knowing misrepresentation of available vehicles is the same as a "bait and switch," and some companies run pictures in their brochures of cars they know will not be in the sale to entice buyers to attend.

Car collecting and the appreciation of fine automobiles shouldn't be a chore or a cold and calculated business transaction. Fun is the name of the game.

If you are just dipping your toes in the car collecting waters, following these guidelines should help you avoid pitfalls that can prove costly.

Of Such Stuff Memories Are Made

Interest in old cars and collecting old cars has never been keener than it is right now. The old-car business/hobby is experiencing unprecedented growth and shows no sign of slowing. Each year more and more of us are buying older cars to either keep or restore or sell. For many, having a car they could only dream about in their youth is a dream fulfilled.

But this isn't a column about collecting cars; it's about collecting memories. And in our memories, what old long-gone car isn't just so much better than the real-life one we now drive?

I wrote the following column over five years ago and won a Moto award for it. A number of you have asked to see it again. With the heightened interest in old cars, I thought now would be the right time.

Psychologists say it's not good to live in the past, that we should let bygones be bygones and get on with the present. Now is what matters.

For the most part, I agree. But I occasionally like to remember the past and when I do, one memory that keeps cropping up is that of my all-time favorite vehicle.

We all have one, that very special vehicle we wish we could have back, that one that served us so well, the one with memories indelibly attached to it.

I grew up with my special vehicle and learned to drive in it. But it wasn't a car, it was a truck—a 1936 Dodge 1-ton.

When my grandfather died, my grandmother, an immigrant who had come to this country by herself at the tender age of 8 to work in a cousin's slaughterhouse, was forced to find a way to support herself. There were no handouts in the late '30s.

Well, the truck my grandparents owned turned out to be her solution and salvation. She used it to haul coal for a living. That's right, haul coal.

Oh, she never did learn to drive the truck, but no matter. She always hired someone to do that for her. But shovel coal she could—and did! Tons and tons of it, day after day, year after year.

And she barely eked out a living doing it, delivering coal on the cuff to families in need and rarely, if ever, getting paid for it. One precious memento I keep in my office is her old coal-smudged logbook, replete with labored handwriting and misspelled words, that shows the many loads she delivered for free.

On special occasions I rode with her and helped her shovel coal off the truck bed and down the chute into western Pennsylvania coal cellars. She would allow me, then a boy of 10 or so with a face dirty from coal dust and sweat—and wearing a red bandanna just like hers around my neck—to ride high and proud atop the mountain of coal in the back of the truck. I was the envy of every kid in town.

There was no greater vehicle anywhere. There still isn't. And I doubt if there ever was another coal-hauling, coal-shoveling grandmother. How grateful I am now for the memories of her and the '36 Dodge.

Eventually, I learned to drive the truck and even took my first driver's test in it, much to the consternation of the examiner.

I drove the truck my entire senior year in high school, but one day, after I returned from my first year of college, I found that my dad had sold it. Impending repair bills had forced the sale.

I remember seeing it around town for a few years after that and resenting the man who had purchased it. After all, what did he know about my truck? I was certain it never ran as well for him.

The truck eventually found its way to a resting place under a large tree in a farmer's field where it spent a number of years. Then one day it was gone, swallowed up somewhere in the western Pennsylvania hills. I never saw it again.

The old '36 Dodge has been gone a long time, but memories of it still hang heavy like the coal dust in the hot, humid autumn air.

Of one thing I'm certain: No matter how big they now make trucks, no matter how powerful the engines or how gripping the 4-wheel drive, there will never be another one as great as my grandmother's—and my—'36 Dodge coal hauler.

Wouldn't you like to bring back that one favorite vehicle of yours, too?

19

All work and no play...

A WONDROUS VARIETY OF DRIVERS fills our city streets. As a courtesy to readers, this column has categorized some (space prohibits a complete list) of these to make identification immediately possible. I suggest you use this list in the same way a bird-watcher uses an identification book. Keep it in the car for quick, easy reference.

Fast-Lane Creepers: Love to drive in the fast lane only. They crawl along, ignoring the traffic buildup behind them and the angry glares of drivers who are forced to pass them on the right.

Slow-Lane Crawlers: Related to the Fast-Lane Creepers, this variety at least picks the correct lane in which to do its crawling. Their sluggish pace provokes much the same reaction from other drivers as the Fast-Lane Creeper. Better have an extra supply of patience if you get caught between a Crawler and a Creeper.

Gawkers: Easily recognizable by their constantly bobbing heads, twisting necks, undulating bodies, and furtive glances out of every window but the front. A distant cousin to the above two. Never seem to find what they are looking for.

In and Outers: A dominating force on city streets, they love to dart in and out of traffic in the race to be first to stop at the next light. Rude to the point of obnoxiousness, these frustrated Indy hopefuls take out their aggressions on the driving public.

Jack Rabbits: One of the oldest breeds known, they love nothing better than to leave an ounce of rubber at each start. A prodigious waster of fuel, the jack rabbit was thought nearing extinction during the last OPEC embargo, but recently has made a dramatic comeback suckled on cheap and deceptively plentiful fuel. A favorite of tire dealers everywhere.

Traveling Testimonials: Put what's on their minds on their bumpers.

Bumper Riders: Also known as Tailgaters, they love to get as close to you as possible and stay there, whether you are moving or not. Psychiatrists say these drivers lack love at home and try to make up for it by getting as close to anything as possible. Can usually be found at the scene of "rear-ender" type accidents. Beware of the hybrid Bumper Rider-Gawker.

Strivers: One of the most aggressive of all, these high-tension drivers are never happy if there is a car in front of them, and will resort to any tactic to be first. Some have been known to actually save a minute or two on a crosstown trip when compared with nonstriving types. As schoolchildren, Strivers always had to be first in any line.

Passing Speed Changers: Can't wait to pass you, and when they finally do, pull in front of you and—you guessed it—slow down. Once believed to populate only the interstate highways, this species is more and more finding its way onto city streets.

Left-Turn-Arrow Ignorers: You must always wait for them to finish their illegal turns long after their green-turn arrow has bid you adieu. Automotive psychological analysts say there is a bit of arrow-ignorer in each of us.

Hand and Mouthers: Usually found cursing and gesticulating at some other driver for something they themselves caused. These crass, tantrum-throwing, pantomime experts can be dangerous and are better left alone in case of a confrontation. Proficient at sign language, too, they are found all over town signaling their IQ with raised digital extremities.

Courteous Drivers: Surface occasionally from the morass of moving steel with an act of graciousness that catches you off-guard and leaves you feeling good all over. Bet you can still remember the last one you encountered. Why not make the next one you?

Take Down the .9 Signs!

Remember when gasoline was 25 cents per gallon? No, I didn't say 24.9 cents per gallon, but an even 25 cents. It's hard to recall gasoline prices without the .9 tacked on. What's even more amazing is that some of our younger drivers have never seen gasoline priced otherwise.

Well, when gasoline was going for about 25 cents, some wise guy decided he would cut the price to 24.9 cents. It looked better than 25 cents, and a lot of people fell for the ruse and scrambled to his station to buy cheaper gas, not really aware of the tiny difference between the two figures. All most people saw was the 24, and to them that meant saving a penny per gallon.

In reality, the saving was negligible. But no harm was done; it was just a bit of good old American ingenuity. Before you knew it, the .9-cent fad hit every gas station across the country, and fractional-cent pricing became as common as the Hula Hoop.

That wasn't bad when gas was cheap and the illusion of saving a penny or two hadn't yet been shattered. But $1.24.9? Ludicrous at best. I think the oil companies still believe we're suckers. Who can possibly be influenced by the .9-cent charade? Be truthful: Does that one-tenth of a cent difference really influence your decision to buy a certain brand? I didn't think so.

But there would be problems if all gasoline stations reverted to pricing on the even penny. One of the problems, perhaps the main one, would be one that has plagued the superpowers on the question of disarmament: Who goes first? You know, the "I'll do it if you do it, but you do it first . . . but if you don't do it then I won't and, of course, you won't if I don't" syndrome. Caught between a Catch and a 22. We can resolve this dilemma by declaring a national "take down the .9 signs" day. Then all gasoline stations would, on cue, remove the offending numbers.

But problems still remain. What will the gas stations do with the hundreds of thousands of .9 numbers scattered throughout the United States? It could be a real problem, but this column has a few suggestions.

If a sequel to Federico Fellini's movie "8½" is made, the promoters could use all the ".9s" for cheap advertising. Or perhaps some company will top Ivory soap's 99.44 percent pure with one that is 99.9 percent pure. That could take care of all the leftover numbers in one fell swoop.

But maybe the best idea is to have Big Oil take the signs and store them in the back rooms of service stations across the nation and keep them there until they are needed again.

Needed again?

Sure. They could hustle them back out and start the whole .9-cent stuff over again after gasoline prices drop to the original 25 cents per gallon. Then I wouldn't mind a bit.

Hey, we can dream, can't we?

Demons of Auto Demise,
Wear and Tear, Hold National Convention

I was driving on a back road in Kentucky not too far south of Cincinnati when a small hand-painted sign caught my eye: "Automotive Specialists Convention, 3 miles" it read. Odd place for a convention I thought as I followed the arrows. Soon I found myself in front of a huge auto junkyard where a large sign proclaimed, "1st Annual Automotive Wear and Tear Convention." I couldn't believe my eyes.

I pulled into the yard, where an attendant greeted me and handed me a large brochure. I eagerly flipped through it—I had to gasp for breath. Wear and Tear, those age-old adversaries of mine, were sponsoring a national get-together of all segments of the auto-destroying fraternity. And what better place to hold it than a junkyard? And could any program chairman pick better keynote speakers than those two demons of auto demise, Wear and Tear?

I crouched behind a rusted '36 Ford and peeked at the proceedings. Lordy, they're all here, I thought. I checked tonight's entertainment schedule. A dance? Nah. Banquet? Nope. A guided tour of surrounding points of interest? No way. There it was in bold print, the main attraction—a demolition derby! I cried. I'd been fighting these wear-and-tear devils for years, but little did I realize they were so organized. And now, a national convention. It was too much.

They were all there, even some I hadn't heard of. There were Wear and Tear, enjoying themselves immensely playing King of the Hill on a pile of old cars. I could see Nasty Corrosion, that promoter of premature engine wear, and his cousin Acidic Oil. And look at this. Scheduled for tomorrow night's entertainment—Shake, Rattle, and Roll, the frame and body destruction specialists, accompanied by Premature Rust and the Oxidizers.

I checked the seminar schedule for the upcoming week. It was ridiculous, too. Keynote speakers: Wear and Tear. Subject: Ways to induce a laissez-faire policy of maintenance in car owners. *Laissez-faire?* Hands off? They were going for the jugular. I checked other seminar topics; they were the antithesis of everything I stood for:

○ How to encourage non-reading of the owner's manual.

○ How to rationalize away prescribed car maintenance, or the don't-disturb-a-sleeping-dog theory of automotive maintenance.

○ Hell-bent-for-leather driving techniques, including how to peel rubber and beat the other driver to the next stoplight.

○ Techniques of non-recordkeeping.

○ How to became irritated at other drivers and release that frustration on one's own car (morning and afternoon sessions).

○ The art of keeping tire pressures low. Ways to encourage drivers to ignore checking their tire pressure.

The list was endless—24 seminars dealing with every possible way to encourage early auto demise.

Well, I thought to myself, if the warriors of the Kingdom of Wear are so organized, I'll just have to fight fire with fire. First, I'll have to let my readers know about this now that there is a never-ending effort afoot to destroy their cars. Then I'll have to keep feeding them anti-wear information, and pray that they heed and read the advice. Knowledge, and a determination to use that knowledge effectively, is necessary for anyone wanting to beat Wear and Tear at their own game. If you read, but don't heed, you'll soon be in need.

But it can be done. Just look at all the members of the High-Mileage Club whose cars have surpassed the 100,000-mile mark without major repairs. Look at all the people who read this column. Indeed, there is reason for optimism. We can win this battle if we want to.

But in the meantime, I thought I'd catch the first Shake, Rattle, and Roll concert—just to see how they sound!

Peepers, Squeezers, and Others

In its ongoing effort to help drivers better understand themselves, their cars, other drivers, and why each acts as he/she does, "Drive It Forever" presents a list of automotive personalities commonly found at various self-service gasoline stations. Perhaps without looking too hard, you can spot yourself here.

Peepers: While filling their tanks, peepers are continually peering into the opening, as if waiting for some giant gas snake to pop out. I know they're looking to see if the tank is getting near full —or are they really Seekers in disguise?

Seekers: Never seem to be able to remember where they placed the gas cap.

Squatters: No, they are not trying to homestead on the station's property. These are the ones who must squat down to get to the tank filler neck concealed behind the rear license plate. Overweight squatters usually head directly to the tailor after gassing up.

Squeezers: A dying breed, remnants of the end of an era. Squeezers usually try to get away with squeezing an extra penny or so from each purchase without paying for it, deriving tremendous satisfaction from the fact that they just put it to old Giant Oil. But Giant Oil isn't taking the antics of squeezers lightly; it is installing digital pumps at an alarming rate; beating squeezers at their own game, and sending the hard-core ones scurrying about town searching for the last of the old-fashioned squeezable, cheatable pumps.

Leakers: They love to fill it to the rim and can easily be spotted after leaving the station because, like giant snails, they leave wet trails in their wake. The number of leakers seems to be directly proportional to the price of gasoline: The higher the price, the fewer the leakers. Some oil-industry analysts actually use the total number of leakers at any given time as an indicator of gasoline supply. Really!

Buck and Go'ers: You'd think they would have long since disappeared, but they're still around. A dollar paid, a quick squeeze of the handle, and they are on their way, usually to look for another gas station. More likely than not they are driving behemoth-like cars.

Protesters: Become furious when the automatic pump is reset and starts off at the 1-cent mark instead of going back to zero. Squeezers are among the most vociferous Protestors, reasoning that it's OK for them to do it, but not for Giant Oil.

Auto Ads Challenge Your Reading Skills

While thumbing through a popular magazine I came across an ad extolling the virtues of a certain European-made car.

The bold type boasted that the cars "are engineered for those who seek out the thrill of driving as well as those who seek to avoid it." That wasn't too clear to me, so I read on. After I finished the ad I still didn't know what they were talking about. The ad came across as stuffy, standoffish, pseudosophisticated, and packed with high-tech talk only an engineer could understand.

In case readers comb across this ad and are unduly confused, Drive It Forever offers its interpretation. What follows are parts of the ad with my comments and/or translation immediately following:

"Consider your favorite twisty bit of road. . . . It probably snakes its way through or around an area of considerable scenic splendor."

Consider the (insert name of local scenic road).

"The road is not without drama. An off-camber curve here, a patch of buckled pavement there."

The (insert name) highway, all right.

"It's challenging . . . but not so hostile to be off-putting."

Off-putting?!? Oh, yeah, right . . . off-putting.

"Perhaps on this particular day you are on this road out of necessity rather than choice. And interested in anything but . . . stimulation."

Damn the weather, you're going skiing. The stimulation can wait.

"You'd want your car's steering to be linear, direct, and highly accurate."

When you turn left, the car goes left.

"One thing you'd find indispensable is a firm but compliant union between your wheels and the road surface."

Tires are standard.

"The curves you love so well are capped with ice."

Your wife or girlfriend is having a tough time changing a flat tire in a snowstorm.

"The precision of its steering can help you avoid obstacles and negotiate slippery conditions while keeping you fully aware of your car's relationship to the direction of the road."

When you turn left, the car goes left.

"The slight understeer of . . . front-wheel drive will prove instrumental in helping prevent a change in your direction of travel when one isn't called for."

If you don't turn left, the car won't go left.

"But of course, there are times when stimulation can go too far."

Especially if you make it to the ski lodge.

"Controls that fall readily to hand as you keep your eyes fixed on the road."

You can shift gears without looking at them.

"On a road such as this, you'd prefer your car to have attributes of a sporting nature."

It will, if the stimulation keeps up.

And lastly, "Manufacturer's suggested retail price for the bottom-of-the-line model: $11,100."

You're lucky if you can get it off the showroom floor for less than 14 thou.

Kind of off-putting, huh?

Dumpies Unite!

Yuppies, yuppies, yuppies. I'm getting tired of hearing and reading about them. In case you've been hiding in a closet and don't know who these creatures are, yuppies are those young, upwardly mobile, urban professionals whose lifestyles have become a national obsession.

These striving young men and women are paid handsome salaries in the $40,000-plus range, and the fruits of their work are reflected in the way they live.

Handsomely. Nice stuff everywhere. High-tech, state-of-the-art goodies in profusion. In the old days this was called living high off the hog. Today, it's more like living a lifestyle commensurate with the position attained on the ladder of success. Grabbing what you can now and enjoying it. I still call it living high off the hog.

Yuppies and their ilk even have flagship cars whose purchase heralds their passage into the upper echelons of the buck brigade. BMW, Honda, and a variety of domestic cars all carry the yuppie banner: official, bona fide yuppiemobiles, if you will.

Now, there is nothing wrong with being young, making money, living the good life, and driving a new high-tech car. But a lot of us aren't, don't, and can't afford to. But it's the car bit that gets me mad. No, not because the yuppies have their own flagship vehicles, but because everyone is ignoring a much larger group and their flagship cars.

Who or what am I talking about?

Why, dumpies, of course. Dumpie—that's my acronym for America's most ignored and taken-for-granted group: Disintegrating, Underpaid, Middle-aged Persons. Five will you get 10 that there are a lot more dumpies than yuppies out there. And we don't even have a flagship car to symbolize our state of affluence. Sure, I said we. You bet, I'm a card-carrying dumpie from way back.

To my way of thinking, dumpies deserve recognition and should have their own flagship cars. Why, without us, who would the yuppies have to trample over in their rush to the top? Our own car is the least we can ask for. Why we haven't had one until now is a mystery to me.

Somewhere out there lurks the ideal dumpmobile. Oh, for sure, it has to be a used one. No respectable dumpie would be caught in a new car. Whether it is foreign or domestic is up for grabs. Myself, I lean toward the domestic side. And the dumpie car, like the dumpies themselves, should fulfill the letters of the acronym. It, too, should be disintegrating, undermaintained, middle-aged, and personable.

So dumpies, unite! There are more of us than them. And a word of caution to all those young, upwardly mobile professionals out there: yuppie or not, here we come!

"Dear Bob: Regarding your column on yuppies and dumpies, I would like to suggest a third group that deserves your recognition. I have been retired five years. The status cars of my era were Cadillacs and Lincoln Continentals. For people such as myself and, I'm sure, many others, may I propose the name "Grumpie"? That's my acronym for America's ignored and sometimes forgotten group—those Geriatric, Retired, Unappreciated, Mature persons.—F.L.B."

Grumpies? I like it. All you grumpies—and your grumpmobiles—have now been officially recognized.

Owed to Billy Joe

Before he passed away recently, Dan Lundberg, publisher of *The Lundberg Letter*, a highly respected oil-industry newsletter that tracks, among other items, the average price of gasoline across the United States, called me with a request. He wanted to reprint a column I had done on gasoline pricing. The request was unusual because *The Lundberg Letter* was all business, while the column in question was tongue-in-cheek. But Lundberg loved it and said my explanation was as good as any he had seen. Of course, he received permission to reprint.

Recently, a number of readers, perhaps prodded by the escalating price of gasoline, have asked me to reprint the column. So here 'tis. Oh yeah, one other note: Contrary to the contention of the town manager of Gila Bend, Arizona, the key character was not shot and killed in a poker game with town officials. That story was circulated to stem the flood of tourists that has inundated Gila Bend since the column first appeared a number of years ago.

I recently spotted a clerk at a convenience mart changing gas-price signs and stopped to ask her how they determined when and how much to raise or lower their prices.

"It's simple," she said. "We just take our cue from the Exxon station across the street. If they raise or lower prices, so do we. All our stores' gas prices are keyed to the prices of other nearby gas stations."

Intrigued by her answer, I sent this column's top investigative reporter—me—to find out more about this unique pricing structure.

I went to the Exxon station and asked how they determine the price of their gasoline. I learned that they, too, were keyed to another station—this time a Texaco just down the road. The Texaco station, it turned out, got its cue from a Shell station a few blocks away. This dominolike structure was prevalent everywhere, each station raising or lowering its prices when its cue station did. Determined to find out where the chain ended, I pushed on, feeling like an automotive Jack Anderson.

My quest led me all over town and eventually took me out of the state, where I discovered many such pricing chains spiraling out over the whole nation like the spokes of a wheel. A few months and a few thousand gas stations later, the answer began to form as I followed these spokes back in the direction I had come from.

I finally found the hub of the price-structuring wheel in a most unlikely place—on a dusty back street in Gila Bend, Arizona. There it was in all its dilapidated glory, Billy Joe's Gas-n-Go Market! I couldn't believe it. What I had discovered was enough to put the lid on any and all international oil conspiracy theories for good. Here, at this old wooden grocery store and gas station, the nation received its cues on when to raise or lower gasoline prices.

I watched as cars from every oil company cruised the street, eyes locked on Billy Joe's gas-price sign. I asked questions. Rumor had it that the late Dan Lundberg, whose *Lundberg Letter* is considered the bible of gasoline-price predictions, had an apartment across the street. A cafe nearby was filled with white-robed, bearded Middle Easterners, oil shieks in a different desert. I jumped out of the way as a Department of Energy car whizzed by, the driver jotting notes on a pad. It was too much; Billy Joe's Gas-n-Go, the hub of the pricing wheel, the place where every oil company and producer got its cue to raise or lower prices.

But what made Billy Joe raise and lower his prices? I had come this far and wasn't about to quit. I just had to find out.

Late one afternoon an opportunity presented itself as I spotted Billy Joe himself rocking away on the rickety front porch of his establishment Billy Joe, a good ol' boy by way of Florida, invited me to set a spell. I accepted, buying a six-pack at inflated prices so we could better ward off the dust cloud generated by all the passing cars. As we chatted and the beer began to loosen up the good ol' boy, I asked him what made him raise and lower his gasoline prices. Billy Joe, unaware that his place was the origination point of international oil- and gasoline-price structuring, thrust forward in his rocker, spewing a stream of Red Man into the dusty parking lot.

"Tain't no secret to it," he explained laconically. "Ya see, I jest loves poker, play two, maybe three times a week. If I lose a little, I raise my prices a little to make up for my loss. If I lose a lot, I raise my prices higher and hold 'em there longer. If I win, which ain't too often," he chuckled, "I lower 'em to celebrate."

I couldn't believe my ears. So much for OPEC and those much-heralded pricing meetings. Forget the Giant Oil greed and conspiracy theory. Throw away supply and demand. The answer was here at Billy Joe's Gas-n-Go.

So the next time you notice gas prices creeping upward don't look to the Department of Energy for an explanation, and don't bury yourself in the financial section of the newspaper or call some professor of economics looking for an answer. Just pray that Billy Joe starts getting some good cards.

If you enjoyed this book of Bob Sikorsky's "Drive It Forever" syndicated newspaper columns and would like to see more of his writings, ask the editor of your local newspaper to contact the New York Times Syndication Sales Corporation for information on how to obtain the column on a weekly basis.

Index